The Association of American University Presses

Directory 2014

The Association of American University Presses
28 W. 36th Street, Suite 602
New York, NY 10018
Phone: 212.989.1010
Fax: 212.989.0275
Website: www.aaupnet.org
Email: info@aaupnet.org

Published by the Association of American University Presses
28 W. 36th Street, #602 New York, NY 10018
© 2013 by the Association of American University Presses, Inc.
All rights reserved.
Printed in the United States of America

International Standard Book Number 13: 9780945103318
Library of Congress Catalog Number 54-43046

Distributed to the Trade by:
The University of Chicago Press
11030 South Langley Avenue
Chicago, Illinois 60628
USA

Publication of this *Directory* was assisted by a generous grant from Thomson-Shore.

Contents

PREFACE

This *Directory* serves as a guide to the publishing programs and personnel of the 131 distinguished scholarly presses that have met the membership standards of the Association of American University Presses. Updated annually, the *Directory* provides the most comprehensive information on these publishers available from any source. It belongs on the reference shelf of anyone connected to scholarly publishing: scholars preparing materials for publication, booksellers, librarians, scholarly presses interested in joining the AAUP, and, of course, AAUP's own members.

The *Directory* is organized particularly for the convenience of authors, librarians, and booksellers who require detailed information about AAUP members and their wide-ranging publishing programs. The "Subject Area Grid," for example, provides a quick overview of the many disciplines published by the presses, indicating those most likely to publish a work in a given area. "On Submitting Manuscripts" gives advice to potential authors on preparing and submitting a scholarly manuscript for publication.

For further detail, individual press listings provide information on their editorial programs, journals published, and key staff members. Addresses, ordering information, and information on sales representation for Canada, the UK, and Europe are also included.

The last section of the *Directory* focuses on the Association and its purposes, and includes its by-laws, guidelines for admission to membership, and the names of the AAUP's Board of Directors, committees, and staff.

GENERAL INFORMATION FOR AUTHORS

What University Presses Do

University Presses perform services that are of inestimable value to the scholarly establishment, and also to the broader world of readers, and ultimately to society. If you are considering publishing with a university or other non-profit scholarly press, the following list should give you a good understanding of the scholarly publishing community.

• University Presses make available to the broader public the full range and value of research generated by university faculty.

• University Press books and journals present the basic research and analysis that is drawn upon by policymakers, opinion leaders, and authors of works for the general public.

• University Presses contribute to the variety and diversity of cultural expression at a time of global mergers and consolidation in the media industry.

• University Presses make common cause with libraries and other cultural institutions to promote engagement with ideas and sustain a literate culture.

• University Presses help to preserve the distinctiveness of local cultures through publication of works on the states and regions where they are based.

• University Presses give voice to minority cultures and perspectives through pioneering publication programs in ethnic, racial, and sexual studies.

• University Presses bring the work of overseas scholars and writers to English-language audiences by commissioning and publishing works in translation.

• University Presses rediscover and maintain the availability of works important to scholarship and culture through reprint programs.

• University Presses encourage cultural expression by publishing works of fiction, poetry, and creative nonfiction and books on contemporary art and photography.

• University Presses sponsor work in specialized and emerging areas of scholarship that do not have the broad levels of readership needed to attract commercial publishers.

• University Presses, through the peer review process, test the validity and soundness of scholarship and thus maintain high standards for academic publication.

• University Presses add value to scholarly work through rigorous editorial development; professional copyediting and design; and worldwide dissemination.

• University Presses are based at a wide array of educational institutions and thus promote a diversity of scholarly perspectives.

• University Presses encourage and refine the work of younger scholars through publication of the first books that establish credentials and develop authorial experience.

• University Presses make the works of English-language scholars available worldwide by licensing translations to publishers in other languages.

• University Presses commit resources to long-term scholarly editions and multivolume research projects, assuring publication for works with completion dates far in the future.

• University Presses add to the richness of undergraduate and graduate education by publishing most of the non-textbook and supplementary material used by instructors.

• University Presses collaborate with learned societies, scholarly associations, and librarians to explore how new technologies can benefit and advance scholarship.

• University Presses extend the reach and influence of their parent institutions, making evident their commitment to knowledge and ideas.

• University Presses demonstrate their parent institutions' support of research in areas such as the humanities and social sciences that rarely receive substantial Federal or corporate funding.

• University Presses help connect the university to the surrounding community by publishing books of local interest and hosting events for local authors.

• University Presses generate favorable publicity for their parent institutions through news coverage and book reviews, awards won, and exhibits at scholarly conferences.

• University Press staff act as local experts for faculty and administrators, providing guidance on intellectual property, scholarly communication, and the publishing process.

• University Presses provide advice and opportunities for students interested in pursuing careers in publishing.

On Submitting Manuscripts

JOURNAL ARTICLES

University presses have always been associated with publishing books of merit and distinction. This remains as true today as in the past, but less well appreciated is the extent to which university presses are active in publishing scholarly journals.

Journals form a major part of the publishing program of many presses, and more than half of the Association's members produce at least one periodical. (See page 18 for a list of presses publishing journals.)

Authors submitting papers to a journal should check a current issue for information on where to submit manuscripts and for guidelines on length and format. Editors of journals often have very precise requirements for manuscript preparation and may return articles that do not meet their specifications.

BOOK MANUSCRIPTS

Selecting a Publisher

If you are looking for a publisher for a book-length manuscript, do some research on which press may be best for your book. You should consider the reputation in your field of various presses and their editors, the design and production quality of their books, and the range and strength of their marketing efforts. To take advantage of group promotions and past experience, presses tend to specialize in certain subjects. Occasionally a press may take on a title in an unfamiliar area, but you are more likely to be successful in your submission if you choose one that knows the field. Use the "Subject Area Grid," which begins on page 9, to find out which presses publish titles in your field. You can then find more specific information about their interests under the listings of individual presses or by consulting their catalogs. If your book has a strong regional interest, consider the lists of the university presses active in your state to determine what types of regional books they publish.

You can also learn more about the list of each publisher by studying brochures received in the mail, reading book advertisements in journals, and by visiting press exhibits at academic meetings. At these exhibits you can meet acquisitions editors from the presses most active in the discipline and talk with them about your manuscript. Such talks can be very helpful to you and the editor in deciding if your manuscript would be suitable for a particular press. If you have already decided which press you would prefer for your book, call the appropriate editor before the meeting to make an appointment.

Preparing a Manuscript Prospectus

If you have selected a publisher but do not know an editor, you can use this directory to find the appropriate editor at that press. If you are not sure which editor to approach, write to the director of the press or to its editor-in-chief. Many AAUP member presses describe their submission guidelines on their Web sites. It is best not to send the complete manuscript until you have been invited to do so. Presses vary in the amount of material they want to receive on a first submission, but some or all of the following materials are usually provided:

- a short, informative cover letter including a clear and concise description of your book and its notable features, your opinion of the audience for the book, information on the current status of the manuscript and expected completion date, and some details on the physical characteristics of the manuscript, such as length, number of illustrations, tables, appendices, etc.

- a table of contents

- a preface, introduction, or other brief sample of your manuscript

- a curriculum vitae or biographical notes

If the press is interested, the editor will invite you to submit the complete manuscript or inform you that he or she can proceed to review the materials you sent.

Preparing Your Manuscript for Review

Presses vary in their requirements for manuscript preparation. In general, the manuscript you submit for review should be as accurate and complete as possible. If a manuscript is carelessly prepared, reviewers may take offense at typographical errors or careless citations and spend precious review space discussing these problems instead of attending to the substance of your manuscript. If, for good reasons, your manuscript is incomplete, you should indicate what material is missing and provide your schedule for completion.

Although some presses will accept a single-spaced manuscript for review, it is best to double-space your text. A double-spaced manuscript is easier to read and may be required when your manuscript reaches the copyediting stage. For book publication, every element of the text should be double-spaced (including quotations, notes, bibliographies, appendices, figure legends, and glossaries). Once your manuscript is accepted for publication, your editor will advise you on any special requirements imposed by that press's house style.

The Review Process

Some university presses may give advance (i.e., conditional) contracts to experienced authors on the basis of incomplete or unreviewed manuscripts. Most, however, must obtain one or more reviews of a completed manuscript before presenting a project for the approval of the press's editorial board. As review procedures differ from press to press, check with the editor when you first submit the manuscript to find out what will be involved. He or she should be able to give you a tentative schedule for the review process. It is difficult to predict exactly how long it will take to reach a decision, since often readers' reports encourage authors to make further revisions to the manuscript and the manuscript is usually reviewed again after the author makes the revisions. If your manuscript is also under review at another publisher, be sure to let the editor know. Some editors will not review manuscripts that are under simultaneous consideration elsewhere; others will not object.

Preparing Your Manuscript for Publication

Most publishers will want an electronic version of your manuscript. Your manuscript should be keyboarded as simply as possible. There is no need to change fonts, type styles, and formats to differentiate between sections; in fact, this is counterproductive. The press's copyediting or production department will insert the proper typesetting codes for formatting extracts, different levels of headings, and so on. And keep in mind that your book will be designed by a professional on the press's staff. Many presses will send you their own guidelines for submitting manuscripts.

FURTHER READING

Abel, Richard, Lyman W. Newlin, Katina Strauch, and Bruce Strauch, eds. *Scholarly Publishing: Books, Journals, Publishers, and Libraries in the Twentieth Century*. Indianapolis: Wiley, 2001.

American Psychological Association. *Publication Manual of the American Psychological Association*. 6th ed. Washington, DC: APA Books, 2009.

Appelbaum, Judith. *How to Get Happily Published: A Complete and Candid Guide*. 5th ed. New York: HarperResource, 1998.

Becker, Howard S. *Writing for Social Scientists: How to Start and Finish Your Thesis, Book, or Article*. 2nd ed. Chicago: University of Chicago Press, 2007.

Belcher, Wendy Laura. *Writing Your Journal Article in Twelve Weeks: A Guide to Academic Publishing Success*. Thousands Oaks, CA: SAGE Publications, 2009

Day, Robert A. and Barbara Gastel *How to Write and Publish a Scientific Paper*. 7th ed. Westport, CT: Greenwood Publishing Group, Inc., 2011.

Derricourt, Robin. *An Author's Guide to Scholarly Publishing*. Princeton: Princeton University Press, 1996.

Germano, William. *From Dissertation to Book*. 2nd ed. Chicago: University of Chicago Press, 2013.

Germano, William. *Getting it Published: A Guide for Scholars and Anyone Else Serious About Serious Books*. 2nd ed. Chicago: University of Chicago Press, 2008.

Hacker, Diana. *A Writer's Reference*. 6th ed. Boston, MA: Bedford Books, 2009.

Harman, Eleanor, Ian Montagnes, Siobhan McMenemy, and Chris Bucci eds. *The Thesis and the Book: A Guide for First-Time Academic Authors*. 2nd ed. Toronto: University of Toronto Press, 2003.

Huff, Anne Sigismund. *Writing for Scholarly Publication*. Thousand Oaks, CA: SAGE Publications, 1998.

Katz, Michael J. *Elements of the Scientific Paper: A Step-by-Step Guide for Students and Professionals*. New Haven: Yale University Press, 1986.

Kasdorf, William E. *The Columbia Guide to Digital Publishing*. New York: Columbia University Press, 2003.

Luey, Beth. *Handbook for Academic Authors*. 5th ed. New York: Cambridge University Press, 2009.

Luey, Beth, ed. *Revising Your Dissertation: Advice from Leading Editors*. 2nd ed. Berkeley: University of California Press, 2007.

Modern Language Association. *MLA Style Manual and Guide to Scholarly Publishing*. 3rd ed. New York: Modern Language Association of America, 2008.

Moxley, Joseph M. and Todd Taylor. *Writing and Publishing for Academic Authors*. 2nd ed. Lanham, MD: Rowman and Littlefield, 1996.

Mulvany, Nancy C. *Indexing Books*. 2nd ed. Chicago: University of Chicago Press, 2005.

Parsons, Paul. *Getting Published: The Acquisition Process at University Presses*. Knoxville: University of Tennessee Press, 1989.

Powell, Walter W. *Getting into Print: The Decision-Making Process in Scholarly Publishing*. Chicago: University of Chicago Press, 1985.

Strong, William S. *The Copyright Book: A Practical Guide*. 6th ed. Cambridge, MA: MIT Press, 2014.

Strunk, William J. and E. B. White. *The Elements of Style*. 4th ed. New York: Pearson Higher Education, 1999.

Swain, Dwight V. *Techniques of the Selling Writer*. Norman: University of Oklahoma Press, 1982.

Thompson, John. *Books in the Digital Age: The Transformation of Academic and Higher Education Publishing in Britain and the United States* Cambridge: Polity Press, 2005.

University of Chicago Press. *The Chicago Manual of Style*. 16th ed. Chicago: University of Chicago Press, 2010.

University of Chicago Press. *The Chicago Manual of Style Online*. 16th ed. Chicago: University of Chicago Press, 2010, http://www.chicagomanualofstyle.org/home.html

Zerubavel, Eviator. *The Clockwork Muse: A Practical Guide to Writing Theses, Dissertations, and Books*. Cambridge, MA: Harvard University Press, 1999.

SUBJECT AREA GRID

This eight-page grid indicates the subject areas in which each press has a particularly strong interest.

Some presses are prepared to consider manuscripts of outstanding quality in areas other than those listed. For more detailed descriptions of press editorial programs, consult the individual listings in the "Directory of Members" section and contact the presses that interest you.

	Abiline Christian	Akron	Alabama	Alaska	Alberta	A. Historical	A. Psychiatric	A. School Classical	Amsterdam	Arizona	Arkansas	Athabasca	Baylor	Beacon	British Columbia	Brookings	Cairo (American)	Calgary	California	Cambridge	Carnegie Mellon	Catholic	Chicago	Chinese	Colorado	Columbia	Cork	Cornell	Duke	Duquesne	Florida
African Studies															●			●	●	●			●						●	●	
African American Studies	●		●							●	●		●		●			●	●				●		●	●			●	●	●
Agriculture									●	●								●	●	●			●						●		
American Indian Studies			●	●					●	●	●		●	●			●	●	●	●			●		●		●		●	●	●
American Studies			●						●	●	●	●	●		●			●	●	●	●		●		●	●		●	●	●	●
Anthropology			●	●					●	●		●		●	●		●	●	●	●			●	●	●	●			●	●	●
Cultural			●	●					●	●				●	●			●	●	●			●	●	●				●	●	●
Physical			●	●														●	●	●			●		●						●
Archaeology			●	●		●	●	●		●		●			●			●	●	●			●		●			●	●	●	●
Architecture			●			●	●	●							●			●	●	●	●		●				●	●	●	●	
Art & Art History			●			●	●	●		●		●		●				●	●	●	●		●				●	●	●	●	
Asian Studies									●				●	●	●			●	●				●		●		●		●	●	
Asian American Studies									●				●				●	●	●				●		●	●		●	●	●	
Bibliography & Reference					●										●		●	●	●			●	●	●	●	●	●	●	●	●	●
Biography	●		●	●	●				●	●		●		●	●		●	●	●	●		●	●	●	●		●				
Business									●						●	●		●	●									●			
Canadian Studies			●	●	●				●				●	●	●		●	●	●				●					●	●		●
Caribbean Studies			●					●					●	●	●			●	●				●		●	●					
Child Development			●			●			●	●			●					●	●		●	●	●			●					
Classics						●	●				●	●	●	●		●	●	●	●				●	●		●		●	●	●	
Communications/Media			●						●		●		●						●	●	●		●								
Computer Sciences																		●	●	●	●										
Creative Nonfiction	●		●	●					●		●		●					●	●				●			●	●				
Criminology									●					●	●	●		●	●				●			●					
Demography			●						●						●	●	●	●	●				●		●		●		●	●	
Economics			●	●		●			●		●		●	●	●	●	●		●	●			●	●		●		●			
Education			●	●									●	●	●						●		●					●	●		
History			●		●		●						●								●		●								
Learning Disabilities	●				●								●					●					●	●							
Theory & Method																			●												
Engineering																			●												
Environment/Conservation		●	●	●					●	●	●	●		●	●	●	●	●	●				●		●	●		●	●		●
ESL																			●												●
Ethnic Studies			●	●				●		●	●	●	●		●	●			●	●			●		●			●	●	●	●
European Studies			●						●		●		●		●		●		●	●			●					●	●	●	●
Fiction			●							●	●		●					●			●										
Film Studies			●		●				●				●		●			●	●	●	●		●			●	●	●	●	●	
Folklore			●						●	●	●	●							●				●			●	●	●	●		
Food Studies									●	●	●		●	●					●				●			●	●	●	●		
Gay and Lesbian Studies		●											●	●				●	●			●	●		●			●	●		
Gender Studies			●			●			●	●			●	●		●	●	●	●				●	●	●		●	●	●		
Geography									●	●	●	●		●				●	●				●		●	●		●			
Gerontology	●							●		●			●					●	●				●		●						
History		●	●	●	●				●	●			●		●			●	●	●		●	●	●	●	●		●	●		●
African					●										●			●	●	●			●								
American	●		●	●					●	●		●	●					●	●	●			●		●	●		●	●		
Asian					●			●					●	●					●	●			●	●	●			●	●		
British					●						●			●					●	●		●	●	●				●	●		
Canadian				●	●	●					●			●				●											●		
Environmental	●	●	●	●					●	●	●		●					●	●				●		●	●		●	●		●
European					●			●					●					●	●		●		●			●	●	●	●		
Latin American			●			●			●				●				●		●	●			●		●			●	●		
Middle Eastern				●			●				●			●			●		●	●			●						●		
Ancient					●	●	●												●	●			●		●				●		
Classical					●	●	●												●	●			●		●				●		

10

	Abilene Christian	Akron	Alabama	Alaska	Alberta	A. Historical	A. Psychiatric	A. School Classical	Amsterdam	Arizona	Arkansas	Athabasca	Baylor	Beacon	British Columbia	Brookings	Cairo (American)	Calgary	California	Cambridge	Carnegie Mellon	Catholic	Chicago	Chinese	Colorado	Columbia	Cork	Cornell	Duke	Duquesne	Florida	Fordham	Gallaudet
Literature			●	●	●				●	●			●						●		●	●	●	●		●		●	●	●	●	●	●
Literary Criticism	●	●	●						●	●			●					●			●	●	●			●	●	●	●	●	●	●	●
Literary History			●						●										●	●	●	●	●		●	●	●	●	●	●	●	●	●
African																			●										●				
African American			●										●						●			●	●		●			●	●		●	●	
American	●	●	●								●	●			●	●			●	●	●	●	●		●	●		●	●		●	●	
Asian																			●			●	●	●	●	●		●	●		●		
British																			●			●	●		●	●		●	●	●			
Canadian					●														●			●			●			●	●			●	
Classical						●	●												●			●	●		●			●	●		●		
Eastern																			●			●			●			●	●				
European									●										●			●	●		●	●		●	●	●	●	●	
Medieval									●										●			●	●		●			●	●	●	●	●	
Renaissance									●										●			●	●		●			●	●	●	●		
Modern	●		●																●	●	●	●	●		●			●	●		●	●	
Contemporary			●						●	●									●	●	●	●	●		●			●	●		●	●	●
Mythology		●	●						●	●									●			●	●			●			●				
Translations				●				●									●		●	●	●	●		●		●	●				●	●	●
Maritime Studies			●	●					●						●				●													●	
Mathematics				●		●				●			●		●				●				●		●			●				●	
Medicine		●	●			●			●		●		●						●					●		●	●	●					
Ethics			●			●												●	●			●			●		●	●	●				
History		●	●						●								●		●			●			●	●	●	●	●				
Medieval Studies									●										●			●	●		●			●	●	●	●	●	●
Middle East Studies									●		●			●		●	●	●	●	●		●	●			●			●	●		●	●
Military Studies			●	●							●	●		●		●	●	●	●	●									●	●		●	●
Near Eastern Studies									●						●		●	●	●	●						●			●	●		●	
Performing Arts									●						●			●	●		●								●	●		●	●
Dance															●							●						●	●			●	●
Music									●						●			●	●	●		●	●					●	●	●	●		
Theory & Method									●			●			●	●				●						●			●	●	●		●
Theatre																			●						●				●				
Pacific Studies			●						●					●	●	●			●				●						●	●		●	
Philosophy									●			●		●	●			●				●	●		●			●	●	●	●		
Ethics									●			●	●	●					●			●	●		●	●		●	●	●	●		
History of Philosophy									●			●	●	●					●			●	●		●			●	●		●		
Photography		●	●	●															●	●	●		●		●				●		●	●	●
Poetry	●	●	●								●	●	●		●							●	●		●			●	●	●		●	●
Political Science/Public Affairs	●		●						●		●	●	●	●	●	●	●	●	●			●	●		●	●		●	●	●	●		
Popular Culture	●	●	●						●			●	●	●				●	●			●	●		●	●		●	●	●		●	●
Psychiatry							●			●													●		●			●	●	●			●
Psychology		●		●		●			●						●	●						●			●	●	●	●	●	●	●		
Public Health			●						●			●		●	●	●						●				●			●	●		●	
Publishing									●													●				●			●				
Regional Studies	●	●	●	●	●				●	●	●	●		●	●	●		●	●		●	●			●	●	●	●	●	●	●	●	●
Religion	●		●						●	●		●	●	●	●		●	●	●	●		●	●			●	●		●	●	●	●	●
Buddhism																		●	●			●	●					●					
Christianity	●													●				●	●	●		●		●			●		●			●	
Islam									●					●				●	●			●				●		●				●	
Judaism									●					●				●	●			●		●			●		●			●	
Science		●		●			●			●		●						●	●			●		●		●			●		●	●	●
Biological Science		●	●		●				●			●	●		●	●			●				●			●	●		●		●	●	
Botany		●	●						●			●	●						●				●			●		●	●				●
Genetics						●													●						●	●	●						
Earth Sciences			●								●			●	●			●	●				●			●				●			
Geology			●								●			●					●				●			●				●			
Physical Science			●						●					●					●				●			●							
Astronomy											●								●				●										
History of Science		●	●						●	●		●							●			●			●			●	●		●	●	
Slavic Studies			●										●	●	●				●				●										
Social Work						●		●		●			●	●					●						●	●	●		●				
Sociology		●	●		●				●			●	●	●			●	●	●	●	●	●		●	●	●		●	●		●	●	●
Sports	●	●	●							●			●						●				●			●	●	●	●		●		
Urban Studies									●			●		●		●	●	●	●	●	●		●						●	●		●	
Veterinary Sciences																									●				●				
Women's Studies			●			●			●	●	●	●	●	●	●	●		●	●	●			●		●	●		●	●		●	●	●

11

Subject	Georgetown	Georgia	Getty	Harvard	Hawaii	Hong Kong	IMF	Illinois	Indiana	Iowa	Island	Johns Hopkins	Kansas	Kent State	Kentucky	Leuven	Lincoln	Liverpool	Louisiana	McGill-Queen's	Manitoba	Marquette	Massachusetts	MIT	Medieval Institute	Mercer	Michigan	Michigan State	Minnesota Hist.	Minnesota	Mississippi	Missouri	MLA	MOMA
African Studies		•	•						•									•					•				•			•		•		
African American Studies		•	•		•			•	•			•		•						•							•	•	•	•	•	•	•	
Agriculture			•						•																									
American Indian Studies		•							•				•										•	•		•		•	•	•	•	•	•	
American Studies		•	•	•		•		•	•	•		•	•	•	•		•		•				•			•	•	•	•	•	•	•	•	
Anthropology			•	•	•		•	•											•				•				•	•	•	•				
Cultural			•	•	•		•	•								•							•				•	•	•	•				
Physical			•																															
Archaeology		•	•	•				•				•		•		•			•	•			•		•								•	
Architecture	•	•		•	•					•			•		•	•		•		•			•			•	•	•	•					•
Art & Art History	•	•	•	•				•				•		•	•	•	•	•		•		•	•	•	•	•				•	•			•
Asian Studies	•		•	•	•			•							•	•				•							•			•		•		
Asian American Studies		•	•	•	•															•						•		•	•	•			•	
Bibliography & Reference			•	•	•			•				•											•	•					•					
Biography	•		•	•	•			•	•	•		•		•	•				•	•		•	•			•	•	•	•		•	•		
Business		•	•	•																				•										
Canadian Studies			•																	•	•												•	
Caribbean Studies	•																	•	•	•										•	•		•	
Child Development		•			•	•									•					•														
Classics		•	•	•	•							•				•		•		•						•				•			•	
Communications/ Media		•	•	•	•	•		•	•							•				•	•		•	•	•	•	•			•	•	•	•	
Computer Sciences		•																						•										
Creative Nonfiction	•			•	•			•	•						•					•									•	•		•	•	
Criminology													•		•			•		•			•			•		•	•					
Demography			•															•		•														
Economics			•	•	•		•		•		•				•		•	•		•			•											
Education			•	•	•			•		•			•				•			•						•			•	•			•	
History			•	•									•				•			•						•			•				•	
Learning Disabilities			•	•																													•	
Theory & Method					•								•							•													•	
Engineering			•		•																													
Environment/Conservation	•	•	•	•	•		•	•			•	•	•	•	•		•		•		•	•			•	•	•	•	•	•	•			•
ESL	•			•																							•			•			•	
Ethnic Studies		•		•	•	•		•	•										•	•	•		•			•	•	•	•	•	•	•	•	
European Studies		•	•					•		•						•	•	•	•	•			•			•		•	•	•	•	•		
Fiction		•	•	•				•	•									•		•			•			•		•	•			•		
Film Studies		•	•	•	•	•			•			•		•	•		•			•						•		•	•	•	•	•	•	•
Folklore		•	•		•			•				•				•				•			•					•	•	•	•	•	•	
Food Studies		•	•		•			•							•				•	•	•		•							•	•		•	
Gay and Lesbian Studies			•	•	•		•													•			•			•			•				•	
Gender Studies		•	•	•	•	•		•	•	•									•	•			•			•			•	•			•	
Geography		•	•		•			•	•	•						•	•			•			•			•			•	•	•			
Gerontology				•																														
History		•	•	•	•		•	•	•	•	•	•	•	•	•				•	•			•	•		•	•	•	•	•	•	•	•	
African			•					•									•		•	•							•							
American		•	•	•	•		•	•	•		•	•	•	•	•		•		•	•			•	•		•	•	•	•	•	•	•	•	
Asian			•	•	•			•							•				•				•									•		
British			•	•	•									•			•		•	•					•				•	•				
Canadian																				•	•								•	•				
Environmental	•		•	•		•		•	•	•		•		•		•		•	•	•			•		•		•	•	•	•		•		
European			•					•			•			•		•	•	•		•		•		•		•			•	•				
Latin American	•	•	•						•						•		•	•	•	•										•	•			
Middle Eastern			•					•							•		•	•																
Ancient		•	•	•	•			•			•		•			•		•		•		•				•						•		
Classical		•	•		•			•			•		•			•		•		•		•				•						•		
Modern		•	•	•	•			•			•		•		•	•	•	•		•						•				•	•			
World			•																	•														
Law		•		•	•	•					•		•		•			•	•				•			•			•		•			
Language	•		•	•	•							•		•			•			•			•			•			•					•
Linguistics	•			•	•												•			•	•		•			•							•	
Speech																							•											
Latin American Studies			•						•								•	•	•										•	•	•	•		
Library Science		•	•			•																												

	Georgetown	Georgia	Getty	Harvard	Hawaii	Hong Kong	Illinois	IMF	Indiana	Iowa	Island	Johns Hopkins	Kansas	Kent State	Kentucky	Leuven	Lincoln	Liverpool	Louisiana	McGill-Queen's	Manitoba	Marquette	Massachusetts	MIT	Medieval Institute	Mercer	Michigan	Michigan State	Minnesota	Minnesota Hist.	Mississippi	Missouri	MLA	MOMA
Literature		●		●	●	●	●		●	●		●			●					●	●				●		●	●	●	●	●	●	●	
Literary Criticism		●		●	●	●	●			●		●		●				●	●	●							●	●	●		●	●	●	●	
Literary History		●		●		●	●			●		●		●	●	●				●	●				●		●	●			●	●	●	
African							●																							●		●	●	
African American		●		●			●	●		●									●					●			●	●			●		●	
American		●		●			●			●		●		●		●			●	●	●			●			●	●	●	●	●	●	●	
Asian				●	●	●	●													●									●			●		
British				●		●				●		●		●		●			●	●				●			●			●	●	●	●	
Canadian																				●	●									●	●		●	
Classical		●	●	●						●						●				●							●				●		●	
Eastern				●																●													●	
European		●		●						●					●	●	●			●							●			●		●	●	
Medieval		●	●	●						●					●	●				●			●							●			●	
Renaissance		●	●	●						●					●					●		●	●		●					●			●	
Modern	●		●	●					●					●		●			●	●							●			●	●	●	●	
Contemporary	●		●	●					●							●		●	●	●							●			●	●	●	●	
Mythology		●		●																●							●						●	
Translations		●		●	●	●			●	●									●	●					●					●		●		
Maritime Studies				●	●													●		●														
Mathematics												●								●														
Medicine	●			●	●				●			●								●							●							
Ethics	●			●		●			●			●								●							●							
History	●			●	●	●	●		●			●							●	●							●		●					
Medieval Studies		●	●	●					●							●				●	●		●		●		●		●				●	
Middle East Studies	●			●					●		●									●							●						●	
Military Studies	●			●	●	●	●			●		●	●	●	●				●	●						●		●		●		●	●	
Near Eastern Studies	●			●					●							●																	●	
Performing Arts				●	●	●	●		●	●										●						●		●		●	●			
Dance				●		●			●											●						●				●				
Music				●		●	●		●							●				●						●			●			●		
Theory & Method				●		●	●		●									●									●		●			●		
Theatre				●		●		●												●						●		●		●				
Pacific Studies				●	●															●									●				●	
Philosophy	●			●	●	●	●		●							●				●		●	●		●			●		●	●		●	
Ethics	●			●		●	●		●							●				●		●		●	●	●					●			
History of Philosophy				●	●	●	●									●				●		●	●		●					●				
Photography	●	●		●	●							●								●	●		●		●		●			●	●	●		●
Poetry				●	●															●	●						●		●			●		
Political Science/Public Affairs	●	●		●	●		●		●		●	●	●	●	●		●			●	●						●	●	●	●	●	●	●	
Popular Culture	●	●		●	●	●	●		●			●	●	●						●							●		●		●	●	●	●
Psychiatry				●	●										●																			
Psychology				●	●					●									●				●				●				●			
Public Health	●			●	●	●			●	●										●							●				●			
Publishing																						●			●									●
Regional Studies	●			●	●	●			●			●	●	●	●	●	●	●	●	●	●		●			●	●	●	●	●	●	●	●	
Religion	●			●	●	●	●			●			●			●	●			●	●		●			●	●	●			●	●		
Buddhism				●																														
Christianity									●											●						●	●							
Islam									●											●														
Judaism									●											●														
Science		●		●	●				●	●	●	●								●						●								
Biological Sciences		●		●	●	●			●	●	●	●								●						●								
Botany	●			●	●				●	●										●														
Genetics				●					●	●	●									●						●								
Earth Sciences				●	●	●			●	●	●									●						●								
Geology				●					●	●	●									●						●								
Physical Science				●	●				●	●	●									●						●								
Astronomy				●	●				●											●						●								
History of Science				●	●		●		●			●	●							●					●	●					●		●	
Slavic Studies				●					●											●									●				●	
Social Work						●	●	●																										
Sociology				●	●	●	●		●							●				●		●						●	●	●	●			
Sports							●					●		●	●					●						●	●	●		●		●	●	
Urban Studies	●	●		●	●	●	●			●		●	●	●			●			●		●	●	●			●			●				
Veterinary Sciences																																		
Women's Studies		●		●	●		●		●	●			●	●						●	●			●			●		●	●	●	●	●	

13

	National Acad.	National Gallery	Naval	Nebraska	Nevada	New England	New Mexico	New York	North Carolina	North Texas	Northern Illinois	Northwestern	Notre Dame	Ohio	Oklahoma	Oregon State	Ottawa	Oxford	Pennsylvania	Penn State	Pittsburgh	PISA	Princeton	Puerto Rico	Purdue	RAND	RIT	Rochester	Rockefeller	Russell Sage	Rutgers	School of Advance	St. Josephs
African Studies			•										•	•									•							•			
African American Studies	•		•	•		•		•	•			•	•		•				•	•	•	•						•			•	•	
Agriculture	•		•							•				•					•				•		•	•	•						
American Indian Studies			•	•	•	•	•		•		•				•	•			•							•					•		•
American Studies			•	•	•	•	•	•	•				•	•	•			•	•	•	•				•	•			•		•		
Anthropology			•	•		•	•			•			•	•	•		•	•		•	•	•			•			•		•	•	•	•
Cultural			•	•	•	•				•			•	•	•			•		•	•	•	•		•		•			•	•	•	
Physical			•	•									•							•											•	•	
Archaeology			•	•	•	•								•	•	•	•		•	•			•	•								•	
Architecture			•	•	•		•		•				•		•	•	•	•	•	•	•			•	•	•							
Art & Art History	•	•		•	•		•		•		•		•		•		•		•	•	•	•	•		•	•							•
Asian Studies			•							•			•			•		•		•		•			•						•		
Asian-American Studies					•		•							•					•		•				•					•	•		
Bibliography & Reference		•		•								•		•	•			•				•	•		•	•	•						
Biography	•		•	•	•	•	•	•	•	•	•	•	•	•	•		•	•	•	•	•		•		•	•	•	•					
Business	•			•	•	•	•	•		•		•			•			•				•	•	•	•	•							
Canadian Studies			•														•																
Caribbean Studies			•					•				•				•		•			•				•					•			
Child Development	•								•					•				•				•	•		•					•	•		
Classics							•				•		•		•		•	•		•		•	•		•						•		
Communications/Media			•	•	•	•		•		•		•			•		•			•		•	•		•					•			
Computer Sciences	•													•				•				•	•		•	•							
Creative Nonfiction	•		•	•	•	•			•	•		•	•			•			•		•		•		•	•							
Criminology	•		•			•		•		•		•				•	•				•	•	•		•					•	•		
Demography	•															•	•			•	•	•	•		•					•			
Economics	•														•	•	•			•		•	•	•	•					•	•		
Education	•			•			•							•			•			•	•	•	•	•	•					•	•		
History	•					•	•			•		•								•		•											
Learning Disabilities																				•		•		•									
Theory & Method																				•		•	•	•	•								
Engineering	•		•									•							•			•	•		•	•							
Environment/Conservation	•			•	•	•	•	•	•	•			•	•	•				•	•	•		•	•	•	•	•						
ESL														•																			
Ethnic Studies				•	•	•	•	•	•	•	•	•		•		•	•		•		•			•				•		•	•	•	
European Studies					•	•	•		•		•	•		•					•	•	•	•	•			•		•			•		
Fiction			•	•		•		•		•			•	•	•	•	•			•	•		•										
Film Studies			•		•	•		•				•				•			•			•			•	•	•				•		
Folklore				•	•	•	•			•			•						•			•			•								
Food Studies	•					•	•	•																									
Gay and Lesbian Studies						•	•	•												•		•				•				•		•	
Gender Studies	•		•	•	•	•	•	•	•		•		•			•			•	•	•	•		•		•		•		•	•	•	
Geography	•		•	•	•	•			•				•				•	•			•		•	•	•		•				•		
Gerontology	•																			•		•	•										
History			•	•	•	•	•	•	•	•	•	•		•	•			•	•	•	•	•	•	•	•	•			•	•	•		
African															•				•												•		
American			•	•	•	•	•	•	•	•	•		•	•	•	•		•	•	•	•		•						•	•	•		
Asian			•			•						•		•	•			•					•										
British			•			•			•		•	•						•	•	•													
Canadian			•	•													•	•															
Environmental			•	•	•	•	•	•	•		•			•	•	•			•	•	•									•			
European			•		•	•		•	•		•			•				•	•	•	•	•	•		•					•			
Latin American			•	•			•		•						•	•			•		•	•		•									
Middle Eastern			•			•			•	•									•					•									
Ancient									•										•	•	•		•	•									
Classical			•						•		•		•		•			•	•				•	•	•								
Modern			•		•	•	•	•	•	•	•			•	•	•			•	•		•		•			•						
World																							•			•							
Law			•			•	•	•	•			•	•		•				•			•	•	•		•					•		
Language			•	•		•				•						•			•		•	•	•										
Linguistics			•		•					•						•		•	•			•	•										
Speech																																	
Latin American Studies			•			•		•					•	•	•				•	•		•			•		•				•	•	
Library Science																											•						

	National Acad.	National Gallery	Naval	Nebraska	Nevada	New England	New Mexico	New York	North Carolina	North Texas	Northern Illinois	Northwestern	Notre Dame	Ohio	Oklahoma	Oregon State	Ottawa	Oxford	Pennsylvania	Penn State	Pittsburgh	PISA	Princeton	Puerto Rico	Purdue	RAND	Rochester	Rockefeller	Russell Sage	Rutgers	School for Advance	St. Josephs
Literature			●	●	●	●		●			●	●	●	●		●		●	●	●			●	●	●					●		
Literary Criticism				●	●	●	●	●				●	●	●				●	●	●			●	●	●	●				●		
Literary History			●	●	●	●			●		●		●						●	●	●		●	●	●							
African													●						●				●									
African American					●			●			●	●	●						●		●		●							●		
American			●	●	●	●	●	●	●		●	●	●	●	●	●			●				●							●		
Asian										●									●				●									
British			●								●	●							●	●			●									
Canadian																		●														
Classical							●	●			●	●		●		●			●	●			●									
Eastern																			●				●									
European			●										●						●	●	●		●	●	●							
Medieval													●					●	●	●	●		●									
Renaissance									●	●			●						●	●	●		●									
Modern						●			●				●						●				●	●	●							
Contemporary				●	●	●	●		●	●			●			●			●				●	●	●							
Mythology				●												●	●		●				●									
Translations	●		●	●		●	●				●	●				●		●	●	●			●	●								
Maritime Studies	●	●		●				●	●							●			●				●	●	●	●						
Mathematics	●				●							●							●				●									
Medicine	●			●	●	●		●			●					●			●		●		●				●		●	●	●	
Ethics	●			●	●	●		●			●				●				●				●					●	●	●		
History				●	●	●		●			●								●		●		●				●	●	●			
Medieval Studies													●						●	●	●	●	●	●								
Middle East Studies						●		●			●		●						●				●	●								
Military Studies	●		●	●			●	●	●	●					●	●			●						●							
Near Eastern Studies											●								●	●	●											
Performing Arts				●			●		●	●		●	●						●				●		●		●					
Dance													●						●								●					
Music				●			●	●	●	●		●	●						●				●	●	●		●					
Theory & Method				●						●		●	●						●				●				●					
Theatre													●	●					●								●					
Pacific Studies													●		●		●		●				●									
Philosophy				●					●	●	●	●	●					●	●		●		●	●	●	●	●		●	●		
Ethics				●					●	●			●						●	●			●	●			●			●		
History of Philosophy									●	●			●						●	●			●	●			●					
Photography		●		●	●			●										●					●	●								
Poetry						●			●	●	●	●	●										●	●								
Political Science/Public Affairs	●		●		●	●		●	●		●			●	●	●	●	●	●	●	●		●	●	●	●	●		●	●		
Popular Culture				●	●	●	●	●					●						●		●		●			●				●		
Psychiatry																			●				●									
Psychology	●						●												●				●		●				●			
Public Health	●			●	●	●		●											●	●			●	●	●	●	●		●	●		
Publishing				●									●										●	●	●							
Regional Studies			●	●	●	●	●	●	●	●		●	●		●	●	●	●	●	●	●		●	●	●	●			●	●		●
Religion			●	●	●	●		●			●		●		●		●	●	●	●			●	●			●					●
Buddhism								●																								
Christianity						●		●	●		●		●																			
Islam						●		●												●												
Judaism						●		●																●								
Science	●		●	●	●	●									●	●			●				●	●	●	●		●	●			
Biological Sciences	●			●	●	●									●	●			●				●	●	●				●			
Botany	●			●	●	●	●									●			●				●	●	●							
Genetics	●																		●				●	●				●				
Earth Sciences	●			●	●	●										●			●				●	●		●						
Geology	●			●	●	●									●	●			●				●	●								
Physical Science	●			●	●	●													●				●	●	●							
Astronomy	●					●													●				●	●								
History of Science	●		●			●	●	●			●		●		●			●	●	●	●		●				●	●				
Slavic Studies									●	●	●		●						●		●		●	●			●					
Social Work	●				●														●		●		●	●						●		
Sociology	●				●	●	●					●							●	●	●		●	●		●			●	●		
Sports	●			●		●		●	●		●								●				●	●				●		●		
Urban Studies	●			●	●	●		●	●		●							●	●	●			●	●	●	●			●	●		
Veterinary Sciences	●																				●			●								
Women's Studies			●	●	●	●	●	●	●	●					●	●	●	●	●	●	●		●		●		●	●		●	●	

Subject index matrix of participating institutions.

Subject	Soc. Biblical Lit.	South Carolina	Southern Illinois	S. Methodist	Stanford	SUNY	Syracuse	Teachers	Temple	Tennessee	Texas	Texas A&M	Texas Christian	Texas Tech	Tokyo	Toronto	U.S. Inst. Peace	Upjohn	Utah	Utah State	Vanderbilt	Virginia	Washington	Wash. State	Wayne State	Wesleyan	West Indies	West Virginia	Wilfrid Laurier	Wisconsin	Woodrow Wilson	Yale
African Studies		•														•		•				•						•		•	•	•
African American Studies		•	•			•	•	•	•	•	•	•				•	•					•	•	•		•	•	•		•		•
Agriculture												•				•								•						•		
American Indian Studies						•	•	•		•	•	•	•	•		•			•	•		•	•	•				•				•
American Studies		•	•		•	•	•		•	•	•	•	•	•		•	•			•	•	•	•	•		•		•		•	•	•
Anthropology					•		•		•	•	•					•	•		•		•	•	•	•	•	•		•		•	•	•
Cultural					•		•		•		•					•	•		•		•	•	•	•	•	•		•		•		•
Physical									•		•					•	•		•							•						•
Archaeology	•	•					•	•	•		•					•	•		•		•	•	•						•			•
Architecture							•	•	•	•	•					•	•				•	•	•				•	•		•	•	•
Art & Art History		•			•		•		•		•					•	•				•	•	•				•	•		•	•	•
Asian Studies	•				•	•		•								•	•	•				•								•	•	•
Asian American Studies					•			•	•							•	•				•									•	•	•
Bibliography & Reference	•		•													•	•				•		•		•					•		•
Biography	•	•				•	•		•	•	•		•	•		•	•		•			•	•					•		•		•
Business		•			•											•	•													•		•
Canadian Studies																•	•				•		•	•	•			•	•			
Caribbean Studies					•			•								•	•				•	•	•					•	•	•		•
Child Development							•									•	•													•		•
Classics	•		•							•						•	•											•		•		•
Communications/Media		•				•		•		•						•	•							•				•		•	•	•
Computer Sciences																•	•															•
Creative Nonfiction	•	•	•	•		•				•		•	•			•	•						•					•	•			
Criminology		•		•				•								•	•				•					•		•				
Demography																•	•									•						
Economics		•								•						•	•	•	•							•		•		•	•	
Education					•		•	•		•		•				•	•		•	•	•		•					•		•		•
History					•		•	•								•	•		•		•		•					•		•		
Learning Disabilities							•									•	•													•		
Theory & Method	•				•		•	•				•				•	•		•				•					•		•		
Engineering																•	•															
Environment/Conservation					•	•		•	•	•	•	•	•	•		•	•		•	•	•	•	•	•	•			•		•	•	•
ESL						•										•	•															•
Ethnic Studies			•	•	•	•		•		•	•		•	•		•	•		•	•	•	•	•	•	•			•		•	•	•
European Studies					•						•			•		•	•				•									•	•	•
Fiction	•	•	•	•		•	•				•	•				•	•										•	•	•	•		•
Film Studies		•				•		•		•						•	•								•	•		•		•		•
Folklore	•					•			•	•	•	•	•			•	•		•	•		•			•			•		•		
Food Studies										•						•	•													•	•	
Gay and Lesbian Studies		•			•		•	•								•	•				•							•		•		•
Gender Studies		•		•	•	•	•		•	•						•	•		•		•	•	•		•			•		•	•	•
Geography					•		•		•	•	•					•	•		•			•						•		•	•	•
Gerontology		•														•	•		•									•				
History		•			•	•	•		•	•	•	•	•	•		•	•	•			•	•	•	•	•	•			•		•	•	•
African		•	•													•	•		•				•					•		•		•
American		•	•		•	•	•		•	•	•	•	•	•		•	•		•	•	•	•	•	•	•			•		•	•	•
Asian					•	•					•	•	•	•		•	•						•					•		•	•	•
British					•						•	•	•	•		•	•								•			•		•	•	•
Canadian																•	•											•	•	•		•
Environmental		•			•	•			•	•		•	•	•		•	•		•	•	•	•	•					•	•	•	•	•
European					•	•					•	•	•	•		•	•			•			•		•			•		•	•	•
Latin American					•	•			•		•	•				•	•		•							•				•	•	•
Middle Eastern	•				•	•		•			•	•	•	•		•	•	•														•
Ancient	•							•			•	•				•	•															•
Classical	•	•	•					•			•	•				•	•											•		•	•	•
Modern		•		•		•		•			•	•	•			•	•											•		•	•	•
World											•	•				•	•											•		•		
Law		•	•		•			•				•	•			•	•		•	•				•				•		•	•	•
Language	•	•	•						•			•				•	•		•			•		•				•		•		•
Linguistics	•										•					•	•		•				•		•			•		•		•
Speech		•														•	•					•		•								
Latin American Studies				•	•			•		•		•	•	•	•		•		•								•		•	•	•
Library Science											•					•	•															•

	Soc. Biblical Lit.	South Carolina	Southern Illinois	S. Methodist	Stanford	SUNY	Syracuse	Teachers	Temple	Tennessee	Texas	Texas A&M	Texas Christian	Texas Tech	Tokyo	Toronto	U.S. Inst. Peace	Upjohn	Utah	Utah State	Vanderbilt	Virginia	Washington	Wash. State	Wayne State	Wesleyan	West Indies	West Virginia	Wilfrid Laurier	Wisconsin	Woodrow Wilson	Yale
Literature		●	●		●	●			●		●	●	●	●	●	●			●		●	●				●	●	●		●		●
Literary Criticism	●	●			●		●			●			●	●	●	●			●	●	●					●	●	●	●	●	●	●
Literary History		●				●			●			●	●	●	●	●			●	●			●					●				●
African																●				●												●
African American		●				●													●	●					●	●	●	●				●
American		●	●		●		●		●	●	●	●	●	●					●	●												●
Asian					●	●						●	●	●							●											●
British		●			●							●	●						●	●							●			●		●
Canadian													●												●					●		
Classical	●					●				●			●																●		●	
Eastern				●									●																			
European		●			●		●					●	●						●	●								●				●
Medieval													●														●		●			●
Renaissance													●																			●
Modern		●	●		●		●		●	●		●	●	●					●	●								●				●
Contemporary		●	●		●		●		●	●		●	●						●									●				●
Mythology					●		●			●			●		●	●	●						●									●
Translations	●				●		●			●		●	●	●					●	●								●	●			●
Maritime Studies		●								●	●	●							●	●												
Mathematics												●																●				●
Medicine			●									●	●						●										●			●
Ethics					●		●					●	●						●						●		●		●			●
History												●	●						●						●		●	●	●			●
Medieval Studies												●	●																●			●
Middle East Studies	●				●	●	●			●		●	●	●	●		●												●		●	●
Military Studies		●	●		●					●	●	●	●	●	●	●													●		●	●
Near Eastern Studies	●				●	●	●			●		●	●	●															●		●	●
Performing Arts			●						●		●		●													●			●			●
Dance																										●			●		●	●
Music						●		●	●		●										●					●		●	●	●		●
Theory & Method			●	●					●				●																●			●
Theatre		●							●							●													●			●
Pacific Studies				●							●	●	●	●									●	●							●	●
Philosophy		●			●	●	●					●	●						●									●		●	●	●
Ethics			●	●	●	●						●	●										●					●		●	●	●
History of Philosophy				●	●	●						●	●	●														●			●	●
Photography		●							●		●		●	●	●								●		●			●		●	●	●
Poetry		●	●			●						●	●						●		●				●	●		●	●	●	●	●
Political Science/Public Affairs			●	●	●	●		●		●		●		●	●	●	●	●			●	●		●			●		●	●	●	●
Popular Culture			●			●				●		●							●	●	●			●	●	●			●	●	●	
Psychiatry												●	●						●										●			●
Psychology					●	●						●	●						●								●		●			●
Public Health												●	●		●				●								●		●			●
Publishing				●								●	●																	●		
Regional Studies		●	●	●	●	●				●		●		●	●	●	●	●	●	●	●		●	●		●	●	●	●	●	● u	●
Religion	●	●			●	●	●		●	●	●					●		●			●			●					●		●	●
Buddhism		●			●	●										●																
Christianity	●	●			●	●										●																
Islam		●			●	●								●	●	●																
Judaism	●	●			●	●						●												●					●			
Science		●							●			●	●	●				●					●	●								●
Biological Sciences		●							●			●	●	●									●				●		●			●
Botany			●			●			●	●		●	●										●			●			●			●
Genetics												●																				●
Earth Sciences					●			●	●	●		●	●					●					●			●			●			●
Geology												●	●					●								●			●			●
Physical Science												●																				●
Astronomy												●																				●
History of Science												●	●								●	●	●					●				●
Slavic Studies												●	●								●									●	●	●
Social Work		●										●	●		●		●		●										●			
Sociology				●		●		●	●			●	●	●	●				●									●	●	●	●	●
Sports			●			●	●	●	●			●	●															●	●	●	●	●
Urban Studies					●			●	●	●		●	●			●					●	●			●			●		●	●	●
Veterinary Sciences												●																				
Women's Studies		●	●		●	●	●		●	●	●		●	●	●	●	●	●	●		●			●	●	●	●		●		●	●

17

PRESSES PUBLISHING JOURNALS

University presses have always been associated with publishing books of merit and distinction. This remains as true today as in the past, but less well appreciated is the extent to which university presses are active in publishing scholarly journals.

Journals form a major part of the publishing program of many presses, and more than half of the association's members produce at least one periodical. University presses publish several hundred scholarly periodicals, including many of the most distinguished in their respective fields.

Each individual press listing also gives the number of journals, if any, that a press publishes and usually lists the titles of journals under the press's editorial program. Many journals are available in both print and electronic versions. For information concerning a specific periodical, readers are advised to consult a copy of the publication before communicating with the press concerned.

The following AAUP member presses publish journals.

University of Akron Press
The University of Alabama Press
American Historical Association
American Psychiatric Press, Inc.
The American School of Classical Studies at Athens
The American University in Cairo Press
Amsterdam University Press
The University of Arkansas Press
Athabasca University Press
Brookings Institution Press
University of California Press
Cambridge University Press
The Catholic University of America Press
The University of Chicago Press
The Chinese University Press
Cork University Press
Duke University Press
Fordham University Press
Gallaudet University Press
Georgetown University Press
University of Hawai'i Press
University of Illinois Press
Indiana University Press
IMF Publications
The Johns Hopkins University Press
The Kent State University Press
Leuven University Press
Lincoln Institute of Land Policy

Liverpool University Press
Marquette University Press
The MIT Press
Medieval Institute Publications
Michigan State University Press
Minnesota Historical Society Press
University of Minnesota Press
Modern Language Association of America
Naval Institute Press
University of Nebraska Press
The University of North Carolina Press
University of North Texas Press
Northern Illinois University Press
Northwestern University Press
University of Ottawa Press
Oxford University Press
University of Pennsylvania Press
Pennsylvania State University Press
Pisa University Press
University of Puerto Rico Press
Purdue University Press
RAND Corporation
RIT Press
The Rockefeller University Press
Society of Biblical Literature
State University of New York Press
University of Texas Press
Texas Tech University Press
University of Toronto Press, Inc.
Washington State University Press
Wayne State University Press
University of the West Indies Press
West Virginia University Press
Wilfrid Laurier University Press
The University of Wisconsin Press

DIRECTORY OF MEMBERS

This section includes a wealth of information on AAUP's member presses, including current street and mailing addresses, phone and fax numbers, email addresses, websites, and social media participation. Most presses also list their sales representatives/distributors for Canada, the UK, and Europe. (Addresses for these representatives are included on page 223)

Each entry contains important information describing that press's editorial program. This includes a list of disciplines published, special series, joint imprints, copublishing programs, and the names of journals published, if any.

Press staff are listed, wherever possible, by the following departments/order: director and administrative staff, acquisitions editorial, electronic publishing, manuscript editorial, design and production, marketing, journals, business, and information systems. In most cases the first person listed within a department is its head. Readers should note, however, that this method of organization is intended to promote ease of use, and is not always indicative of the lines of authority within an individual press.

Information on each press's membership status follows the staff listing. This includes date of press founding, type of membership (full, international, associate, or introductory), year admitted to AAUP, title output for 2012 and 2013 the number of journals published, and the total number of titles currently in print.

Abilene Christian University Press

1626 Campus Court
Abilene, TX 79601

Phone: 325.674.2720
Fax: 325.674.6471

Orders:
Phone: 325.674.2720 or 877.816.4455
Email: orders@acupressbooks.com

Websites and Social Media:
Website: www.abilenechristianuniversitypress.com;
www.leafwoodpublishers.com; www.acupressbookclub.com
Facebook: Facebook.com/ACUPress
Twitter: ACUPress
YouTube: www.youtube.com/user/leafwoodpublishers

Staff

Director & Acquisitions Editor: C. Leonard Allen (325.674.2720; email:
  leonardallen1@cox.net)
Managing Editor: Mary Hardegree (325.674.2761; email: mary.hardegree@acu.edu)
Director of Sales & Operations: Duane Anderson (325.674.2720;
  email: duane.anderson@acu.edu)
Director of Trade Sales & Special Acquisitions: Gary Myers (325.674.2720;
  email: gary.myers@leafwoodpublishers.com)
Marketing Manager: Seth Shaver (325.674.4978; email: seth.shaver@acu.edu)
Publicist: Ryan Self (325.674.4976; email: ryan.self@acu.edu)
Sales Associate: Philip Dosa (325.674.2731; email: phil.dosa@acu.edu)
Office Manager: Lettie Morrow (325.674.2720; email: lettie.morrow@acu.edu)

Full Member

Established: 1984

Title output 2012: 36
Titles currently in print: 491

Admitted to AAUP: 2008 (intro. member)
Admitted to AAUP: 2012 (full member)
Title output 2013: 35

Editorial Program

Religion in American culture; biblical studies and Christian theology; Texas regional studies;
history and theory of higher education (with an emphasis on faith-based education);
international and multicultural studies; literary works.
Special series: Christianity and Literature; Faith-Based Higher Education; History and
Theology of the Stone-Campbell Movement; Texas History and Culture

The University of Akron Press

120 E. Mill Street, Suite 415
Akron, OH 44308

Phone: 330.972.6953
Fax: 330.972.8364

Customer Service/Order Fulfillment:
Phone: 419.281.1802
Toll-free: 800.247.6553
Fax: 419.281.6883
Email: orders@atlasbooks.com

Websites and Social Media:
Website: www.uakron.edu/uapress
Blog: uakronpress.wordpress.com
Facebook: www.facebook.com/UAkronPress
Twitter: uakronpress

Staff

Director & National Marketing: Thomas Bacher (330.972.6202; email: bacher@uakron.edu)
Editorial & Design: Amy Freels (330.972.5342; email: afreels@uakron.edu)
Production & Manufacturing: Carol Slatter (330.972.2795; email: slatter@uakron.edu)

Full Member

Established: 1988

Title output 2012: 15

Titles currently in print: 163

Admitted to AAUP: 1997

Title output 2013: 9

Journals published: 2

Editorial Program

Regional trade books, scholarly books, and poetry, with special interests in applied politics, business, multi-disciplinary studies, and regional culture and history. The Press distributes the publications of Principia Press and The University of Göttingen Press.

Journals: *The International Journal of Ethical Leadership*; *Journal of Economics and Politics*
Special series: Akron Series in Poetry; Akron Series in Poetics; Center for the History of Psychology Series; Critical Editions in Early American Literature; & Law: Legal Issues Across Disciplines; Ohio History and Culture; and Ohio Politics
Other imprints: Buchtel Books and Ringtaw Books

The University of Alabama Press

Street Address:
200 Hackberry Lane
Tuscaloosa, AL 35401

Mailing Address:
Box 870380
Tuscaloosa, AL 35487-0380

Phone: 205.348.5180
Fax: 205.348.9201
Email: (user I.D.)@uapress.ua.edu

Website and Social Media:
Website: www.uapress.ua.edu
Facebook: www.facebook.com/
   UniversityALPress
Twitter: univofalpress

Order Fulfillment:
The University of Alabama Press
Chicago Distribution Center
11030 South Langley Avenue
Chicago, IL 60628
Phone: 773.568.1550
Fax: 773.660.2235

UK/European Distributor:
Eurospan

Canadian Representative:
Codasat Canada

Staff

Director: Curtis L. Clark (205.348.5180; email: cclark)
   Assistant to the Director: Blanche Sarratt (205.348.5180; email: bsarratt)
   Rights and Permissions Coordinator: Claire Lewis Evans (205.348.1561; email: cevans)
Acquisitions Editorial: Dan Waterman, Editor-in-Chief and Acquisitions Editor, Humanities
   (literature and criticism, rhetoric and communication, African American studies, public
   administration, theater, environmental studies) (205.348.5538; email: waterman)
   Senior Acquisitions Editor: Wendi Schnaufer (archaeology, anthropology, ethnohistory,
   Native American studies) (205.348.1568; email: wschnaufer)
   Acquisitions Editors: Elizabeth Motherwell (natural history and the environment)
   (205.348.7108; email: emother); Donna Cox Baker (history) (205.348.7471; email:
   donna.baker@ua.edu)
Electronic Publishing: Claire Lewis Evans, Associate Editor for Digital and Electronic
   Publishing (205.348.1561; email: cevans)
Manuscript Editorial: Vanessa Lynn Rusch, Managing Editor (205.348.9708; email: vrusch)
   Assistant Managing Editor: Joanna Jacobs (205.348.1563; email: jjacobs)
   Project Editor: Jon Berry (205.348.1565; email: jberry)
   Editorial Assistant: Carol Connell (205.348.5183; email: cconnell)
Design and Production: Rick Cook, Production Manager (205.348.1571; email: rcook)
   Designer: Michele Quinn (205.348.1570; email: mquinn)
Marketing: J. D. Wilson, Sales and Marketing Director (205-348-1566; email: jdwilson)
   Sales Manager: Shana Rivers (205.348.9534; email: srrivers)
   Marketing Coordinator: Latasha Watters (205.348.5181; email: lwatters)
Business: Rosalyn Carr, Business Manager (205.348.1567; email: rcarr)
   Accounting Specialist: Allie Harper (205.348.1564; email: aharper)

Full Member

Established: 1945
Title output 2012: 52
Titles currently in print: 1,800

Admitted to AAUP: 1964
Title output 2013: 82
Journals published: 3

Editorial Program

African American studies; American history; American literature and criticism; American religious history; American social and cultural history; anthropology; archaeology, American, Caribbean, southern and historical; creative non-fiction; ethnohistory; Judaic studies; Latin-American studies; linguistics, esp. dialectology; military history; Native American studies; natural history and environmental studies; public administration; regional studies; rhetoric and communication; southern history and culture; sports history; theatre. Submissions are not invited in poetry, fiction, or drama. The Press distributes for Samford University Press.
Journals: *Journal of Community Engagement and Scholarship*; *Theatre History Studies*; *Theatre Symposium*
Special series: Alabama: The Forge of History; American Writers Remembered; Atlantic Crossings; Caribbean Archaeology and Ethnohistory; Classics in Southeastern Archaeology; Contemporary American Indian Studies; Gosse Nature Guides; Jews and Judaism: History and Culture; Library of Alabama Classics; Modern and Contemporary Poetics; The Modern South; NEXUS: New Histories of Science, Technology, the Environment, Agriculture, and Medicine; Public Administration: Criticism and Creativity; Religion and American Culture; Rhetoric, Culture, and Social Critique; Studies in American Literary Realism and Naturalism
Imprints: Fiction Collective 2

University of Alaska Press

Mailing Address:
PO Box 756240
Fairbanks, AK 99775-6240

Street Address:
1760 Westwood Way
Fairbanks, AK 99709

Phone: 888.252.6657; 907.474.5831
Fax: 907.474.5502

Orders:
Chicago Distribution Center
11030 South Langley Avenue
Chicago, IL 60628-3892
Phone: 800.621.2736
Fax: 800.621.8476

Website and Social Media:
Website: www.uaf.edu/uapress
Facebook: www.facebook.com/pages/
   University-of-Alaska-Press/44832289241
Twitter: ualaskapress

Staff

Director: Joan Braddock (907.474.2776; email: jfbraddock@alaska.edu)
Assistant to the Director/Marketing Manager: Amy Simpson (907.474.5832;
   email: amy.simpson@alaska.edu)
Acquisitions Editor: James Engelhardt (907.474.6389; email: james.engelhardt@alaska.edu)
Production Editor: Sue Mitchell (907.474.6413; email: sue.mitchell@alaska.edu)
Marketing Assistant: Dawn Montano (907.474.6544; email: dawn.montano@alaska.edu)

Sales and Distribution Coordinator: Laura Walker (907.474.5345;
    email: laura.walker@alaska.edu)

Full Member

Established: 1967   Admitted to AAUP: 1992
Title output 2012: 20   Title output 2013: 16
Titles currently in print: 234

Editorial Program

The University of Alaska Press is recognized as the premier scholarly publisher of books
relating to Alaska, the Pacific Rim, and circumpolar North. The Press publishes on topics
that include history, politics, and literature; anthropology; Native American studies
and art; science and natural history; energy and conservation; environmental studies;
geography; biography and memoir; humanities and health; poetry and international poetry;
photography; field guides; and children's literature. Submissions are invited in poetry, fiction,
and literary nonfiction and should have a strong connection to Alaska or the circumpolar
North.

The Press distributes publications for the following University of Alaska entities: UA
Foundation; UA Museum of the North; Alaska Sea Grant College Program; Alaska Native
Knowledge Network; and Alaska Native Language Center. The Press also serves as a
distributor for various independent publishers.

Special series: Alaska Literary Series, Alaska Writer Laureate; Classic Reprint; Oral
Biography; and Rasmuson Library Historical Translation

Special imprints: Snowy Owl (trade books)

The University of Alberta Press

Ring House 2   Canadian Distributor:
Edmonton, AB T6G 2E1   GTW Limited
Canada   34 Armstrong Avenue
                                            Georgetown ON L7G 4R9 Canada
Phone: 780.492.3662   Phone: 905.873.9781
Fax: 780.492.0719   Fax: 905.873.6170
Email: (user I.D.)@ualberta.ca   Email: orders@gtwcanada.com

Website and Social Media: US Distributor:
Website: www.uap.ualberta.ca   Wayne State University Press
Blog: holeinthebucket.wordpress.com   The Leonard N. Simons Building
Facebook: www.facebook.com/pages/   4809 Woodward Avenue
    University-of-Alberta-Press-UAP/   Detroit MI 48201-1309
    18764314500   Phone: 800.978.7323
Twitter: UAlbertaPress   313.577.6120
                                            Fax: 313.577.6131
UK/European Distributor: Email: bookorders@wayne.edu
Gazelle Academic

Staff

Director: Linda D. Cameron (780.492.0717; email: linda.cameron)
    Administrative Assistant: Sharon Wilson (780.492.3662; email: sharon.wilson)

Senior Editor (Acquisitions): Peter Midgley (780.492.7714; email: peter.midgley)
Editor (Production): Mary Lou Roy (780.492.9488; email: marylou.roy)
Digital Coordinator: Duncan Turner (780.492.4945; email: duncan.turner)
Design/Production: Alan Brownoff (780.492.8285; email: alan.brownoff)
Sales & Marketing Manager: Cathie Crooks (780.492.5820; email: cathie.crooks)
  Sales/Marketing Assistant: Monika Igali (780.492.7493; email: monika.igali)

Full Member

Established: 1969   Admitted to AAUP: 1983
Title output 2012: 17   Title output 2013: 16
Titles currently in print: 412

Editorial Program

The University of Alberta Press (UAP) publishes in the areas of Canadian biography, history, literature, natural history, regional interest, travel narratives, and reference books.
Special series: Mountain Cairns—a series on the history and culture of the Canadian Rockies; Wayfarer—a literary travel series

American Historical Association

400 A Street, S.E.
Washington, DC 20003-3889

Phone: 202.544.2422
Fax: 202.544.8307
Email: aha@historians.org

Website and Social Media:
Website: www.historians.org
Blog: blog.historians.org
Facebook: www.facebook.com/AHAhistorians
Twitter: AHAhistorians

Staff

Executive Director: James R. Grossman (202.544.2422 ext. 100; email:
  jgrossman@historians.org)
Controller: Randy Norell (202.544.2422 ext.109; email: rnorell@historians.org)
Editor, American Historical Review: Robert A. Schneider (812.855.7609;
  email: raschnei@indiana.edu)
Director of Scholary Communications and Digital Initiatives: Seth Denbo (ext. 118;
  email: sdenbo@historians.org)
Internet Projects Coordinator: Vernon Horn (202.544.2422 ext. 122;
  email: vhorn@historians.org)
Editor, *Perspectives on History*: Pillarisetti Sudhir (202.544.2422 ext. 121;
  email: psudhir@historians.org)
Production Manager: Christian A. Hale (202.544.2422 ext. 133;

email: chale@historians.org)
Publication Sales: Matt Burruss (202.544.2422 ext. 108; email: mburruss@historians.org)

Associate Member

Established: 1884

Admitted to AAUP: 2005

Title output 2012: NR

Title output 2013: NR

Titles currently in print: 102

Journals published: 2

Editorial Program

The AHA publishes a wide variety of periodical, annual, and other publications of service and interest to the historical profession and the general public. Primary publications are the journals, the *American Historical Review* (published by the Journals Division of the University of Chicago Press) and the monthly news magazine *Perspectives on History*. The Association's other major publication is the annual Directory of History Departments, Historical Organizations, and Historians. Beyond that, the AHA publishes a wide range of topical booklets on the practice of history and historical topics. On the Web, the Association publishes articles, directories, and documentary materials. The AHA also maintains a daily blog for those interested in the study of the past and the practice of history, and a wiki on archives for history researchers.

American Psychiatric Publishing

1000 Wilson Blvd., Suite 1825
Arlington, VA 22209

Orders:
Phone: 800.368.5777; 703.907.7322
Fax: 703.907.1091

Phone: 703.907.7322
Fax: 703.907.1092
Email: appi@psych.org
Indiv: (user I.D.)@psych.org

Website and Social Media:
Website: www.appi.org
Facebook: www.facebook.com/AmericanPsychiatricPublishing
Twitter: APP_Publishing

European Distributor:
NBN International

Canadian Representative:
Login Brothers Canada

Staff

Publisher: Rebecca D. Rinehart (703.907.7876; email: rrinehart)
　Executive Assistant: Bessie Jones (703.907.7892; email: bjones)
Editor-in-Chief: Robert E. Hales (703.907.7892)
Editorial Director, Books: John McDuffie (703.907.7871; email: jmcduffie)
Book Acquisitions Coordinator: Bessie Jones (703.907.7892; email: bjones)
e-Publishing Manager: Melissa Coates (703.907.7870; email: mcoates)
Managing Editor, Books: Greg Kuny (703.907.7872; email: gkuny)
Director of Production: Andrew Wilson (703.907.7882; email: awilson)
Director of Marketing and Sales: Patrick Hansard (703.907.7893; email: phansard)

Associate Director of Marketing: Christie Couture (703.907.7877; email: ccouture)
Editorial Director, Journals: Michael Roy (703.907.7894; email: mroy)
Director of Finance and Business Operations: Kathy Stein (703.907.7875; email: kstein)

Associate Member

Established: 1981   Admitted to AAUP: 1993
Title output 2012: 21   Title output 2013: 27
Titles currently in print: 745   Journals published: 5

Editorial Program

Clinical books and monographs in psychiatry and related fields; research monographs;
medical textbooks; study guides; nonfiction trade books in mental health; annual review; and
journals.
Journals: *American Journal of Psychiatry*; *FOCUS*; *Journal of Neuropsychiatry*; *Psychiatric
News*; *Psychiatric Services*
Special series: Concise Guides, Clinical Manuals
Special imprints: American Psychiatric Association; Group for the Advancement of
Psychiatry; American Psychopathological Association
Copublishing programs: The World Health Organization

The American School of Classical Studies at Athens

Publications Office: Orders:
6–8 Charlton Street   Phone: 800.791.9354
Princeton, NJ 08540-5232   Fax: 860.945.9468
Phone: 609.683.0800   Email: queries@dbbconline.com
Fax: 609.924-0578
Email: areinhard@ascsa.org
Website: www.ascsa.edu.gr/publications

UK Representative: Canadian Representative:
Oxbow Books   David Brown Book Company

Staff

Director of Publications: Andrew Reinhard (ext. 21; email: areinhard@ascsa.org)
Managing Editor: Carol A. Stein (ext. 16; email: castein@ascsa.org)
Editor of Hesperia: Susan Lupack (ext. 22; email: slupack@ascsa.org)
Editor of Monographs: Michael A. Fitzgerald (ext. 17; email: maf@ascsa.org)
Production Manager: Sarah George Figueira (ext. 18; email: sgf@ascsa.org)
Print Designer and Website Managing Editor: Mary Jane Gavenda (ext. 20;
    email: mjgavenda@ascsa.org)

Associate Member

Established: 1881

Title output 2012: 4
Titles currently in print: 140

Admitted to AAUP: 2008 (intro. member)
Admitted to AAUP: 2012 (assoc. member)
Title output 2013: 4
Journals published: 2

Editorial Program

All fields of Greek archaeology, art, epigraphy, history, materials science, ethnography, and literature, from earliest prehistoric times onward. A particular focus is on publishing the work of the American School of Classical Studies at Athens, a research and teaching institutions founded in 1881 and based in Athens, Greece.

Journals: *Hesperia, The New Griffon*

Special series: Agora Picture Books; Ancient Art and Architecture in Context; The Argive Heraion; The Athenian Agora; Corinth; Gennadeion Monographs; Hesperia Supplements; Isthmia; Lerna

The American University in Cairo Press

113 Kasr el Aini Street
PO Box 2511
Cairo, Egypt 11511

Phone: 202.2797.6926
Fax: 202.2794.1440
Email: aucpress@aucegypt.edu
Indiv: (user I.D.)@aucegypt.edu

US Office:
420 Fifth Avenue
New York, NY 10018-2729

Phone: 212.730.8800
Fax: 212.730.1600

Website and Social Media:
Website: www.aucpress.com
Facebook: www.facebook.com/pages/Cairo-Egypt/The-American-University-in-Cairo-Press-
   AUC-Press/26100067607

North American Distributor:
Oxford University Press
2001 Evans Road
Cary, NC 27513
Phone: 800.445.9714
Email: custserv.us@oup.com

UK and European Distributor:
Eurospan

Staff

Director: Nigel Fletcher-Jones (202.2797.6888; email: nigel)
   Assistant to the Director: Tawhida Sherif (202.2797.6926; email: tina)
Associate Director for Editorial Programs: Neil Hewison (202.2797.6892;
   email: rnh)
Senior Development Editor: Randi Danforth (202.2797.6642; email: randi)
Managing Editor: Nadia Naqib (202.2797.6887; email: nnaqib)
Production Manager: Miriam Fahmy (202.2797.6937; email: miriam)

Associate Director of Sales and Marketing: Trevor Naylor (202.2797.5759;
   email: trevornaylor)
Sales Manager: Tahany el-Shammaa (202.2797.6985; email: tahanys)
Promotion Manager: Nabila Akl (202.2797.6896; email: akl)
Contracts and Rights Manager: Yasmine Gado (202.2797.6820; email: yasmine.gado)
   Assistant Publishing Manager (New York City): Tarek El-Elaimy (212.730.8800; email:
   telaimy)

International Member

Established: 1960	Admitted to AAUP: 1986
Title output 2011: 100	Title output 2012: 70
Titles currently in print: 1,500	Journals published: 2

Editorial Program
The Press is recognized as the leading English-language publisher in the Middle East, and
publishes a wide range of scholarly monographs, texts and reference works, and general
interest books on ancient and modern Egypt and the Middle East, as well as Arabic literature
in English translation, most notably the works of Egyptian Nobel laureate Naguib Mahfouz.
Journals: *Alif: Journal of Comparative Poetics; Cairo Papers in Social Science*
Copublishing programs: Numerous copublishing programs with US, UK, and European
universities and trade publishers

Amsterdam University Press

Herengracht 221
1016 BG Amsterdam
The Netherlands

Phone: +31.20.4200050
Fax: +31.20.4203214
Email: info@aup.nl
Indiv: (user I.D.)@aup.nl

Website and Social Media:
Website: www.aup.nl
Facebook: www.facebook.com/
   AmsterdamUPress
Twitter: AmsterdamUPress

US and Canadian Sales Representative:
University of Chicago Press
Phone: 773.702.7700

Australia/New Zealand Representative:
Footprint Books Pty Ltd.
Phone: +61(0) 2 9997 3973

China and Hong Kong Representative:
China Publishers Service
Phone: +86 852 24911 436

Japan Representative:
Tim Burland
Phone: +81(0)3-3424 8977

India Representative:
MAYA Publishers PVT Ltd.
Phone: + 91 9811 555 197

Staff

Director: Jan-Peter Wissink (email: wissink)

Finance and Administration: Judith van Jaarsveld (email: jvanJaarsveld@holding.uva.nl); Daniela Pinnone (email: d.pinnone)

Senior Acquisitions Editor: Simon Forde (head of Acquisitions) (email: s.forde)

Acquisition Editors: Maaike Groot (humanities) (email: m.groot); Saskia Gieling (Asian studies and social sciences) (email: s.gieling); Jeroen Sondervan (film & media) (email: j.sondervan); Inge van der Bijl (email: i.vd.bijl)

Editorial Assistant: Atie Vogelenzang (email: a.vogelenzangdejong)

Project Manager Digital Publications: Ronald Snijder (email: r.snijder)

Manuscript Editorial: Chantal Nicolaes, Chief Editor (email: c.nicolaes); Jaap Wagenaar (social sciences) (email: j.wagenaar)

Head of Production: Rob Wadman (email: r.wadman)

Production: Paul Penman (email: p.l.penman)

Head of International Sales and Marketing: Magdalena Hernas (email: m.hernas)

Orders: Michiel van der Drift (email: m.vander.drift)

Marketing & PR: Ebisse Rouw (email: e.rouw)

International Marketing & PR: Vanessa de Bueger (email: v.de.bueger); Valeria Mecozzi (email: v.mecozzi)

Office Manager: Jacqueline Wippo (email: info@aup.nl)

International Member

Established: 1992

Title output 2012: 140

Titles currently in print: 1,050

Admitted to AAUP: 2000

Title output 2013: 215

Journals published: 10

Editorial Program

Scholarly and trade titles (English and Dutch language) in archaeology; art and art history; Asian studies; classical studies; cultural studies; film and television studies; history; language and linguistics; law; literature; music; philosophy; political science; social sciences; regional titles. Textbooks for universities and higher education.

Journals: *Mens & Maatschappij (People and Society); Journal of Archeology in the Low Countries (JALC); Internationale Neerlandistiek (International Dutch Studies); Tijdschrift voor Genderstudies (Journal for Gender Studies); Tijdschrift voor Zeegeschiedenis (Journal of Maritime History); Tijdschrift voor Sociale en Economische Geschiedenis (Journal of Social and Economic History); Taal & Tongval (Language and Dialects); International Journal for History, Culture and Modernity; Journal of Comparative Migration Studies; NECSUS, European Journal for Media Studies*

English series: American Studies; Amsterdam Archaeological Studies; Amsterdam Studies in the Golden Age; Asia Studies; Care & Welfare; Changing Welfare States; European Film Studies - The Key Debates; Film Culture in Transition; Islam & Society; Landscape & Heritage Research; Law, Governance and Development; MediaMatters; Studies In Language and Literature; German series: Justiz und NS-Verbrechen (A collection of postwar German trial judgments concerning Nazi crimes of a homicidal nature committed during World War II)

Copublications: Princeton University Press (USA); University of California Press (USA); MIT Press (USA); Thames & Hudson (UK); Brandeis University Press (USA); Actes Sud (France); Lannoo Uitgeverij (Belgium); Uitgeverij Davidsfonds (Belgium); Mercatorfonds (Belgium)

The University of Arizona Press

1510 E. University, 5th Floor
P.O Box 210055
Tucson, AZ 85721-0055

Orders:
Chicago Distribution Center
Phone: 800.621.2736
Email: orders@press.uchicago.edu

Phone: 520.621.1441
Fax: 520.621.8899
Email: uapress@uapress.arizona.edu
Indiv: (user I.D.)@uapress.arizona.edu

Canadian Representative:
University of British Columbia Press

European Representative:
Eurospan

Website and Social Media:
Website: www.uapress.arizona.edu
Facebook: www.facebook.com/AZpress
Twitter: AZpress

Staff

Director: Kathryn M. Conrad (520.621.1441; email: kconrad)
  Assistant to the Director/Permissions: Julia Balestracci (520.621.3911; email: julia)
Editor-in-Chief: Allyson Carter (anthropology, archaeology, ecology, natural history, Native American studies, Latin American studies, environmental science, astronomy and space sciences, geography, regional) (520.621.3186; email: acarter)
  Acquiring Editor: Kristen Buckles (Native American literature and studies, Latin American studies, Border studies, Chicano/Latino studies and literature, environmental and western history, regional) (520.621.7921; email: kbuckles)
  Editorial Assistant: Scott DeHerrera (520.621.5919; email: scott)
Editing, Design, and Production Manager: Sylvia Mendoza (520.621.5916)
  Production Editor: Amanda Piell (520.621.5915; email: apiell)
  Production Coordinator: Miriam Warren (520.621.7916; email: mwarren)
  Book Designer: Leigh McDonald (520.621.5824; email: lmcdonald)
Marketing Manager: Abby Mogollon (520.621.8656; email: amogollon)
  Publicity Manager: Holly Schaffer (520.621.3920; email: hollys)
  Sales and Exhibits Manager: Lela Scott MacNeil (520.621.4913; email: lela)
Senior Accountant: Sarah Trotta (520.621.0064; email: trottas)
  Accounts Payable: Melissa Sotomayor (520.626.3041; email: msotomayor)

Full Member

Established: 1959
Title output 2012: 71
Titles currently in print: 1,345

Admitted to AAUP: 1962
Title output 2013: 60

Editorial Program

Specialties strongly identified with the universities in the state and other significant nonfiction of regional and national interest. Especially strong fields include the American West; anthropology and archaeology; Chicano/Latino studies and literature; ecology and environmental sciences; environmental studies and literature; Latin American studies; Native American studies and literature; space sciences; western and environmental history.

The Press also distributes titles from Ironwood Press; the Arizona State Museum; Statistical Research, Inc.; SWCA, Inc.; Northern Arizona University Bilby Research Center; Center for Desert Archaeology; Center for Sustainable Environments; Crow Canyon Archaeological Center; The University of Arizona Critical Languages Program; U.S. Department of Interior Bureau of Reclamation; Grand Canyon Association; and Oregon State University Press.

Special series: Amerind Studies in Archaeology; Anthropological Papers of the University of Arizona; The Archaeology of Colonialism in Native North America; Arizona Sonora Desert Museum Studies In Natural History; Camino del Sol; Critical Green Engagements; Critical Issues in Indigenous Studies; First Peoples; La Frontera: People and Their Environments in the U.S.-Mexico Border; Latin American Landscapes; The Mexican American Experience; Modern American West; Native Peoples of the Americas; Society, Environment, and Place; Southwest Center Series; Space Science; Sun Tracks; Women's Western Voices

The University of Arkansas Press

McIlroy House
105 North McIlroy Avenue
Fayetteville, AR 72701-1201

Phone: 800.626.0090; 479.575.3246
Fax: 479.575.6044
Email: uapress@uark.edu
Indiv: (user I.D.)@uark.edu

Website and Social Media:
Website: www.uapress.com
Blog: uapress.blogspot.com
Facebook: www.facebook.com/UARKPRESS
Twitter: uarkpress

Customer Service/Orders:
1580 West Mitchell Street
Fayetteville, AR 72701
Phone: 800.626.0090
Fax: 479.575.5538

Canadian Representative:
Scholarly Book Services

UK/European Representative:
Eurospan

Staff
Director and Editor: Lawrence J. Malley (479.575.3096; email: lmalley)
Acquisitions Editor: Julie Watkins (479.575.7242; email: jewatki)
   Editorial Assistant: Tyler Lail (479.575.4724; email: tlailwh)
Manuscript Editorial, Design, and Production: Brian King, Assistant Director and Director of Editorial, Design, and Production (479.575.6780; email: brking)
   Project Editor: David-Scott Cunningham (479.575.5767; email: dscunni)
Marketing: Melissa King, Director of Marketing and Sales (479.575.6657; email: mak001)
   Assistant Marketing Manager: Charlie Shields (479.575.7258; email: cmoss)
Business: Mike W. Bieker, Assistant Director and Business Manager (479.575.3859; email: mbieker)
   Assistant Business Manager: Sam Ridge (479.575.3459; email: sridge)
   Ordering & Customer Service: Kathleen Z. Willis (479.575.3634; email: kwillis)
UAP Distribution Services:
Distribution Services Manager: Mike W. Bieker (479.575.3859; email: mbieker)
Distribution Services Operations Manager: Sam Ridge (479.575.3459; email: sridge)

Full Member

Established: 1980

Title output 2012: 15

Titles currently in print: 612

Admitted to AAUP: 1984

Title output 2013: 22

Journals published: 1

Editorial Program

African American history; civil rights studies; Civil War studies; cultural studies; history; Middle East studies; regional studies; southern history; and women's studies. Submissions are not invited in general fiction, textbooks, or children's books. The Press also publishes the winner and three finalists of the Miller Williams Arkanas Poetry Prize competition.

Journal: *Philosophical Topics*

Special series: Arkansas Classics; The Carter Collection; The Civil War in the West; The Histories of Arkansas; Portraits of Conflict; Arkansas Poetry; The William Gilmore Simms Collection; World of Voices

Athabasca University Press

Peace Hills Trust Tower

1200, 10011 – 109 Street

Edmonton, AB T5J 3S8 Canada

Phone: 780.497.3412

Fax: 780.421.3298

Email: aupress@athabascau.ca

Website and Social Media:

Website: www.aupress.ca

Facebook: www.facebook.com/AUPress1

Twitter: au_press

YouTube: www.youtube.com/user/aupresst

Blog: aupressblog.com

Canadian Orders:

University of British Columbia Press

c/o UTP Distribution

Phone: 800.565.9523/416.667.7791

Fax: 800.221.9985/416.667.7832

Email: utpbooks@utpress.utoronto.ca

US Orders:

University of Washington Press

c/o Hopkins Fulfillment Service

Phone: 800.537.5487/410.516.6965

Fax: 410.516.6998

Email: hfscustserv@press.jhu.edu

UK, Europe, Middle East, & Africa Orders:

Eurospan

c/o Turpin Distribution

Phone: 44.0(20).1767-604972

Email: eurospan@turpin-distribution.com

Staff

Acting Director: Kathy Killoh (780.421.2528; email: kathyk@athabascau.ca)

Administrative Assistant: Rosie Pucci (780.497.3412; email: rosiep@athabascau.ca)

Senior Editor: Pamela Holway (780.428.7278; email: pholway@athabascau.ca)

Associate Editor: Connor Houlihan (780.392.1204; email: connorh@athabascau.ca)

Journals and Digital Coordinator: Kathy Killoh (780.421.2528;
  email: kathyk@athabascau.ca)

Marketing & Production Coordinator: Megan Hall (780.428.2067;
  email: mhall@athabascau.ca)

Digital Design Technician: Sergiy Kozakov (780.421.5846; email: sergiyk@athabascau.ca)
IT Systems Administrator/Coordinator: Shubhash Wasti (780.421.2526;
  email: shubhash@athabascau.ca)
Fulfillment Administrator: Linda Kadis (780.421.5062; email: lkadis@athabascau.ca)

Full Member

Established: 2007	Admitted to AAUP: 2008 (intro. member)
	Admitted to AAUP: 2011 (full member)
Title output 2012: 13	Title output 2013: 19
Titles currently in print: 84	Journals published: 7

Editorial Program

Our geographical focus is on Canada, the North American West, and the Circumpolar North. One of our mandates is to publish innovative and experimental works (in both fiction and non-fiction) that challenge established canons, subjects, and formats. As we are dedicated to making AU Press publications accessible to a broad readership through open access technologies, we cultivate the areas of open, distance, and e-learning. We promote forms such as diary, memoir, and oral history. AU Press also publishes websites (under its imprint) with content that has scholarly parameters and standards, especially grey literature on distance learning; and primary sources in labour studies, Métis and Aboriginal Studies, gender studies, and the environment.

Journals: *The Canadian Journal of Learning and Technology (CJLT)*; *Canadian Folk Music/ Musique folklorique canadienne*; *International Review of Research in Open and Distance Learning (IRRODL)*; *The Journal of Distance Education*; *Journal of Research Practice (JRP)*; *Labour/Le Travail*; *Oral History Forum d'histoire orale*; *The Trumpeter*

Web-based Publications: Aurora; Canadian Theatre Encyclopedia

Special series: Canadian Plays; Cultural Dialectics; Fabriks: Studies in the Working Class; Global Peace Studies; Issues in Distance Education; Mingling Voices; OPEL: Open Paths to Enriched Learning; Our Lives: Diary, Memoir, and Letters; The West Unbound: Social and Cultural Studies; Working Canadians: Books from the CCLH

Baylor University Press

Street Address:
1920 South 4th Street
Waco, TX 76706-2529

Mailing Address:
One Bear Place # 97363
Waco, TX 76798-7363

Phone: 254.710.3164
Fax: 254.710.3440
Email: (user I.D.)@baylor.edu

Orders:
Baylor University Press
c/o Hopkins Fulfillment Service
P.O. Box 50370
Baltimore, MD 21211-4370
Phone: 800.537.5487 or 410.516.6956
Fax: 410.516.6998

Website and Social Media:
Website: www.baylorpress.com
Facebook: www.facebook.com/BaylorPress
Twitter: Baylor_Press
YouTube: www.youtube.com/user/baylorpress
Instagram: baylor_press

UK Representative:
Gazelle

Staff

Director: Carey Newman (254.710.3522; email: carey_newman)
Design and Production: Diane E. Smith, Associate Director/Production Manager
  (254.710.2563; email: diane_smith)
    Associate Production Manager and Electronic Publishing Manager: Jenny Hunt
    (254.710.3236; email: jenny_hunt)
Sales and Publicity Manager: David Aycock (254.710.1465; email: david_aycock)
Business: Karla Garrett, Finance and Operations Manager (254.710.1285;
  email: karla_garrett)

Full Member

Established: 1897   Admitted to AAUP: 2007
Title output 2012: 40   Title output 2013: 35
Titles currently in print: 355

Editorial Program

Established in 1897, Baylor University Press publishes forty new titles each year in the
following academic areas: religion & public life; rhetoric & religion; religious studies
& theology; religion & literature; religion & philosophy; religion & higher education.
In accordance with Baylor University's mission, the Press strives to serve the academic
community by producing works of excellent quality that integrate faith and understanding.
Special series: Baylor Handbook on the Greek New Testament; Baylor Handbook on
the Hebrew Bible; Charles Edmondson Historical Lectures; Documents of Anglophone
Christianity Series; The Making of the Christian Imagination; New Perspectives on Latina/o
Religion; Provost's Series; Studies in Christianity and Literature; Studies in Religion and
Higher Education; Studies in Rhetoric and Religion; World Christianity

Beacon Press

Mailing Address:
25 Beacon Street
Boston, MA 02108-2892

Phone: 617.742.2110
Fax: 617.723.3097
Marketing/Publicity/Subsidiary
Rights Fax: 617.742.2290
Email: (user I.D.)@beacon.org

Website and Social Media:
Website: www.beacon.org
Blog: www.beaconbroadside.com
Facebook: www.facebook.com/beaconpress
Twitter: BeaconPressBks
YouTube: www.youtube.com/user/BeaconBroadside

Street Address:
41 Mt. Vernon Street
Boston, MA 02108

UK Representative:
Publishers Group UK

Canadian Representative:
Random House Canada

Staff

Director: Helene Atwan (email: hatwan)
  Assistant to the Director: Alice Li (email: ali)
Editorial: Gayatri Patnaik, Executive Editor (email: gpatnaik)
  Executive Editor: Amy Caldwell (email: acaldwell)
  Editor: Alexis Rizzuto (email: arizzuto)
  Associate Editor: Joanna Green (email: jgreen)
Production: Marcy Barnes, Production Director & Digital Publishing Director (email: mbarnes)
  Managing Editor: Susan Lumenello (email: slumenello)
  Creative Director: Bob Kosturko (email: bkosturko)
Marketing: Tom Hallock, Associate Publisher, Director of Sales, Marketing, and SubRights (email: thallock)
  Publicity Director: Pamela MacColl (email: pmaccoll)
  Publicist: Caitlin Meyer (email: cmeyer)
  Sales & Marketing Associate: Jenah Blitz-Stoehr (email: jblitzstoehr)
  Rights & Permissions Associate: Ryan Mita (email: rmita)
Business: Mike Lindgren, Chief Financial Officer (email: mlindgren)
  Director of Business Operations: Greg Kanter (email: gkanter)
  Accounts Payable/Receivable: Irene Huang (email: ihuang)

Associate Member

Established: 1854
Title output 2012: 39
(64 with paperback reprints)
Titles currently in print: 956)

Admitted to AAUP: 1988
Title output 2013: 61

Editorial Program

Beacon Press, the non-profit publisher affiliated with the Unitarian Universalist Association, publishes works for the general reader, specializing in African American, Native American, and Asian American studies; anthropology; current affairs; education; environmental studies; gay and lesbian studies; nature writing; personal essays; philosophy; regional books; religion; and women's studies.

Special series and joint publishing programs: The Beacon Press/Simmons College Series on Race, Education, and Democracy; The Concord Nature Library; The King Legacy; Queer Action/Queer Ideas

University of British Columbia Press

2029 West Mall
University of British Columbia
Vancouver, BC V6T 1Z2 Canada

Phone: 604.822.5959
Toll-free (in Canada): 877.377.9378
Fax: 604.822.6083
Toll-free (in Canada): 800.668.0821
Email: (user I.D.)@ubcpress.ca

Website and Social Media:
Website: www.ubcpress.ca
Twitter: UBCPress
Facebook: UBC Press

UK Distributor:
Eurospan

Canadian Orders and Returns:
University of Toronto Press
5201 Dufferin Place
Toronto, ON M3H 5T8 Canada
Phone: 416.667.7791
Fax: 416.667.7832
Email: utpbooks@utpress.utoronto.ca

US Orders and Returns:
University of Washington Press
C/O Hopkins Fulfillment Service
PO Box 50370
Baltimore, MD 21211-4370 USA
Phone: 800.537.5487; 410.516.6956
Email: hfscustserv@press.jhu.edu

Staff

Director: Melissa Pitts (604.822.6376; email: pitts)
  Assistant to the Publisher: Valerie Nair (604.822.4161; email: nair)
Acquisitions Editorial: Emily Andrew (Toronto) (Asian studies, communications, military history, political science and political philosophy, political and diplomatic history, sociology, transnational and multicultural studies) (416.429.0322; email: andrew); Randy Schmidt (Kelowna) (environmental studies, forestry, geography, law and society, sustainable development, urban studies and planning) (250.764.4761; email: schmidt); Darcy Cullen (Canadian history and regional history [BC and other regions], food studies, health studies, Native studies, Northern and Arctic studies, sexuality studies) (604.822.5744; email: cullen)
Production Editorial: Holly Keller, Assistant Director—Production and Editorial Services (604.822.4545; email: keller)
  Editors: Ann Macklem (604.822.0093; email: macklem); Lesley Erickson (604.822.4548; email: lerickson); Megan Brand (604.822.5885; email: brand)

Marketing: Laraine Coates, Marketing and Operations (604.822.6486; email: coates)
  Academic Sales and Marketing Manager: Harmony Johnson (604.822.1978; email: johnson)
  Bibliographic Data Coordinator: Murray Tong (604.822.5790; email: tong)
  Exhibits, Reviews, and Awards Manager: Kerry Kilmartin (604.822.8244; email: kilmartin)
  Advertising Manager: Alexa Love (604.822.4546; email: love)
Agency Marketing Coordinator: Emily Rielly (604.822.8226; email: rielly)
  Director Emeritus: Peter Milroy (email: milroy)
  Marketing Assistant: Megan Malashewsky (604.822.5959; email: malashewsky)
Finance/Distribution: Devni De Silva, Finance Manager (604.822.8938; email: desilva)
  Finance Assistant: Caitlin Kopperson (604.822.5370; email: kopperson)
  Inventory, Data, and Distribution Manager: Shari Martin (604.822.1221; email: martin)

Full Member

Established: 1971   Admitted to AAUP: 1972
Title output 2012: 52   Title output 2013: 59
Titles currently in print: 922

Editorial Program

Scholarly books and serious nonfiction, with special interest in First Nations culture politics and linguistics, Canadian history, environmental history and policy, resources, Canadian politics, globalization, multiculturalism, urban planning, Asian studies, and sexuality and gender studies

Special series: Asia Pacific Legal Culture and Globalization Series; Asian Religions and Society; Brenda and David McLean Canadian Series; Canada and International Relations; Canadian Democratic Audit; Canadian Yearbook of International Law; Contemporary Chinese Studies; Ethnicity and Democratic Governance Series; Equality|Security|Community; First Nations Languages; Globalization and Autonomy; Law and Society; Legal Dimensions; Nature|History|Society; Pacific Rim Archaeology; Pioneers of British Columbia; Sexuality Studies; Studies in Canadian Military History; Sustainability and the Environment; Urbanization in Asia; Women and Indigenous Studies Series

Brookings Institution Press

1775 Massachusetts Avenue, N.W.
Washington, DC 20036-2103

Phone: 202.536.3600
Email: bibooks@brookings.edu
Indiv: firstinitiallastname@brookings.edu

Website and Social Media:
Website: www.brookings.edu/press
Facebook: www.facebook.com/brookingspress
Twitter: BrookingsInst

UK Representative:
University Presses Marketing

Customer Service/Orders:
Hopkins Fulfillment Service
P.O. Box 50370
Baltimore, MD 21211-4370
Phone: 800.537.5487 or 410.516.6956
Fax: 410.516.6998

Warehouse (RETURNS ONLY):
Brookings Press—Book Returns
c/o Maple Press Distribution
704 Legionaire Drive
Fredericksburg, PA 17026

Canadian Representative:
UBC Press

Staff

Director: Valentina Kalk (202.536.3629)
Director of Finance and Administration: Renuka Deonarain (202.536.3637)
Electronic Media Coordinator: Steven Roman (202.536.3609)
Rights Coordinator & Assistant to the Director: Kristen Harrison (202.536.3604)
Associate Director/Senior Acquisitions Editor: Christopher Kelaher (202.536.3606)
Manuscript Editorial: Janet Walker, Managing Editor (202.536.3613)
Editor: Eileen Hughes (202.536.3614)
Design and Production: Lawrence Converse, Production Manager (202.536.3618)
Art Coordinator: Susan Woollen (202.536.3619)
Marketing Director: Rebecca Campany (202.797.2492)
Direct Marketing Manager: Thomas Parsons (202.536.3610)
Publicity: Natalie Fullenkamp (202.536.3607)
Exhibits and Marketing Specialist: Anthony Nathe (202.536.3608)
Distribution Services Manager: Terrence Melvin (202.797.6429)
Distribution Services Assistant: Frederick King (202.797.6311)

Full Member

Established: 1916
Title output 2012: 38
Titles currently in print: 1,261

Admitted to AAUP: 1958
Title output 2013: 29
Journals published: 2

Editorial Program

Economics, government, and international affairs, with emphasis on the implications
for public policy of current and emerging issues confronting American society. The Press
publishes books written by the Institution's resident and associated staff members employed
or commissioned to carry out projects defined by the directors of Brookings research
programs, as well as manuscripts acquired from outside authors.

The Institution also publishes Brookings Papers on Economic Activity and Economia
(copublished with the Latin American and Caribbean Economic Association).

The Press distributes publications for organizations such as the American Chamber of Commerce to the European Union, the Bertelsmann Foundation, the Carnegie Endowment for International Peace, the Centre for Economic Policy Research, the Century Foundation Press, Economica, the Center for Global Development, the Institute for the Study of the Americas, the International Labor Organization, the Japan Center for International Exchange, the OECD, the Royal Institute for International Affairs, the Trilateral Commission, the United Nations University Press, and the World Trade Organization.

University of Calgary Press

2500 University Drive N.W.
Calgary, AB T2N 1N4 Canada

Phone: 403.220.7578
Fax: 403.282.0085
Email: ucpress@ucalgary.ca
Indiv: (user I.D.)@ucalgary.ca

Website and Social Media:
Website: www.uofcpress.com
Facebook: www.facebook.com/UCalgaryPress

US Orders:
Michigan State University Press
c/o Chicago Distribution Center
11030 South Langley Ave
Chicago, IL 60628
Phone: 800.621.2736
Fax: 800.621.8476
Email: orders@press.chicago.edu

Canadian Distribution & Orders:
uniPRESSES
c/o Georgetown Terminal Warehouses
34 Armstrong Avenue
Georgetown, ON L7G 4R9 Canada
Phone (toll-free): 877.864.8477
Fax (toll-free): 877.864.4272
Email: orders@gtwcanada.com

UK/European Distributor:
Gazelle Book Services, Ltd.

Staff
Interim Director: John Wright (403.220.3511; email: jpwright)
Operations Manager: Michelle Lipp (403.220.2606; email: mlipp)
Editorial Secretary & Marketing Associate: Karen Buttner (403.220.3979; email: kbuttner)
Senior Editor (Acquisitions) & Project Coordinator: John King (403.220.4208; email: jking)
Graphic Design & Print Management: Melina Cusano (403.220.8719; email: mcusano)

Full Member
Established: 1981

Title output 2012: 5
Titles currently in print: 324

Admitted to AAUP: 2002
(Affiliate member: 1992-95)
Title output 2013: 9

Editorial Program
University of Calgary Press publishes books that explore a sense of place in western Canada, the relevance of history in our lives, and our impact on the world around us. We disseminate research that makes us think, that moves the conversation forward. To ensure that the research of our authors is accessible to its widest possible audience, we strive to make

available as many of our publications as possible as open-access ebooks.
Publishing interests include: contemporary Canadian art & architecture; African studies;
energy, environment & ecology; Latin American & Caribbean studies; Western Canada;
Aboriginal and Métis studies; Arctic and Northern studies; film & television; history &
environment; women's studies; and public policy.
Special series: Africa: Missing Voices; Art in Profile; Beyond Boundaries (Canadian Defence
and Strategic Studies); Canadian History and Environment; Cinemas Off Centre; Energy,
Ecology, and Environment; Latin American and Caribbean Studies; Northern Lights; The
West
Copublishing programs: The Arctic Institute of North America; Latin American Research
Centre

University of California Press

2120 Berkeley Way
Berkeley, CA 94704-1012

Phone: 510.642.4247
Fax: 510.643.7127
Email: askucp@ucpress.edu
Indiv: firstname.lastname@ucpress.edu

Order Fulfillment:
California Princeton Fulfillment Services
1445 Lower Ferry Road
Ewing, NJ 08618-1424
Orders: 800.777.4726
Fax: 800.999.1958
Customer Service: 609.883.1759

Website and Social Media:
Website: www.ucpress.edu
Journals website: www.ucpress.edu/journals
Blog: www.ucpress.edu/blog/
Facebook: www.facebook.com/ucpress
Twitter: ucpress

UK/European Office:
John Wiley & Sons Ltd
European Distribution Centre
New Era Estate,
Oldlands Way Bognor Regis
West Sussex PO22 9NQ UK
Phone: +44 (0) 1243 843291
Fax: +44 (0) 1243 843302
Email: customer@wiley.com

Staff
Director: Alison Mudditt (510.642.5393)
   Assistant to the Director: Susan Owen (510.642.2102)
   Chief Financial Officer: Todor Grigorov (510.643.7993)
Chief Administrative Officer: Anna Weidman (510.642.4388)

Director Publishing Operations: Erich van Rijn (510.643.8915)

Executive Director of UC Press Foundation: May Hu (510.643.7704)

Science Publisher: Denise Penrose (510.642.4246)

Social Science and Humanities Publisher: Kim Robinson (regional studies) (510.643.3741)

  Executive Editors: Naomi Schneider (sociology, public anthropology, contemporary social issues, Latin American studies, global health) (510.642.6715); Niels Hooper (US History, American studies, Pacific world, western history, world history, Middle East studies) (510.643.8331); Mary Francis (music, cinema, media studies, Mark Twain) (510.643.5558)

  Sponsoring Editors: Kari Dahlgren (art history, museum copublications) (510.642.6733); Blake Edgar (ecology, earth science, wine and viticulture) (510.643.4643); Reed Malcolm (anthropology, Asian studies, global studies) (510.643.1812); Kate Marshall (food studies, Latin American studies, environmental history) (510.642.4147); Eric Schmidt (classical studies, the ancient world to late antiquity, religion) (510.643.3826); Maura Roessner (criminology, law and society, criminal justice) (510.643.9793); Peter Richardson (economics, environmental and natural resource management) (510.642.4244)

Director of Editing, Design, and Production: Scott Norton (510.643.1335)

Managing Editor: Kate Warne (510.643.6858)

  Manufacturing Manager: Janet Villanueva (510.642.9805)

Art Director: Lia Tjandra (510.643.7982)

Journals Production & Publishing Technology Manager: Gabe Alvaro (510.642.4961)

Director of Marketing & Sales: Rebekah Darksmith (510.643.0952)

  Assistant Director of Marketing: Deb Nasitka (510.642.0378)

  Publicity Director: Alexandra Dahne (510.643.5036)

Journals Publishing Manager: Hannah Love (510.643.1094)

Human Resources: Doris Floyd (510.642.5338)

Full Member

Established: 1893	Admitted to AAUP: 1937
Title output 2012: 225	Title output 2013: 200
Titles currently in print: 4,729	Journals published: 32

Editorial Program

Anthropology, art history, Asian studies, Latin American studies, Middle Eastern studies, biology, classical studies, environmental and earth sciences, film, food studies, history, media studies, music, natural history, global health, criminology, criminal justice, economics, regional studies, religion, sociology, wine and viticulture. Submissions are not invited in original poetry or fiction.

Journals: *The American Biology Teacher; Asian Survey; Boom; California History; California Management Review; Classical Antiquity; Federal Sentencing Reporter; Film Quarterly; Gastronomica: Historical Studies in the Natural Sciences; Huntington Library Quarterly; International Review of Qualitative Research; Journal of Empirical Research on Human Research Ethics; The Journal of Musicology; Journal of Palestine Studies; Journal of the American Musicological Society; Journal of the Society of Architectural Historians; Journal of Vietnamese Studies; Mexican Studies/Estudios Mexicanos; Music Perception; New Criminal Law Review; Nineteenth-Century Literature; 19th-Century Music; Nova Religio; Pacific Historical Review; The Public Historian; Qualitative Communication Research; Religion and American Culture; Representations; Rhetorica; Social Problems; Southern California Quarterly*

Special series: American Crossroads; Ancient Philosophies; Asia Pacific Modern; Asia: Local

Studies/Global Themes; California Natural History Guides; California/Milbank Books on Health and the Public; California Series in Law, Politics, and Society; California Series in Public Anthropology; California Series in Urban Development; California Studies in 19th-Century Music; California Studies in 20th-Century Music; California Studies in Critical Human Geography; California Studies in Food and Culture; California World History Library; Classics in Urban History; Encyclopedias of the Natural World; Ernest Bloch Lectures; Ethnographic Studies in Subjectivity; Experience the California Coast; Freshwater Ecology Series; From Indochina to Vietnam: Revolution and War in a Global Perspective; Global, Area, and International Archive; Hellenistic Culture and Society; Jumping Frogs: Undiscovered, Rediscovered, and Celebrated; Writings of Mark Twain; Mark Twain Library; Mark Twain Papers; Music of the African Diaspora; New California Poetry; Organisms and Environments; Origins of Human Behavior and Culture; Sather Classical Lectures; South Asia Across the Disciplines; Species and Systematics; Sport in World History; Studies in Avian Biology; The Anthropology of Christianity; The Clark Kerr Lectures On the Role of Higher Education in Society; The Collected Writings of Robert Duncan; The Huntington Library Children's Classics; The Huntington Library Classics; The Huntington Library Garden Series; The Marcus Garvey and Universal Negro Improvement Association Papers; The Middle Awash Series; The Norman and Charlotte Strouse Edition of the Writings of Thomas Carlyle; The Works of Mark Twain; The World's Finest Wines; Transformation of the Classical Heritage; Treasures from the Huntington Library; UC Publications in Anthropological Records; UC Publications in Anthropology; UC Publications in Botany; UC Publications in Catalogs and Bibliographies; UC Publications in Classical Studies; UC Publications in Entomology; UC Publications in Folklore and Mythology Studies; UC Publications in Geological Sciences; UC Publications in Ibero-Americana; UC Publications in Linguistics; UC Publications in Modern Philology; UC Publications in Zoology; Weimar and Now: German Cultural Criticism; Western Histories; Wildavsky Forum Series

Cambridge University Press

North American Branch
32 Avenue of the Americas
New York, NY 10013-4211

Distribution Center (West Nyack, NY)
Phone: 845.353.7500
Fax: 845.353.4141

Phone: 212.337.5000
Fax: 212.691.3239
Email: firstinitiallastname@cambridge.org

Website and Social Media:
Website: www.cambridge.org
Blog: www.cambridgeblog.org

Head (UK) Office:
The Edinburgh Building
Cambridge CB2 2RU UK

Staff
Chief Executive: Peter Phillips (UK)
NY Office: 212.337.5000
Managing Director, Americas and ELT: Michael Peluse (212.337.6551)
Managing Director, Academic Publishing, MD Journals: Simon Ross (212.337.5090)

Academic Publishing:
Director of Publishing, Humanities: Beatrice Rehl (212.337.5096)
Director of Publishing, STM: Elaine Stott (212.337.5964)
Publishing Director, STM: Matt Lloyd (212.337.5956)
Academic Editors: Lewis Bateman (political science) (212.337.5965); Matthew Bennett
    (psychology); John Berger (law) (212.337.5958); Lauren Cowles (math, computer
    science) (212.337.5962); Robert Dreesen (politics, sociology) (212.337.5981); Deborah
    Gershenowitz (American and Latin American history and politics) (212.337.5950);
    Diana Gillooly (mathematical sciences); Peter Gordon (engineering) (212.337.5944);
    Anastasia Graf (archaeology and Renaissance studies) (212.337.6598); William Hammel
    (Middle Eastern and African studies) (212.337.6598); Vince Higgs (astronomy, physics)
    (212.337.5081); Karen Maloney (economics and finance) (212.337.5958); David Repetto
    (psychology); Ray Ryan (literature) (212.337.5760); Laura Morris (religious studies)
    (212.337.5066)
Academic Content Manager: Catherine Friedl (212.337.5049)
Sales Director, Americas: Andrea Cernichiari (212.337.5022)
    Associate Sales Director, Retail: Melissanne Scheld (212.337.5988)
    Institutional Sales Managers: Ruth Melchionne (212.337.6535), Kellie O'Rourke
    (212.337.6577)
    Marketing Director, Retail: Al Cascio (212.337.5066)
    College Marketing Manager: Thomas DeMarco (212.337.6505)
    Retail Marketing Manager, STM: Gary Suarez (212.337.5085)
    Retail Marketing Manager, Social Sciences: Michael Duncan (212.337.6548)
    Library Marketing Manager: Keiko Hirano (212.337.5983)
    Exhibits Manager: James Murphy (212.337.5074)
    Rights and Permissions Manager: Marc Anderson (212.337.5048)
Production: Michael Esposito, Global Supply Chain Director (212.337.5094)
Journals Director: John Pescatore (212.337.5993)
    Senior Editor, STM Journals: Aaron Johnson (212.337.6595)
    Publisher, HSS Journals: Mark Zadrozny (212.337.5012)
    Associate Director, Journals Production: Edward Carey (212.337.5985)
    Head of Journals Marketing: Alex Engel (212.337.5967)
    Advertising Sales & Commercial Reprints: Adam Schubak (212.337.5053)
ELT Publishing
    Publishing Director: Janet Aitchison (212.337.6574)
    Associate Publishing Director: Jeff Krum (adult courses) (212.337.5005)
    Global Digital Operations Manager: Jeff Chen (212.337.5971)
    Operations Manager-Production/Manufacturing: Tami Savir (212.337.5968)
    Adaptations & Versioning Unit Manager: Danielle Power (212.337.5989)
    US/Canada Sales Director: Kenneth Clinton (212.337.5010)
    Marketing Manager: Carine Mitchell (212.337.5006)
    Associate Director, Product Marketing: Pierre Montagano (212.337.5007)
    Senior National Sales Manager: James Anderson
    Business Manager: Aniko Banfi (212.337.5030)
Information Services: David Kwederis, IT Director (212.337.5060)
HR: Judith Grace, Human Resources Director, Americas (212.337.5045)
Distribution and Chief Administrative Officer: Steve Miller (845.348.4323)
    Controller, Americas: Thomas Vitkowski (ext. 4326)

Credit & Collections Manager: Lydia Rodrigues (ext. 4314)
Associate Director Customer Services: Marianne Headrick (ext. 4409)
Senior Manager, Inventory Operations & Third Party Logistics: Holly Verrill (ext. 4306)
Third Party Logistics Coordinator: William Morrison (ext. 4391)

Full Member

Established: 1534

American Branch: 1949   Admitted to AAUP: 1950
Title output 2012: over 3900   Title output 2013: 4000
Titles currently in print: about 45,000   Journals published: 330

Editorial Program

A broad range of academic books, journals, digital and online products in the humanities,
social sciences, science, engineering, technology, engineering, medical and health sciences;
including pre-eminent lists in social and political sciences; biological, physical and earth
sciences; mathematics; psychology, psychiatry and neuroscience; law, history and religious
studies; and a premier global English language teaching program.

Carnegie Mellon University Press

5032 Forbes Avenue   Order Fulfillment/Customer Service:
Pittsburgh, PA 15289-1021   Carnegie Mellon University Press
                                      c/o University Press of New England
                                      1 Court Street
Phone: 412.268.2861   Lebanon, NH 03766
Fax: 412.268.8706   Phone: 800.421.1561
Email: Fax: 603.448.9429
cmupress@andrew.cmu.edu.com
Website: www.upne.com/distributed/dist_cmu.html

Website and Social Media:
Website: www.cmu.edu/universitypress
Facebook: www.facebook.com/CarnegieMellonUniversityPress
Twitter: CMUPress

Staff

Director: Gerald Costanzo (poetry editor) (email: gc3d@andrew.cmu.edu)
Senior Editor: Cynthia Lamb (nonfiction acquisitions) (email: cynthial@andrew.cmu.edu)
Production Coordinator: Connie Amoroso (email: camoroso@andrew.cmu.edu)
Accounts Administrator: Anna Houck (email: am2x@andrew.cmu.edu)

Full Member

Established: 1972   Admitted to AAUP: 1991
Title output 2012: 11   Title output 2013: 14
Titles currently in print: 261

Editorial Program

Carnegie Mellon University Press' particular strength lies in literary publishing: Carnegie Mellon Poetry Series, Carnegie Mellon Classic Contemporaries Series (the reissuing of significant early poetry and fiction collections by important contemporary writers), Carnegie Mellon Series in Short Fiction, Poets in Prose Series (memoir in the form of poets writing about their writing lives, poetry criticism, guidebooks and handbooks about the writing of poetry, and Carnegie Mellon Series in Translation. Additionally, the Press publishes in regional social history (titles that explore the rich history of Pittsburgh and Western Pennsylvania), art history, the performing arts (original plays and adaptations), literary analysis, education, and Carnegie Mellon University history.

The Catholic University of America Press

240 Leahy Hall
620 Michigan Avenue, N.E.
Washington, DC 20064

Phone: 202.319.5052
Fax: 202.319.4985
Email: (user I.D.)@cua.edu

Website and Social Media:
Website: cuapress.cua.edu
Facebook: www.facebook.com/pages/
   The-Catholic-University-of-America-Press/232124655084
Twitter: CUAPress

Warehouse (Returns only):
HFS
RETURNS
c/o Maple Press Co.
Lebanon Dist. Center
704 Legionaire Drive
Fredericksburg, PA 17026

Customer Service:
HFS
PO Box 50370
Baltimore, MD 21211
Phone: 800.537.5487
Fax: 410.516.6998

UK Representative:
Eurospan

Canadian Representative:
Scholarly Book Services

Staff

Director: Trevor Lipscombe (email: lipscombe)
   Assistant to the Director: Libby Newkumet (email: newkumet)
Acquisitions Editors: James C. Kruggel (philosophy, theology) (email: kruggel);
   Trevor Lipscombe (all other fields)
Managing Editor: Theresa Walker (email: walkert)
   Editorial Assistant: Tanjam Jacobson (email: jacobsot)
Design and Production: Anne Kachergis (Kachergis Book Design, 14 Small Street North,
   Pittsboro, NC 27312)
Marketing Manager: Brian Roach (email: roach)
   Journals: Hubert Ngueha, Administrative Assistant (email: ngueha)

Full Member

Established: 1939
Title output 2012: 38
Titles currently in print: 1,010

Admitted to AAUP: 1985
Title output 2013: 38
Journals published: 5

Editorial Program

American and European history (both ecclesiastical and secular); American and European literature; philosophy; political theory; theology. Periods covered range from late antiquity to modern times, with special interest in late antiquity, early Christianity, and the medieval period.

Journals: *The Catholic Historical Review; Pierre d'Angle; The Jurist: Studies in Church Law and Ministry; U.S. Catholic Historian; and The Bulletin of Medieval Canon Law*

Special series: Catholic Moral Thought; The Fathers of the Church: A New Translation; Library of Early Christianity; Medieval Texts in Translation; Patristic Monograph Series of the North American Patristics Society (distributed); Publications of the American Maritain Association (distributed); Studies in Philosophy and the History of Philosophy; Thomas Aquinas in Translation; IPS Monograph Series of the Institute for the Psychological Sciences (distributed); Sapientia Press (distributed)

The University of Chicago Press

1427 E. 60th Street
Chicago, IL 60637-2954

Phone: 773.702.7700
Fax: 773.702.2705 (Books Acquisitions)
      773.702.9756 (Books Marketing)
      773.834.3480 (Journals Marketing)
      773.753.4247 (Journals Production)
Email: firstinitiallastname@press.uchicago.edu

Chicago Distribution Center:
11030 South Langley Avenue
Chicago, IL 60628
Phone: 773.702.7000
Fax: 773.702.7212

Website and Social Media—Books:
Website www.press.uchicago.edu;
Chicago Blog: pressblog.uchicago.edu
Twitter: UChicagoPress
Facebook: facebook.com/UniversityofChicagoPress
Tumblr: uchicagopress.tumblr.com
Goodreads: goodreads.com/UChicagoPress
LibraryThing: www.librarything.com/profile/UChicagoPress

Website and Social Media—Journals:
Website: www.journals.uchicago.edu
Blog: pressblog.uchicago.edu
Facebook: www.facebook.com/UChicagoJournals
Twitter: ChicagoJournals

UK Representative: Canadian Representative:
University Press Marketing   The University Press Group

Staff

Director: Garrett P. Kiely (773.702.8878)
  Deputy Director: Christopher Heiser (773.702.2998)
  Assistant to the Director and Deputy Director: Ellen M. Zalewski (773.702.8879)
  Executive Director of Information Technology: Patti O'Shea (773.702.8521)
  IT Operations Manager Information Technology Support: Derek Simmons (773.702.0510)
  Human Resources Manager: Alice Lloyd (773.702.7303)
  Digital Publishing Manager: Krista Coulson (773.702.5862)
Books Division
Acquisitions Editorial:
  Editorial Directors: Christie Henry (sciences and social sciences) (773.702.0468); Alan Thomas (humanities and social sciences) (773.702.7644)
  Editors: Susan Bielstein (art, architecture, ancient archeology, classics, film studies) (773.702.7633); T. David Brent (anthropology, philosophy, psychology, psychiatry) (773.702.7642); Abby Collier (geography and cartography) (773.702.6691); Christopher Chung (life sciences evolutionary biology, ecology, and conservation biology) (773.702.3145); Timothy Mennel (American history, regional publishing) (773.702.0158); Elizabeth Branch Dyson (ethnomusicology, education, philosophy) (773.702.7637); Marta Tonegutti (music) (773.702.0427); Christie Henry (life sciences, geography, cartography) (773.702.0468); Douglas Mitchell (history, sociology, sexuality studies, rhetoric) (773.702.7639); Randolph Petilos (medieval studies, poetry in translation) (773.702.7647); Karen Darling (history, philosophy, and social studies of science)(773.702.7641); Joe Jackson (economics, business) (773.702.7638); Alan Thomas (literature, religion) (773.702.7644); John Tryneski (political science, law and society) (773.702.7648) Chris Rhodes (law and linguistics) (773.702.4517); Priya Nelson (anthropology, Asian studies)(773.702.4759)
  Managing Editor, Phoenix Poets: Randolph Petilos (773.702.7647)
  Paperback Editor: Margaret Hivnor (773.702.7649)
  Assistant Paperback Editor: Janet Deckenbach (773.702.7034)
  Senior Editor: David Morrow (773.702.7465)
  Senior Project Editor: Mary Laur (773.702.7326)
  Contracts and Subsidiary Rights Manager: Perry Cartwright (773.702.6096)
  Foreign Rights Manager: Ines ter Horst (773.702.7741)
Manuscript Editorial: Anita Samen, Managing Editor (773.702.5081)
Design and Production: Jill Shimabukuro, Design and Production Director (773.702.7653)
Marketing Director: Carol Kasper (773.702.7733)
  Promotions Director: Levi Stahl (773.702.0289)
  Promotions Managers: Margaret Hagan (773.702.0279); Micah Fehrenbacher (773.702.7717); Laura Avey (773.702.0376); Melinda Kennedy (773.702.2945); Nick Lilly (773.702.7740); Kristen Raddatz (773.702.1964)
  Marketing and Sales Specialist-Ref, Library: James Lilly (773.702.7957)
  Online Publicity Managers: Kristi McGuire (773.702.2548); Ryo Yamaguchi (773.834.8708)

Advertising Manager: Anne Osterman (773.702.7897)
Exhibits Coordinator: Eric DeTratto (773.834.7201)
Marketing Design Manager: Mary Shanahan (773.702.7697)
Senior Marketing Designer: Alice Reimann (773.702.7849)
Sales: John Kessler, Associate Marketing Director/Sales Director (773.702.7248)
  Sales and Distribution Associate: Robert Hoffman (773.702.0340)
  Sales and Inventory Associate: Joseph Peterson (773.702.7723)
  Sales Representatives: Bailey Walsh (Midwest); Blake Delodder (East Coast); Gary Hart (West Coast)
  Sales Assistant: Vertelle Kanyama (773.702.7899)
  International Sales Manager: Saleem Dhamee (773.702.7898)
E-commerce/Direct-to-Consumer Sales: Dean Blobaum, Electronic Marketing and E-commerce Manager (773.702.7706)
  Marketing Systems Coordinator: Tom McGraw (773.702.6674)
  Associate Direct Marketing Manager: Stuart Kisilinsky (773.702.8924)
  Direct Mail Associate: Casimir Psujek (773.702.7887)
  Reference Marketing: Ellen Gibson, Reference Marketing Manager (773.702.3233)
  Reference Special Sales and Promotions Manager: Lauren Salas (773.702.0890)
Marketing Client Distribution: Carol Kasper, Director (773.702.7733)
  Distributed Books Manager: Teresa Fagan (773.834.1916)
  Publicity Manager: Carrie Adams (773.702.4216)
Journals Division
Director, Journals Division: Michael Magoulias (773.753.2669)
  Publisher, Journals Acquisitions: Kari Roane (773.702.7362)
  Publishers: Tess Mullen (773.702.7442); Gordon Rudy (773.702.2448)
  Publishing Operations Manager: Ashley Towne (773.753.4241)
  Manager of Electronic Publishing Technology: Michael Boudreau (773.753.3298)
  Manager of Subscription Fulfillment: Rich Connelly (773.753.3601)
  Manager of Editorial Processes: Mary E. Leas (773.702.7961)
  Chief Manuscript Editor, Science Journals: Mary Nell Hoover (773.702.7679)
  Chief Manuscript Editor, General Journals: Jane Jiambalvo (773.702.7689)
Chicago Distribution Center Services
President of Chicago Distribution Services: Don Linn (773.702.7020)
  Senior Operations Manager: Mark Stewart (773.702.7024)
  Distribution Services Coordinator: Sue Tranchita (773.702.7014)
  Customer Service Manager: Karen Hyzy (773.702.7109)
  Asst. Manager, Customer Service/Instructor Trainer Title Management: Latrice Allen (773.702.7112)
  Credit and Collections, A/R Manager: Nick Cole (773.702.7164)
  Director of Accounting: Bob Peterson (773.702.7036)
Manager, Chicago Digital Distribution Center: Kewon Bell (773.702.7238)
  M.I.S. Manager: Christopher Jones (773.702.7229)
  Royalty/Rights Manager: Cassandra Wisniewski (773.702.7062)
  Warehouse Office Manager: Gail Candreva-Szwet (773.702.7080)

Assistant Supervisor: Tammy Paul (773.702.7081)
Journals Warehouse Manager: Don P. Collins (773.702.7245)
Returns Manager: Jenn Stone (773.834.3687)
Inventory Control Manager: Dennis Kraus (773.834.3499)
BiblioVault
BiblioVault Manager: Kate Davey (773.834.4417)

Full Member

Established: 1891	Admitted to AAUP: 1957
Title output 2012: 300	Title output 2013: 334
Titles currently in print: 5,000	Journals published: 51

Editorial Program

Scholarly, course, and general-interest works in: Anthropology; Art and Architecture; Asian Studies; Business; Cartography and Geography; Classics; Economics and Finance; Education; History; Law; Life Sciences; Linguistics; Literary Criticism; Musciology; Philosophy; Political Science; Reference; Religious Studies; Science Studies; Sociology; Writing and Publishing. Closed to submissions in fiction and poetry.

Journals: *Afterall; American Art; American Journal of Education; American Journal of Sociology; The American Naturalist; American Political Thought; Art Documentation; The China Journal; Classical Philology; Comparative Education Review; Critical Historical Studies; Critical Inquiry; Current Anthropology; Economic Development and Cultural Change; The Elementary School Journal; Ethics; Freshwater Science; Gesta; History of Religions; HOPOS; Infection Control and Hospital Epidemiology; International Journal of American Linguistics; International Journal of Plant Sciences; Isis; Journal of Consumer Research; The Journal of Geology; Journal of Human Capital; Journal of Labor Economics; Journal of Law and Courts; The Journal of Law and Economics; The Journal of Legal Studies; The Journal of Modern History; Journal of Near Eastern Studies; Journal of Political Economy; The Journal of Religion; The Journal of the Association of Environmental and Resource Economists; Journal of the Society for Social Work and Research; Library Quarterly; Metropolitan Museum Journal; Modern Philology; Philosophy of Science; Physiological and Biochemical Zoology; Publications of the Astronomical Society of the Pacific; The Quarterly Review of Biology; Renaissance Drama; Renaissance Quarterly; Schools; Signs; Signs and Society; Social Service Review; I Tatti Essays in the Italian Renaissance; West 86th; Winterthur Portfolio*

Annuals: *Crime and Justice; Innovation Policy and the Economy; NBER International Seminar on Macroeconomics; NBER Macroeconomics Annual Tax Policy and the Economy; OSIRIS; Supreme Court Economic Review; The Supreme Court Review*

The Chinese University Press

The Chinese University of Hong Kong
Sha Tin
New Territories, Hong Kong

North American Distributor:
Columbia University Press
c/o Perseus Distribution
Phone: 800.944.8648/731.988.4440
Email: cup_book@columbia.edu

Phone: +852 39439800
Fax: +852 2603.7355
Email: cup@cuhk.edu.hk
Indiv: (user I.D.)@cuhk.edu.hk

UK and European Distributor:
Eurospan Group
c/o Turpin Distribution
Phone: +44 (0) 1767 604972
Email: eurospan@turpin-distribution.com

Website and Social Media:
Website: www.chineseupress.com
Facebook: www.facebook.com/
   home.php#!/TheChineseUniversityPress
Weibo: weibo.com/cupress
Twitter: twitter.com/CUHKPress

Other Areas
(Customer Service and Orders)
The Chinese University Press
Phone: +852 39439800
Fax: +852 26037355
Email: cup-bus@cuhk.edu.hk

Staff
Director: Qi GAN (+852 39439818; email: ganqi)
Secretary to the Director: Tina Chan (+852 39439810; email: tinachan)
Editorial: Ying LIN, Managing Editor (+852 39439811; email: linying)
Production: Kingsley Ma, Manager (+852 39439808; email: kwaihungma)
Business/Marketing: Angelina Wong, Manager (+852 39439822; email: laifunwong)

International Member
Established: 1977
Title output 2012: 50
Titles currently in print: 946

Admitted to AAUP: 1981
Title output 2013: 52
Journals published: 7

Editorial Program
Bilingual publication of academic and general trade titles. Areas of interest include Chinese studies in literature, history, philosophy, languages, and the arts. The Press also publishes books on business, government, medicine, as well as dictionaries and general books in both the English and Chinese languages.

Journals: *Asian Journal of English Language Teaching; The China Review; Communication & Society; Daoism: Religion, History and Society; Journal of Chinese Studies; Journal of Translation Studies, International Journal for the Study of Humanistic Buddhism*

Special series: Bibliography and Index Series; Bilingual Series on Modern Chinese Literature; Ch'ien Mu Lectures in History and Culture; Educational Studies Series; Hong Kong Taxation; Institute of Chinese Studies Monograph Series; Jintian Series of Contemporary Chinese Writing; Young Scholars Dissertation Awards, Translation Series

University Press of Colorado/Utah State University Press

Colorado Address:
5589 Arapahoe Avenue
Suite 206C
Boulder, CO 80303

Phone: 720.406.8849
Fax: 720.406.8849
Email: (user I.D)@upcolorado.com

Utah Address:
3078 Old Main Hill
Merrill-Cazier Library
Logan, UT 84322-3078

Phone: 720.406.8849
Fax: 720.406.8849

Distributor:
Chicago Distribution Center
11030 South Langley Ave.
Chicago, IL 60628

Phone: 800.621.2736
Fax: 800.621.8476

European and International Representative:
National Book Network International

Websites and Social Media:
Websites: www.upcolorado.com; www.usupress.org
Facebook: www.facebook.com/pages/The-University-Press-of-Colorado/347439013387
www.facebook.com/pages/Utah-State-University-Press/164439110276267
Twitter: UPColorado

Staff
Director: Darrin Pratt (email: darrin)
Associate Director: Michael Spooner (email: michael@usupress.com)
Acquisitions Editor: Jessica d'Arbonne (email: jessica)
Managing Editor: Laura Furney (email: laura)
Production Manager: Dan Pratt (email: dan)
Marketing & Sales Manager: Beth Svinarich (email: beth)
Marketing Manager & Production (USUP): Dan Miller (email: danmiller@usupress.com)

Full Member
Established: 1965
Title output 2012: 41
Titles currently in print: 667

Admitted to AAUP: 1982
Title output 2013: 41

Editorial Program
Physical sciences; natural history; ecology; American history; Western history; anthropology; archaeology; composition studies; folklore studies; Native American studies; Western women's history; Mormon history; and regional (Mountain West) titles. Submission by invitation only in fiction and poetry for the Utah State University Press imprint.

The Press also copublishes with and distributes titles for the Denver Museum of Natural History, the Colorado Historical Society Colorado State University's Cooperative Extension, the Center for Literary Publishing, and the Institute for Mesoamerican Studies.

Special series: Atomic History & Culture; The George and Sakaye Aratani Nikkei in the Americas Series; Leonard J. Arrington Lecture Series; Life Writings of Frontier Women; May Swenson Poetry Award Series; Mesoamerican Worlds; Mining the American West; Timberline Books

Columbia University Press

61 West 62nd Street
New York, NY 10023-7015

Phone: 212.459.0600
Fax: 212.459.3677
Email: (user I.D.)@columbia.edu

Website and Social Media:
Website: www.columbia.edu/cu/cup
Blog: cupblog.org
Facebook: www.facebook.com/
  ColumbiaUniversityPress
Twitter: ColumbiaUP
YouTube: www.youtube.com/CUPvideos

Perseus Distribution Warehouse:
193 Edwards Drive
Jackson, TN 38301

Orders and Customer Service:
Phone: 800.944.8648
Fax: 800.944.1844

UK Office:
University Press Group
Southern Cross Trading Estate
Southern Cross Trading Estate
1 Oldlands Way, Bognor Regis
West Sussex PO22 9SA
Phone: +44 1243 842165
Fax: +44 1243 842167

Staff

Interim Director: Jennifer Crewe (ext. 7145; email: jc373)
  Assistant to the Director: Jonathan Fiedler (ext. 7142; email: jf2801)
    Chief Financial Officer: Richard G. Gehringer (ext. 7112; email: rg2665)
    Manager of Manager of Rights and Contracts: Justine Evans (ext. 7128; email: je2217)
Acquisitions Editorial: Jennifer Crewe, Associate Director and Editorial Director (Asian humanities, film studies, food studies) (ext. 7145; email: jc373)
  Publisher for the Life Sciences: Patrick Fitzgerald (ext. 7136; email: pf2134)
  Publisher for Finance and Economics and Columbia Business School Publishing: Myles Thompson (ext. 7161; email: mt2312)
  Publisher for Philosophy and Religion: Wendy Lochner (ext. 7121; email: wl2003)
  Senior Executive Editor: Jennifer Perillo (social work, criminology, psychology) (ext. 7107; email: jp3187)
  Senior Editor: Anne Routon (Asian history, international relations, Middle East studies) (ext. 7116; email: akr36)
  Editors: Philip Leventhal (literary studies, journalism, American history) (ext. 7159; email: pl2162); Bridget Flannery-McCoy (economics) (ext. 7136; email: bmf7136)
Manuscript Editorial: Anne McCoy, Managing Editor (ext. 7111; email: aam10)
  Assistant Managing Editors: Leslie Kriesel (ext. 7110; email: lrk11); Ron Harris (ext. 7155; email: rh182)
  Senior Production Editor: Irene Pavitt (ext.7138; email: ip126)

Senior Manuscript Editors: Roy Thomas (ext. 7160; email: ret12); Susan Pensak (ext. 7139; email: srp4)
Electronic Manuscripts Administrator: Michael Haskell (ext. 7162; email: mh2100)
Director of Design and Production: Jennifer Jerome (ext. 7177; email: jj352)
  Art Director: Julia Kushnirsky (ext. 7102; email: jk3151)
  Senior Designers: Lisa Hamm (ext. 7105; email: lh400); Milenda Lee (ext. 7103; email: ml2657); Chang Jae Lee (ext. 7140; email: chl32)
Marketing: Brad Hebel, Associate Director, Director of Marketing and Sales (ext. 7130; email: bh2106)
  Assistant Marketing Director/Publicity Director: Meredith Howard (ext. 7126; email: mh2306)
  Electronic Marketing Manager: Philip Leventhal (ext. 7159; email: pl2164)
  Assistant Marketing Director/Direct Marketing Manager: Todd Lazarus (ext. 7152; email: tdl10)
  Advertising Manager: Elena Iaffa (ext. 7124; email: ei2131)
  Sales Consortium Manager: Catherine Hobbs (ext. 7809; email: chobss@rlc.net)
  Mid-West Sales Representative: Kevin Kurtz (ext. 7806; email: kkurtz5@earthlink.net)
  West Coast Sales Representative: William Gawronski (ext. 7807; email: wgawronski@earthlink.net)
Business: Robert Abrams, Controller (ext. 7119; email: ra2555)
  Director of Human Resources: James Pakiela (ext. 7109; email: jp2483)
  Accounts Payable & Royalty Manager: Frederick Stokes (ext. 7108; email: fs2445)
IT Director: Greg Lara (ext. 7132; email: gl2298)
  Systems Support Specialist: Sean Chen (ext. 7106; email: sc2566)
  Publishing Systems Manager: Michael Haskell (ext. 7162; email: mh2100)
  Managing Editor for Reference and Electronic Publishing: Stephen Sterns (ext. 7148; email: ss724)

Full Member

Established: 1893

Admitted to AAUP: 1937

Title output 2012: 160

Title output 2013: 140

Titles currently in print: 3,360

Editorial Program

General reference works in print and electronic formats. Scholarly, general interest, and professional books, and upper-level textbooks in the humanities, social sciences, and earth and life sciences, business and social work. Subjects include animal studies; Asian Studies; botany; conservation and environmental science; criminology; ecology; evolutionary studies; film; finance and business economics; gender studies; history; international relations; journalism; literary and cultural studies; media studies; Middle East studies; philosophy; political philosophy; political science; religion; and social work. The Press publishes poetry, fiction, and drama in translation only and is the publisher of Wallflower Press titles worldwide.

Columbia University Press is the distributor in the United States, Canada, and Latin America for American Institute of Buddhist Studies, Auteur Publishing, Chinese University Press, Dalkey Archive Press, East European Monographs, , European Consortium for Political Research Press, Harrington Park Press, Hong Kong University Press, Ibidem Press, Jagiellonian University Press, Transcript Verlag, and University of Tokyo Press.

Special series, joint imprints, and/or co-publishing programs: American Academy of Religion Lectures on the History of Religions; Arts and Traditions of the Table; Asia Perspectives; Bampton Lectures in America; Biology and Resource Management; CERI Series in Comparative Politics and International Studies; Columbia Business School Publishing; Columbia Classics in Philosophy; Columbia Classics in Religion; Columbia History of Urban Life; Columbia Readings of Buddhist Literature; Columbia Series in Science and Religion; Columbia Studies in International History; Columbia Studies in Terrorism and Irregular Warfare; Columbia Themes in Philosophy, Social Criticism and the Arts; Complexity in Ecological Systems; Contemporary Asia In the World; Critical Moments in Earth History; Critical Perspectives on Animals; Cultures of History; Empowering the Powerless; End of Life Care; European Perspectives; Film and Culture; Foundations of Social Work Knowledge; Gender and Culture; Gender, Theory and Religion; Global Chinese Culture; History and Society of the Modern Middle East; Hurst Books; Initiative for Policy Dialogue at Columbia; Introduction to Asian Civilizations; Insurrections: Critical Studies in Religion, Politics, and Culture; Leonard Hastings Schoff Lectures; Modern Asian Literature; Modern Chinese Literature from Taiwan; The Neurosciences, Social Sciences, and the Arts; New Directions in Critical Theory; Political Thought/Political History; Records of Western Civilization; Religion and American Culture; Social Science Research Council Books; Translations from the Asian Classics; Weatherhead Books on Asia; Wellek Library Lectures

Cork University Press

Youngline Industrial Estate, Pouladuff Road
Cork, Ireland

Phone: +353 21 490 2980
Fax: + 353 21 431 5329
Email: corkuniversitypress@ucc.ie

<u>Website and Social Media:</u>
Website: www.corkuniversitypress.com
Blog: corkuniversitypress.org
Facebook: www.facebook.com/CorkUP
Twitter: CorkUP

<u>US Representative:</u>
Stylus Publishing
22883 Quicksilver Drive
Sterling, VA 20166-2012
Phone: 703.661.1504
Fax: 703.661.1501
Email: stylusmail@presswarehouse.com

<u>UK Representative:</u>
Marston Book Services

<u>Irish Representative:</u>
Gill & MacMillan

Staff
Director: Mike Collins (email: mike.collins@ucc.ie)
Editorial and Production: Maria O'Donovan (email: maria.odonovan@ucc.ie)

International Member
Established: 1925
Title output 2012: 20
Titles currently in print: 200

Admitted to AAUP: 2002
Title output 2013: 14
Journals published: 1

Editorial Program

While the Press specializes in the broad field of Irish Culture, its subject range extends across the fields of music, art history, literary criticism and poetry. However, the focus of our list is in the areas of Irish cultural history, archaeology and landscape studies.

Journal: *Irish Review*

Special series: Field Day Monographs; Ireland into Film

Cornell University Press

Street Address:
Sage House
512 East State Street
Ithaca, NY 14850

Phone: 607.277.2338
Fax: 607.277.2374
Email: (user I.D.)@cornell.edu

Website and Social Media:
Website: www.cornellpress.cornell.edu
Blog: cornellpress.wordpress.com
Facebook: www.facebook.com/CornellUP
Twitter: CornellPress
YouTube: www.youtube.com/user/CornellPressNews

UK Representative:
University Presses Marketing

Canadian Representative:
Lexa Publishers' Representatives

Mailing Address:
Sage House
512 East State Street
Ithaca, NY 14850

Order Fulfillment:
CUP Services
750 Cascadilla Street
Ithaca, NY 14850
Phone: 800.666.2211
Fax: 800.688.2877
Email: orderbook@cupserv.org

UK/European Distributor:
NBN International

Staff

Director: John G. Ackerman (ext. 209; email: jga4)
　Assistant Director & CFO: Roger A. Hubbs (607.277.2696; email: rah9)
　Assistant to the Director: Michael Morris (ext. 210; email: mam278)
Acquisitions Editorial: Peter J. Potter, Editor-in-Chief (classics, medieval studies, literature) (ext. 241; email: pjp33)
　Editorial Director, ILR Press: Frances Benson (labor studies and workplace issues, health care, sociology, business) (ext. 222; email: fgb2)
　Executive Editor: Roger Haydon (politics, international relations, Asian studies) (ext. 225; email: rmh11)
　Editors: John G. Ackerman (European history, Russian/East European/Eurasian history and literature) (ext. 209; email: jga4); TBA (science: entomology, herpetology, natural history, ornithology, plant sciences); Michael J. McGandy (American history, U.S. politics, urban studies, New York state and regional books) (ext. 233; email: mjm475)
Manuscript Editorial: Ange Romeo-Hall, Managing Editor (ext. 243; email: asr8)
　Manuscript Editors: Karen T. Hwa (ext. 260; email: kth9); Karen Laun (ext. 236; email: kml35); Susan Specter (ext. 245; email: sps19)

Design and Production: Karen Kerr, Manager (ext. 235; email: kg99)
  Senior Designers: Scott Levine (ext. 263; email: sel37); Lou Robinson (email: lr11); George
  Whipple (email: gtw2)
  Designer: Richanna Patrick (ext. 240; email: rp12)
  Senior Production Coordinator: Diana Silva (ext. 257; email: drs68)
  Production Coordinator: Jessica A. Venezia (ext. 239; email: jav85)
Marketing: Mahinder Kingra, Marketing Director (ext. 255; email: msk55)
  Sales Manager: Nathan Gemignani (ext. 251; email: ndg5)
  Publicity Manager: Jonathan Hall (ext. 252; email: jlh98)
  Subsidiary Rights Manager: Tonya Cook (email: tcc6)
  Advertising Coordinator: Amelia Wise (ext. 256; email: arw45)
  Publicity Coordinator: Jennifer Longley (ext. 254; email: jal225)
  Exhibits/Awards Coordinator: David Mitchell (ext. 248; email: dwm23)
  Copy Supervisor/Grant Writer: Susan Barnett (ext. 259; email: scb33)
  Permissions Coordinator: Stephanie Munson (ext. 231; email: sm120)
Business: (607.277.2696)
  Chief Financial Officer: Roger A. Hubbs (ext. 132; email: rah9)
  Accounting & Operations Coordinator: Cindy Snyder (ext. 133; email: chs6)
  Procurement, Disbursements & Title Accounting: Laurie McGuire (ext. 139; email: lam35)
CUP Services Distribution Center:
  CUP Services Manager: Christopher Quinlan (607.277.2211, ext. 125;
  email: cq@cupserv.org)
  Customer Service, Client Services, Accounts Receivable: Christine Jolluck (607.277.2037,
  ext. 126; email: cj@cupserv.org)
  MIS: Patrick Garrison (607.277.2969, ext. 149; email: plg6@cupserv.org)
  Warehouse and Shipping: Christopher Quinlan (607.277.2211, ext. 125;
  email: cq@cupserv.org)

Full Member

Established: 1869   Admitted to AAUP: 1937
Re-established in present form: 1930
Title output 2012: 145   Title output 2013: 131
Titles currently in print: 2,573

Editorial Program

Serious nonfiction, with particular strengths in anthropology; Asian studies; classics; German
studies, history; industrial and labor relations; life science; literary criticism and theory;
music; natural history; politics and international relations; race studies; Slavic studies;
sociology; and women's studies. Submissions are not invited in poetry or fiction.

  Cornell University Press is the distributor for Cornell University's Southeast Asia Program
Publications and distributes in North America for Leuven University Press.

Special imprints: Comstock Publishing Associates; Cornell Selects; Fall Creek Books; ILR
Press

Special series, joint imprints and/or copublishing programs: Agora Editions; American
Institutions and Society; Ancient Commentators on Aristotle; Cornell Hospitality
Management; Cornell Studies in Classical Philology/Townsend Lectures; Cornell Studies in

the History of Psychiatry; Cornell Studies in Money; Cornell Studies in Political Economy; Cornell Studies in Security Affairs; The Cornell Yeats; The Culture and Politics of Health Care Work; Culture and Society after Socialism; Cushwa Center Studies of Catholicism in Twentieth-Century America; Expertise—Cultures and Technologies of Knowledge; Islandica; Religion and American Public Life; Signale—Modern German Letters, Cultures, and Thought; The United States in the World.

Duke University Press

Street Address:
905 West Main Street
Suite 18-B
Durham, NC 27701

Mailing Address:
Box 90660
Durham, NC 27708- 0660

Phone: 919.687.3600
Faxes: 919.688.4574 (general)
919.688.3524 (journals)
919.688.4391 (marketing/production-books)
Email: info@dukepress.edu
Indiv:
firstinitiallastname@dukepress.edu or
firstname.lastname@dukepress.edu
(unless otherwise indicated)

Orders and Customer Service:
Phone: 888.651.0122; 919.688.5134
Fax: 888.651.0124; 919.688.2615

Warehouse:
Duke University Press
Distribution Center
120 Golden Drive
Durham, NC 27705
Phone: 919.384.0733

Website and Social Media:
Website: www.dukepress.edu
Blog: www.dukepress.typepad.com
Facebook: www.facebook.com/DukeUniversityPress
Twitter: DUKEpress

UK/European Representative:
Combined Academic Publishers

Canadian Representative:
Lexa Publishers' Representatives

Staff
Director: Stephen A. Cohn (919.687.3606)
  Assistant to the Director/Development Coordinator: Bonnie Perkel (919.687.3685)
  Assistant Director for Digital Publishing: Allison Belan (919.687.3683)
  Manager, Rights and Permissions: Diane Grosse (919.687.8020)
Central Administration: Robyn L. Miller, Manager (919.687.3633)
  Assistant Manager: Starr Loftis (919.687.3609)
  Logistics Coordinator: Bonnie Conner (919.687.3693)
Books
Acquisitions Editorial: Ken Wissoker, Editorial Director (anthropology, cultural studies, Asian Studies, post-colonial theory, lesbian and gay studies, construction of race, gender and national identity, new media, literary criticism, film and television, popular music, science studies, visual studies) (919.687.3648; email: kwiss@duke.edu)
  Editors: Courtney Berger (political theory, sociology and social theory, geography, American studies, literary theory and criticism, cultural studies, gender studies, Asian

American studies, Native American & indigenous studies, film and television, science and technology studies, food studies) (919.687.3652); Gisela Fosado (anthropology, history, Latin American studies, Latin American history, U.S. history, African American studies, women's history, social movements, gender studies, environmental studies) (919.687.3632)
    Associate Editor: Miriam Angress (religion, world history, women's studies, World Readers) (919.687.3601)
Books Editing, Design, and Production Manager: Nancy Hoagland (919.687.3629)
    Book Designers: Amy Buchanan (919.687.3651); Heather Hensley (919.687.3658)
    Managing Editor: Jessica Ryan (919.687.3666)
    Project Editors: Susan Albury (919.687.3669); Sara Leone (919.687.3681); Elizabeth Smith (919.687.8006); Danielle Szulczewski (919.687.8016)
    Production Manager: Patty Chase (919.687.3622)
    Production Specialists: Tanya Davis (919.687.8019); Venus Bradley (919.687.3643)
Marketing: Emily Young, Books Marketing Manager (919.687.3654)
    Books Marketing Metadata and Digital Systems Manager: H. Lee Willoughby-Harris (919.687.3646)
    Associate Marketing Manager and Sales Manager: Michael McCullough (919.687.3604)
    Publicity and Advertising Manager: Laura Sell (919.687.3639)
    Copywriter: Katie Courtland (919.687.3663)
    Direct Marketing Manager and Sales Associate: Julie Thomson (919.687.3603)
    Exhibits Manager: Helena Knox (919.687.3647)
    Publicity and Advertising Assistant: Emily Estelle Lawrence (919.687.3650)
Journals
Editorial & Administrative Manager: Rob Dilworth (919.687.3624)
    Senior Managing Editor, H&SS: Charles Brower (919.687.3688)
    Senior Managing Editor, STM: Ray Lambert (919.687.3625)
    Senior Editor Journal Acquisitions: Erich Staib (919.687.3664)
    Project Euclid Manager: Mira Waller (919.687.3630)
Production and Finance Manager: Michael Brondoli (919.687.3605)
    Assistant Production Manager: Terri Fizer (919.687.3619)
    Art Director/Journals Designer: Sue Hall (919.687.3620)
    Digital Publishing Technologists: Bendte Fagge (919.687.3674); Rebekah Kati (919.687.8011)
    Digital Content Developer: Steve Grathwohl (919.687.3634)
Marketing Manager: Cason Lynley (919.687.3631)
    Assistant Marketing Manager: Jocelyn Dawson (919.687.3653)
    Library Relations Manager: Kim Steinle (919.687.3655)
    Library Relations Coordinator: Beth Hoskins (919.687.3627)
    Data and Projects Specialist: Kendall McKenzie (919.687.3636)
    Academic Exhibits & Publicity Coordinator: Katie Smart (919.687.8029)
    Web & Advertising Coordinator: Kevin Woodcock (919.687.3687)
    Institutional Exhibits & Direct Marketing Coordinator: Leslie Eager (919.687.8027)
Customer Service Manager: Lesley Jones (919.687.3684)
    Customer Service—Assistant Manager: Amanda Kolman (919.687.3602)
    Customer Service—Digital Access and Journals Specialist: Shannon Harvey

(919.687.8010)

Customer Service—Digital Access and Books Specialist: Cynthia Morgia (919.687.3617)

Business Office and Distribution: Norris Langley, Chief Financial Officer (919.687.3607)

Warehouse Manager: Don Griffin (919.384.1244)

Information Systems: Pamela Spaulding, Manager (919.687.3641)

Assistant Manager: Sonya Johnson (919.687.3662)

Database Administrator/Advantage Programmer: Ling Mao (919.687.3665)

System Administrator: Michael Brennan (919.687.3679)

Enterprise System Integrator—Programmer: Ariel Dela Fuente (919.687.3611)

Help Desk Manager: Marcus Butts (919.687.3635)

Full Member

Established: 1921 (as Trinity College Press)	Admitted to AAUP: 1937
Title output 2012: 130	Title output 2013: 120
Titles currently in print: 2,634	Journals published: 48

Editorial Program

Scholarly books in the humanities and social sciences, with lists in art criticism and history; visual studies; cultural studies; gay and lesbian studies; gender studies; American studies; American history; African American studies; Asian American studies; Native American & indigenous studies; cultural anthropology; minority politics and post-colonial issues; Latin American studies: Asian studies; South Asian studies; African studies; Middle East studies; Slavic studies; European studies; music; film, TV and media studies; literary theory and history; environmental studies; political science and political theory; legal studies; religion; sociology and social theory; and science studies.

Journals: *American Literary Scholarship; American Literature; American Speech; boundary 2; Camera Obscura; Collected Letters of Thomas and Jane Welsh Carlyle; Common Knowledge; Comparative Literature; Comparative Studies of South Asia, Africa and the Middle East; Cultural Politics; differences; Duke Mathematical Journal; East Asian Science, Technology and Society; Eighteenth-Century Life; Ethnohistory; French Historical Studies; Genre; GLQ: A Journal of Lesbian and Gay Studies; Hispanic American Historical Review; History of Political Economy; Journal of Chinese Literature and Culture; Journal of Health Politics, Policy and Law; Journal of Medieval and Early Modern Studies; Journal of Music Theory; Kyoto Journal of Mathematics; Labor; Limnology and Oceanography: Fluids and Environments; Mediterranean Quarterly; minnesota review; Modern Language Quarterly; Nagoya Mathematical Journal; New German Critique; Nka; Notre Dame Journal of Formal Logic; Novel; Pedagogy; Philosophical Review; Poetics Today; positions; Public Culture; Radical History Review; Small Axe; Social Science History; Social Text; South Atlantic Quarterly; Theater; Tikkun; TSQ: Transgender Studies Quarterly*

Special series, joint imprints and/or copublishing programs: American Encounters: Global Interactions; Asia-Pacific: Culture, Politics and Society; Collected Letters of Thomas and Jane Welsh Carlyle; C. L. R. James Archives; Console-ing Passions; Body/Commodity/Text; Ecologies for the Twenty-First Century; Experimental Futures; Improvisation, Community, and Social Practice; Latin America in Translation; Latin America Otherwise: Languages, Empires, Nations; Latin America Readers; Narrating Native Histories; New Americanists; Next Wave: New Directions in Women's Studies; Objects/Histories: Perverse Modernities; Post-Contemporary Interventions; Public Planet; Radical Perspectives: A Radical History Review Book Series; Refiguring American Music; Science and Cultural Theory; SIC; Sign, Storage, Transmission; Social Text Books; Theory Q; World Readers

Duquesne University Press

600 Forbes Avenue
Pittsburgh, PA 15282

Phone: 412.396.6610
Fax: 412.396.5984

Website and Social Media:
Website: www.dupress.duq.edu

UK Representative:
Gazelle Book Sevices

Distribution/Orders:
CUP Services
Box 6525
750 Cascadilla Street
Ithaca, NY 14851-6525

Orders only: 800.666.2211
Fax: 607.272.6292
Customer Service: 607.277.2211

Staff

Director: Susan Wadsworth-Booth (412.396.6610; email: wadsworth@duq.edu)
Office Assistant: Mei Yi Lim (412.396.6610)
Production Editor: Kathy McLaughlin Meyer (412.396.1166; email: meyerk@duq.edu)
Editorial Assistant: Kasey Dickinson (412.396.4866)
Marketing & Business Manager: Lori R. Crosby (412.396.5732; email: crosbyl@duq.edu)
Promotions/Marketing Assistant: Tara Majdalani (412.396.4863)

Full Member

Established: 1927

Title output 2012: 10
Titles currently in print: 195

Admitted to AAUP: 1995
(Former membership: 1962-72)

Title output 2013: 10

Editorial Program

Literary studies, specifically of late medieval, Renaissance and seventeenth-century literature; ethics; philosophy; psychology; religious studies. The Press does not publish fiction, poetry, or unrevised dissertations.

Special series: Levinas Studies: An Annual Review; Medieval & Renaissance Literary Studies; Milton Studies; A Variorum Commentary on the Poems of John Milton; Philosophy/Communication

University Press of Florida

15 N.W. 15th Street
Gainesville, FL 32611-2079

Phone: 352.392.1351
Fax: 352.392.0590
Email: (user I.D.)@upf.com

Orders:
Phone: 800.226.3822
Fax: 352.392.7302
Toll free fax: 800.680.1955

Website and Social Media:
Website: www.upf.com
Blog: floridacurrent.wordpress.com
Facebook: www.facebook.com/pages/University-Press-of-Florida/257714960219
www.facebook.com/pages/The-Florida-Bookshelf/158260221214
Twitter: floridapress

UK Representative:
Eurospan

Canadian Representative:
Scholarly Book Services

Staff

Director: Meredith Morris Babb (ext. 204; email: mb)
  Assistant to the Director: Cindy Laukert (ext. 201; email: cl)
  Deputy Director: Dennis Lloyd (ext. 206; email: dl)
Interim Editor-in-Chief: Meredith Morris Babb (ext. 204; email: mb)
  Assistant Editor-in-Chief: Sian Hunter (919.428.8813; email: sian)
  Rights and Permissions Manager: Carmen Dolling (ext. 200; email: carmen)
  Acquisitions Editor: Sonia Dickey (ext. 232; email: sonia)
  Acquisitions Assistant: Shannon McCarthy (ext. 236; email: smccarthy)
Editorial, Design & Production: Lynn Werts, Associate Director & EDP Manager
  (ext. 222; email: lw)
  Managing Editor: Michele Fiyak-Burkley (ext. 212; email: mf)
  Editorial Assistants: Marthe Walters (ext. 217; email: marthe); Eleanor Deumans (ext. 216;
  email: eleanor); Nevil Parker (ext. 213; email: np)
  Design Manager: Larry Leshan (ext. 221; email: ll)
  Designer/Compositor: Robyn Taylor (ext. 218; email: rt)
Marketing Manager: Teal Amthor-Shaffer (ext. 209; email: tas)
  Advertising and Direct Mail Manager: Romi Gutierrez (ext. 235; email: rg)
  Sales and Marketing Assistant: Ale Gasso (ext. 233; email: ale)
  Awards and Exhibits: Rachel Doll (ext. 238; email: rd)
Business: Kim Lake, Associate Director for Finance (ext. 207; email: kl)
  Accounting/Order Fulfillment Manager: Sandra Dyson (ext. 210; email: sd)
  Credit Manager: Jackie Harvey (ext. 211; email: jackie)
  Order Entry: Chris Warner (352.392.6867; email: orders)
  Warehouse and Shipping Manager: Charles Hall (352.392.6867; email: charles)
Information Technology: Bryan Lutz, Manager (ext. 215; email: bryan)

Full Member

Established: 1945   Admitted to AAUP: 1950
Title output 2012: 86   Title output 2013: 88
Titles currently in print: 2,805

Editorial Program

Floridiana; New World archaeology; conservation biology; Latin American studies;
Caribbean studies; Middle East studies; African American studies; American history and
culture; Native American studies; dance; natural history; humanities. Submissions are not
invited in prose fiction or poetry.

Fordham University Press

Street Address: Mailing Address:
Canisius Hall   University Box L
2546 Belmont Avenue   Bronx, NY 10458-5172
Bronx, NY 10458-5172

Phone: 718.817.4795   Orders:
Fax: 718.817.4785   Oxford University Press, Inc.
Email: (user I.D.)@fordham.edu   2001 Evans Road
                                                    Cary, NC 27513
Website and Social Media: Phone: 800.445.9714
Website: www.fordhampress.com   Fax: 919.677.0977
Blog: www.fordhamimpressions.com   Email: custserv.us@oup.com
Facebook: www.facebook.com/FordhamUP
Twitter: fordhampress
Pinterest: www.pinterest.com/fordhampress
Empire State Editions: empirestateeditions.com/
Empire State Editions Twitter: www.twitter.com/E_S_Editions
Empire State Editions Facebook: www.facebook.com/EmpireStateEditions

European Representative: Canadian Representative:
Combined Academic Publishers Ltd.   Oxford University Press, Inc.

Staff

Director: Fredric W. Nachbaur (718.817.4789; email: fnachbaur)
   Editorial Associate and Assistant to the Director: Will Cerbone (718.817.4781;
   email: wcerbone)
Editorial Director: Helen Tartar (718.817.4787; email: tartar)
   Assistant Editor: Thomas Lay (718.817.4790; email: tlay)
Managing Editor: Eric Newman (718.817.4786; email: ernewman)
Production Editor: Loomis Mayer (718.817.4788; email: lmayer)
Marketing Director: Kate O'Brien-Nicholson (718.817.4782; email: bkaobrien)
   Assistant Marketing Manager: Kathleen A. Sweeney (718.817.4791; email: kasweeney)
Business Manager: Margaret M. Noonan (718.817.4780; email: mnoonan)
   Assistant Business Manager: Marie Hall (718.817.4783; email: mhall21)

Full Member

Established: 1907
Title output 2012: 71
Titles currently in print: 965

Admitted to AAUP: 1938
Title output 2013: 101
Journals published: 3

Editorial Program

Fordham University Press publishes primarily in the humanities and social sciences, with emphasis on the fields of philosophy, religion, theology, history, anthropology, and literature. Additionally, the Press publishes books focusing on the New York region and books of interest to the general public.

The Press distributes the publications of Creighton University Press; University of San Francisco Press; St. Joseph's University Press; Rockhurst University Press; the Institution for Advanced Study in the Theater Arts (IASTA); The Reconstructionist Press; Center for Migration Studies; and St. Bede's Publications.

Journals: *Dante Studies; Joyce Studies Annual; Traditio: Studies in Ancient and Medieval History, Thought, and Religion*

Imprints: Empire State Editions: Dedicated to publishing books about the New York Region.

Series: American Philosophy; Bordering Religions: Concepts, Conflicts, and Conversations; Catholic Practice in North America; Commonalities; Critical Studies in Italian America; Donald McGannon Research Center's Everett C. Parker Book Series; Fordham Series in Medieval Studies; Forms of Living; The Future of the Religious Past; Groundworks: Ecological Issues in Philosophy and Theology; Historicizing Dante; International Humanitarian Affairs; Just Ideas; Meaning Systems; Medieval Philosophy: Texts and Studies; The North's Civil War; Orthodox Christianity and Contemporary Thought; People and the Environment; Perspectives in Continental Philosophy; Psychoanalytic Interventions; Poets Out Loud; Reconstructing America; Thinking Out Loud; Townsend Papers in the Humanities; Transdisciplinary Theological Colloquia; Verbal Arts: Studies in Poetics; and World War II: The Global, Human, and Ethical Dimension.

Gallaudet University Press

800 Florida Avenue, N.E.
Washington, DC 20002-3695

Phone: 202.651.5488
Fax: 202.651.5489
Email: (user I.D.)@gallaudet.edu

Website and Social Media:
Website: gupress.gallaudet.edu

European Distributor:
University Chicago Press/John Wiley

Orders:
Gallaudet University Press
Chicago Distribution Center
11030 South Langley Avenue
Chicago, IL 60628
Phone: 800.621.2736
TTY: 888.630.9347
Fax: 800.621.8476

Pacific-Asian Area Representative:
East-West Export Books, Inc.

Staff

Executive Director: Gary Aller (202.651.5488; email: gary.aller)
Editorial: Ivey Pittle Wallace, Assistant Director and Acquisitions (202.651.5662;
  email: ivey.wallace)
Managing Editor: Deirdre Mullervy (202.651.5967; email: deirdre.mullervy)
Production: Donna Thomas, Coordinator (202.651.5488; email: donna.thomas)
Marketing: Dan Wallace, Assistant Director (202.651.5661; email: daniel.wallace)
  Marketing Assistant: Valencia Simmons (202.651.5488; email: valencia.simmons)
Business: Frances W. Clark (202.651.5455; email: frances.clark)

Full Member

Established: 1980   Admitted to AAUP: 1983
Title output 2012: 13   Title output 2013: 10
Titles currently in print: 278   Journals published: 2

Editorial Program

Scholarly books and serious nonfiction from all disciplines as they relate to the interests and
culture of people who are deaf, hard of hearing, or experiencing hearing loss. Particular areas
of emphasis include signed languages, linguistics, deaf culture, deaf history, disability studies,
biography and autobiography, parenting, and special education, as well as instructional works
and children's literature with sign language or deafness themes.

The Press distributes select titles from Signum Verlag (Hamburg, Germany).

Journals: *American Annals of the Deaf; Sign Language Studies*
Special imprints: Kendall Green Publications; Clerc Books
Special series: Deaf Lives; Deaf Education Series; Gallaudet Classics in Deaf Studies;
Interpreter Education; Sociolinguistics in Deaf Communities; Studies in Interpretation

Georgetown University Press

3240 Prospect Street NW, Suite 250
Washington, DC 20007

Phone: 202.687.5889
Fax: 202.687.6340
Email: gupress@georgetown.edu
Indiv: (user I.D.)@georgetown.edu

Orders:
US: c/o Hopkins Fulfillment Service
PO Box 50370
Baltimore, MD 21211
Phone: 800.537.5487
Fax: 410.516.6998
Email: hfscustserv@press.jhu.edu

Website and Social Media:
Website: www.press.georgetown.edu
Blog: georgetownuniversitypress.tumblr.com
Facebook: www.facebook.com/georgetownup
News blog: georgetownup.wordpress.com
Pinterest: pinterest.com/georgetownup
Twitter: gupress
YouTube: www.youtube.com/user/GeorgetownUP

UK/European Distributor:
NBN International

Canadian Representative:
Scholarly Book Services

Staff

Director: Richard Brown (202.687.5912; email: reb7)
  Publishing Assistant and Permissions Coordinator: Milica Cosic (202.687.4462; email: mc1794)
Director, Georgetown Languages: Hope LeGro (202.687.4704; email: hjs6)
Digital Editor, Georgetown Languages: Kyle Kuhn (202.687.2988; email: kdk40)
Acquisitions Editor, Political Science and International Affairs: Donald Jacobs (202.687.5218; email: dpj5)
Acquisitions Editor, Languages: David Nicholls (202.687.6263; email: dgn5)
Editorial and Production Manager: Deborah Weiner (202.687.6251; email: weinerd)
  Editorial and Production Coordinator: Nancy Driver (202.687.0159; email: njd23)
Assistant Director and Marketing and Sales Director: John W. Warren (202.687.9856; email: jww55)
  Marketing Coordinator: Maureen Mills (202.687.3671; email: mm634)
  Publicist: Jacqueline Beilhart (202.687.9298; email: jb594)
  Intellectual Property Manager: Laura Leichum (202.687.7687; email: lal75)
  Marketing Assistant: Miriam McPhie (202.687.8170; email: mhm56)
Business Manager: Ioan Suciu (202.687.5641; email: suciui)
  Accountant: Sulah Kim (202.687.8151; email: slk33)

Full Member

Established: 1964
Title output 2012: 39
Titles currently in print: 675

Admitted to AAUP: 1986
Title output 2013: 40
Journals published: 2

Editorial Program

Disciplines: bioethics; international affairs; languages and linguistics; political science, public policy, and public management; and religion and ethics.

Journals: *Al-cArabiyya: Journal of the American Association of Teachers of Arabic and Journal of the Society of Christian Ethics*

Special series: Advancing Human Rights; American Governance and Public Policy; Georgetown Classics in Arabic Language and Linguistics; Georgetown Studies in Spanish Linguistics; Georgetown University Round Table on Languages and Linguistics; Moral Traditions; Public Management and Change; Religion and Politics; South Asia in World Affairs; Working Languages

University of Georgia Press

Main Library, Third Floor
320 S. Jackson Street
Athens, GA 30602

Phone: 706.542.1007
Fax: 706. 542.2558
Email: books@ugapress.uga.edu
Indiv: (user I.D.)@ugapress.uga.edu
(unless otherwise indicated)

Distribution Center:
University of Georgia Press
Distribution Center
4435 Atlanta Highway West Dock
Bogart, GA 30622

Orders and Customer Service:
Phone: 800.266.5842
Fax: 706.425.3061

Website and Social Media:
Website: www.ugapress.org
Blog: ugapress.blogspot.com
Facebook: www.facebook.com/UGAPress
Goodreads: www.goodreads.com/UGAPress
Instagram: instagram.com/ugapress
Twitter: UGAPress
YouTube: UGAPress

UK Distributor:
Eurospan

Staff

Director: Lisa Bayer (706.542.0027; email: lbayer)
  Assistant to the Director and Development Coordinator: Elizabeth Crowley (706.542.1007; email: ecrowley)
  Intellectual Property Manager (Contracts & Rights): Sean Garrett (706.542.7175; email: sgarrett)
  Director of Development: Chantel Dunham (706.542.0628; email: cdunham@uga.edu)
Acquisitions Editorial: Mick Gusinde-Duffy, Assistant Director and Editor-in-Chief (706.542.9907; email: mgd)
  Senior Acquisitions Editor: Walter Biggins (702.542.4728; email: wbiggins)
  Acquisitions Editor: Patrick Allen (706.542.6004; email: pallen)

Assistant Acquisitions Editors: Beth Snead (706.542.7613; email: bsnead); Sydney Dupre (706.542.1903; email: sdupre)
Manuscript Editorial: Jon Davies, Assistant Director and Managing Editor (706.542.2101; email: jdavies)
Project Editor: John Joerschke (706.542.5137; email: johnj)
Design and Production: Kathi Dailey Morgan, Assistant Director and Design and Production Manager (706.542.2491; email: kdmorgan)
Production Editor: Rebecca Norton (706.542.4643; email: rnorton)
Senior Designer and Production Manager: Kaelin Broaddus (706.542.3889; email: kbroaddus)
Senior Designer and Art Director: Erin Kirk New (706.769.0879; email: ekirknew)
Reprints Coordinator: Melissa Bugbee Buchanan (706.542.4488; email: mbuchanan)
Marketing and Sales: David Des Jardines, Marketing and Sales Director (706.542.9758; email: ddesjard)
Publicity Manager: Amanda Sharp (706.542.4145; email: asharp)
Direct Mail Manager: Jason Bennett (706.542.9263; email: jbennett)
Marketing Designer and Advertising Manager: Jacqueline Baxter (706.542.4674; email: jbaxter)
Exhibits and Awards Manager: Christina Cotter (706.542.0134; email: ccotter)
Business: Phyllis Wells, Assistant Director and Business Manager (706.542.7250; email: pwells)
Senior Accountant: Marena Smith (706.542.0753; email: msmith)
Accounts Payable and Permissions Coordinator: Stacey Hayes (706.542.2606; email: shayes)
Distribution Center Manager: Jeri Headrick (706-369-6146, email: jheadrick)
Customer Service Assistant: Betty Downer (706.369.6148; email: bddowner)
Administrative and Shipping Clerk: Pam Bond (706.369.6149; email: pbond)
Shipping Clerk: Mark Jenkins (email: mjenkins)
IT Professional Associate: Matthew Tyler (email: mwtyler@uga.edu)
The New Georgia Encyclopedia Project (www.georgiaencyclopedia.org)
Editor: John Inscoe (706.542.8848; email: jinscoe@uga.edu)
Project Director and Managing Editor: Kelly Caudle (404.523.6220, ext. 18; email: kcaudle@uga.edu)
Project Editor: Sarah McKee (404.523.5702; email: semckee@uga.edu)

Full Member

Established: 1938   Admitted to AAUP: 1940
Title output 2012: 92   Title output 2013: 81
Titles currently in print: 1,939

Editorial Program

Humanities and social sciences with particular interests in Atlantic world, American, and southern history; civil rights history; legal history; environmental history; African American studies; geography; urban studies; international relations and security studies; natural history; environmental studies; nature writing; American and southern literature; American studies; cinema and media studies; food studies; popular culture; and regional trade titles.
Special series and imprints: Brown Thrasher Books; Center Books on the American South;

Early American Places; Environmental History and the American South; Geographies of Justice and Social Transformation; The New Southern Studies; Politics and Culture in the Twentieth-Century South; Publications of the Southern Texts Society; Race in the Atlantic World, 1700-1900; Since 1970: Histories of Contemporary America; Southern Foodways Alliance Studies in Culture, People, and Place, Southern Women: Their Lives and Times; The Spirit of the Laws; Studies in Security and International Affairs; Studies in the Legal History of the South; UnCivil Wars; The United States and the Americas; The Works of Tobias Smollett; A Wormsloe Foundation Nature Book; A Wormsloe Foundation Publication
Literary competitions: Flannery O'Connor Award for Short Fiction; The Association of Writers and Writing Programs Award for Creative Nonfiction; Cave Canem Poetry Prize; National Poetry Series
Lecture series: Mercer University Lamar Memorial Lectures; George H. Shriver Lecture Series in Religion in American History

Getty Publications

1200 Getty Center Drive
Suite 500
Los Angeles, CA 90049-1682

Phone: 310.440.7365
Fax: 310.440.7758
Email: pubsinfo@getty.edu
Indiv: (user I.D.)@getty.edu

Orders:
Chicago Distribution Center
11030 South Langley Avenue
Chicago, IL 60628
Phone: 800.621.2736
Fax: 800.621.8476
Email: custserv@press.uchicago.edu

Website and Social Media:
Website: www.getty.edu/publications
Facebook: www.facebook.com/GettyPublications
Tumblr: gettypubs.tumblr.com
Twitter: GettyPubs

UK/European Distributors:
Orca Book Services

UK/Sales Representative:
Roundhouse Group

Canada Sales Representative:
Canadian Manda Group

Staff
Publisher: Kara Kirk (310.440.6066; email: kkirk)
Getty Research Institute: Michele Ciaccio (310.440.7453; email: mciaccio)
Getty Conservation Institute: Cynthia Godlewski (310.440.6805; email: cgodlewski
Rights & Permissions: Leslie Rollins (310.440.7102; email: lrollins)
Editor-in-Chief: Robert T. Flynn (310.440.6486; email: rflynn)
Production: Karen Schmidt (310.440.6504; email: kschmidt)
Marketing & Sales: Mark Heineke (310.440.6117; email: mheineke)
General Manager: Carolyn Simmons (310.440.7130; email: csimmons)

Associate Member

Established: 1982
Title output 2012: 36
Titles currently in print: 545

Admitted to AAUP: 1989
Title output 2013: 31

Editorial Program
Scholarly and general interest publications on the visual arts; conservation and the history of art and the humanities; and areas related to the work of the Getty Research Institute, the Getty Conservation Institute, and the collections of the J. Paul Getty Museum: antiquities, decorative arts, drawings, manuscripts, paintings, photographs, and sculpture.

Harvard University Press

79 Garden Street
Cambridge, MA 02138-1499

Phone: 617.495.2600
Faxes: 617.495.5898 (General)
617.495.2611 (Editorial)
617.495.2606 (Sales/Marketing)
Email:
firstname_lastname@harvard.edu

Customer Service/Orders:
Harvard University Press
c/o TriLiteral-LLC
100 Maple Ridge Drive
Cumberland, RI 02864-1769
Phone: 800.405.1619 (US & Canada)
401.531.2800 (all others)
Faxes: 800.406.9145 (US & Canada)
401.531.2801 (all others)

Website and Social Media:
Website: www.hup.harvard.edu
Blog: harvardpress.typepad.com
Facebook: www.facebook.com/HarvardPress
Twitter: Harvard_Press
YouTube: www.youtube.com/user/harvardupress

European Office:
Harvard University Press
Vernon House
23 Sicilian Avenue
London WC1A 2QS United Kingdom
Email: info@harvardup.co.uk
Phone: 011.44.20.3463.2350

Staff
Director: William P. Sisler (617.495.2601)
Director of Intellectual Property and Subsidiary Rights: Stephanie Vyce (617.495.2603)
CFO/COO: Dan Wackrow (617.495.2613)
Assistant Director for University Relations/Executive Editor for Science and Medicine: Michael G. Fisher (617.495.2674)
Editor-in-Chief: Susan Wallace Boehmer (617.495.2624)
Executive Editor for Social Sciences: Michael Aronson (617.495.1837)
Executive Editor-at-Large: Elizabeth Knoll (617.495.0486)
Executive Editor-at-Large: John Kulka (203.227.4706)

Executive Editor-at-Large (Europe): Ian Malcolm (44 7843 301 029)
Executive Editor for History: Kathleen McDermott (617.495.4703)
Senior Executive Editor for History and Contemporary Affairs: Joyce Seltzer (212.337.0280)
Executive Editor-at-Large: Sharmila Sen (617.495.8122)
Executive Editor for the Humanities: Lindsay Waters (617.495.2835)
Senior Editor for Digital Publications Development: Emily Arkin (617.496.4690)
Managing Editor: Mary Ann Lane (617.495.1846)
Editorial Manager: David Foss (617.496.8170)
Director of Design and Production: Tim Jones (617.495.2669)
  Assistant Production Director: Abigail Mumford (617.496.9421)
  Design Manager: Lisa Roberts (617.495.5129)
Assistant Director/Sales and Marketing Director: Susan Donnelly (617.495.2606)
  Sales Manager/Digital Content Manager: Vanessa Vinarub (617.495.2650)
  Publicity Manager: Phoebe Kosman (617.495.0303)
  Senior Publicist: Lisa LaPoint (617.495.1284)
  Web Marketing Manager: Gregory Kornbluh (617.496.3281)
  Promotion Manager: Sheila Barrett (617.495.2618)
  Special Sales: Briana Ross (617.384.7515)
  Exhibits Manager: Val Hunt (617.495.2607)
  Sales Manager (Europe): Richard Howells (011.44.20.3463.2350)
  Marketing Manager (Europe): Rebekah White (011.44.20.3463.2350)

Full Member

Established: 1913	Admitted to AAUP: 1937
Title output 2012: 267	Title output 2013: 290
Titles currently in print: 8,000	

Editorial Program

Scholarly books and serious works of general interest in the humanities, the social and behavioral sciences, the natural sciences, and medicine. The Press does not normally publish poetry, fiction, festschriften, memoirs, symposia, or unrevised doctoral dissertations.

The Press distributes publications for a number of Harvard University departments and affiliates: Archaeological Exploration of Sardis, Center for Hellenic Studies, Center for the Study of World Religions, David Rockefeller Center for Latin American Studies, Department of Celtic Languages and Literatures, Department of the Classics, Department of Comparative Literature, Department of English, Department of Music, Department of Near Eastern Languages and Civilizations, Department of Sanskrit and Indian Studies, Derek Bok Center, Dumbarton Oaks Research Library and Collection, FXB Center for Health and Human Rights, Harvard Center for Middle Eastern Studies, Harvard College Library, Harvard Divinity School, Harvard Global Equity Initiative, Harvard University Asia Center, Harvard University Center for Jewish Studies, Harvard University Graduate School of Design, Houghton Library of the Harvard College Library, Ilex Foundation, Islamic Legal Studies Program, Harvard Law School, Peabody Museum Press, School of Public Health, the Ukrainian Research Institute of Harvard University, and Villa I Tatti.

Special imprints: The Belknap Press

Special series, joint imprints, and/or copublishing programs: The Adams Papers; Bernard Berenson Lectures; Carl Newell Jackson Lectures; Charles Eliot Norton Lectures; Dumbarton Oaks Medieval Library; Edwin O. Reischauer Lectures; Godkin Lectures; Harvard Historical Studies and Monographs; Harvard Studies in Business History; I Tatti Renaissance Library; I Tatti Renaissance Monographs; John Harvard Library; Loeb Classical Library; Loeb Classical Monographs; Nathan I. Huggins Lectures; Oliver Wendell Holmes Lectures; Revealing Antiquity; Tanner Lectures; W.E.B. Du Bois Lectures; William E. Massey Sr. Lectures

University of Hawai'i Press

2840 Kolowalu Street
Honolulu, HI 96822-1888

Phone: 808.956.8257
Fax: 808.988.6052
Email: (user I.D.)@hawaii.edu

Orders:
Phone: 888.UHPRESS; 808.956.8255
Fax: 800.650.7811; 808.988.5203

Website and Social Media:
Website: www.uhpress.hawaii.edu
Blog: uhpress.wordpress.com
Facebook: www.facebook.com/pages/University-of-Hawaii-Press/200519105362
Twitter: UHPRESSNEWS

European Distributor:
Eurospan

Staff

Director: Michael Duckworth (808.956.6218; email: mpd4)
  Secretary to the Director: Cheryl Reyes (808.956.8257; email: cherylre)
Acquisitions Editorial: Patricia Crosby, Executive Editor (808.956.6209; email: pcrosby)
  Editors: Pamela Kelley (808.956.6207; email: pkelley); Nadine Little (808.956.6208; email: nlittle); Masako Ikeda (808.956.8696; email: masakoi)
  Editorial Associates: Stephanie Chun (808.956.6426; email: chuns); Debra Tang (808.956.8694; email: dtang)
Managing Editors: Cheri Dunn (808.956.6210; email: cheri); Ann Ludeman (808.956.8695; email: aludeman)
Design and Production: Santos Barbasa, Manager (808.956.8877; email: barbasa)
  Production Editors: Julie Matsuo-Chun (808.956.8276; email: jsmatsuo); Mardee Melton (808.956.2858; email: mmelton); Lucille Aono (808.956.6328; email: lucille)
  Fiscal Support Specialist: Terri Miyasato (808.956.8275; email: terrimiy)
Marketing and Sales: Colins Kawai, Director (808.956.6417; email: ckawai)
  Sales Manager: Royden Muranaka (808.956.6214; email: royden)
  Product Manager: Steven Hirashima (808.956.8698; email: stevehir)
  Promotion Manager: Carol Abe (808.956.8697; email: abec)
  E-Marketing Specialist: TBA

Journals: TBA, Manager (808.956.6790)
  Journals Managing Editor: TBA
  Production Editor: Cindy Chun (808.956.8834; email: cindychu)
  Administrative Assistant: Norman Kaneshiro (808.956.8833; email: uhpjourn)
East-West Export Books: Royden Muranaka, International Sales Manager (808.956.6214;
  email: royden)
  Assistant: Kiera Nishimoto (808.956.8830; email: eweb)
Business: Joel Cosseboom, CFO (808.956.6292; email: cosseboo)
  Credit Manager: Kyle Higa (808.956.6228; email: kshiga21)
  Order Processing: Cindy Yen (808.956.8256; email: cyen); Danny Li (808.956.6279;
  email: wingon)
  Warehouse: Kyle Nakata, Clifford Newalu (808.956.3357; email: uhpwhse)

Full Member

Established: 1947   Admitted to AAUP: 1951
Title output 2012: 74   Title output 2013: 62
Titles currently in print: 1,653   Journals published: 20

Editorial Program

Asian, Pacific, and Asian American studies in history; art; anthropology; architecture;
economics; sociology; philosophy and religion; languages and linguistics; law; literature;
performing arts; political science; physical and natural sciences; regional studies.
Journals: *Archives of Asian Art; Asian Perspectives; Asian Theatre Journal; Azalea; Biography;
Buddhist-Christian Studies; China Review International; The Contemporary Pacific; Cross-
Currents; Journal of Korean Religions; Journal of World History; Korean Studies; Language
Documentation and Conservation; Manoa; Oceanic Linguistics; Pacific Science; Philosophy East
and West; Review of Japanese Culture and Society; U.S.-Japan Women's Journal; Yearbook of the
Association of Pacific Coast Geographers*
Special series, joint imprints, and/or copublishing programs: ABC Chinese Dictionary;
ASAA (Asian Studies Association of Australia) Southeast Asia Publications; Biography
Monographs; Critical Interventions; Dimensions of Asian Spirituality; Hawai'i Studies
on Korea; Hawai'inuiakea Series (Hawai'inuiakea School of Hawaiian Knowledge);
Intersections: Asian and Pacific American Transcultural Studies; KLEAR Textbooks in
Korean Language (Korean Language Education and Research Center/Korea Foundation);
Korean Classics Library: Historical Materials; Korean Classics Library: Philosophy and
Religion; Kuroda Institute Classics in East Asian Buddhism; Kuroda Institute Studies in
East Asian Buddhism; Modern Korean Fiction; Nanzan Library for Asian Religion and
Culture; National Foreign Language Resource Center Monographs; Oceanic Linguistics
Special Publications; Pacific Islands Monographs; PALI Language Texts; Perspectives on the
Global Past; Pure Land Buddhist Studies; Social Process in Hawaii Monographs; Society for
Asian and Comparative Philosophy; Southeast Asia: Politics, Meaning, and Memory; Spatial
Habitus: Making and Meaning in Asia's Architecture; Topics in Contemporary Buddhism;
The World of East Asia; Writing Past Colonialism

Hong Kong University Press

The University of Hong Kong
Run Run Shaw Heritage House
Pokfulam Road
Hong Kong

Phone: +852 39177815
Fax: +852 28581655
E-mail: hkupress@hku.hk
Indiv: (user I.D.)@hku.hk

Website and Social Media:
Website: www.hkupress.org

North American Distributors:
Columbia University Press
61 West 62nd Street
New York, NY 10023

Phone: 212.459.0600
Fax: 212.459.3678

UK/European Distributor:
Columbia University Press

Staff
Publisher: TBA
Administration: Maria Yim (+852 39177815; email: hkupress)
Acquisitions: Christopher Munn, Associate Publisher (+852 39177805; email: cmunn)
   Editorial: Clara Ho, Managing Editor (+852 39177814; email: cscho)
Production: Jennifer Flint, Design & Production Manager (+852 39177809; email: jbflint)
Marketing: Winnie Chau, Sales & Marketing Manager (+852 39177803; email: wywchau)
Business: Connie Yip, Business & Warehouse Manager (+852 25502703; email: uporders)
Rights: Christy Leung, Assistant Editor & Rights Manager (+852 39177812; email:
   leungsyc)

International Member
Established: 1956
Title output 2012: 55
Titles currently in print: 925+

Admitted to AAUP: 2009
Title output 2013: 51

Editorial Program
English and Chinese scholarly books in humanities, art, social sciences, law, medicine,
education, science, architecture/urban planning; particular strengths in Asian film and
cultural studies, China studies, gender studies, linguistics and language training, as well as
Asian law, history, politics, economics, photography, natural history, and Hong Kong/Macau
studies.
Special series: Asian Englishes Today; Global Connections; Echoes: Classics of Hong
Kong Culture and History; Education in China: Reform and Diversity; HKU Press Law
Series; The New Hong Kong Cinema; Hong Kong Culture and Society; Hong Kong
Teacher Education; Queer Asia; Royal Asiatic Society Hong Kong Studies Series; Studying
Multicultural Discourses; Traces: A Multilingual Series of Cultural Theory and Translation;
TransAsia: Screen Cultures; Understanding China: New Viewpoints on History and Culture

University of Illinois Press

1325 S. Oak Street
Champaign, IL 61820-6903

Phone: 217.333.0950
Fax: 217.244.8082
Email: uipress@uillinois.edu
Journals: journals@uillinois.edu
Indiv: (user I.D.)@uillinois.edu

Website and Social Media:
Website: www.press.uillinois.edu
Blog: www.press.uillinois.edu/wordpress
Facebook: www.facebook.com/UniversityofIllinoisPress
Twitter:@IllinoisPress

Warehouse Address and Orders:
University of Illinois Press
c/o Chicago Distribution Center
11030 South Langley Avenue
Chicago, IL 60628

Orders:
Books: 800.621.2736
Email: orders@press.uchicago.edu
Journals: 866.244.0626

UK/European Representative:
Combined Academic Publishers

Canadian Representative:
Scholarly Book Services

Staff

Director: Willis G. Regier (217.244.0728; email: wregier)
  Assistant to the Director: Kathy O'Neill (217.244.4691; email: oneill2)
  Rights, Permissions, and Awards Manager: Angela Burton (217.244.0820;
  email: uip-rights, alburton)
Acquisitions Editors: Laurie Matheson, Editor-in-Chief (American history, Appalachian
  studies, labor studies, music, folklore) (217.244.4685; email: lmatheso); Willis G. Regier
  (ancient religion, literature, translations, sports history, Lincoln studies, Nietzsche studies,
  classics) (217.244.0728; email: wregier); Larin McLaughlin (African American studies,
  Asian American studies, women's studies, American studies, religion) (217.244.8978;
  email: larinmc); Daniel Nasset (communication studies, anthropology, film studies,
  military history) (217.244.5182; email: dnassset)
  Assistant Editors: Marika Christofides; Dawn Durante (Women in American History)
  (217.265.8491; email: durante9)
Electronic Publisher: Paul Arroyo (217.244.7147; email: parroyo)
Editorial, Design, and Production Manager: Jennifer Reichlin (217.244.3279;
  email: reichlin)
  Assistant Managing Editor: Jennifer Clark (217.244.8041; email: jsclark1)
  Copyeditor: Tad Ringo (217.265.0238; email: tringo)
  Production: Kristine Ding, Production Manager (217.244.4701; email: kding)
  Production Coordinator: Tamara Shidlauski (217.265.0940; email: shidlaus)
  Art Director: Dustin Hubbart (217.333.9227; email dhubbart)
  Designer: Kelly Gray (email: kellyg)
Marketing: Michael Roux, Marketing Manager (217.244.4683; email: mroux)
  Publicity Manager: Steven Fast (217.244.4689; email: sfast)
  Sales Manager: Lynda Schuh (217.333.9071; email: lschuh)
  Exhibits Manager: Margo Chaney (217.244.6491; email: mechaney)
  Direct Marketing & Advertising Manager: Denise Peeler (217.244.4690; email: dpeeler)

Catalog & Copywriting Coordinator: Kevin Cunningham (217.244.5069; email: rkcunnin)

Journals: Clydette Wantland, Journals Manager (217.244.6496; email: cwantlan)
  Associate Journals Manager: Jeff McArdle (217.244.0381; email: jmcardle)
  Journals Production Editors: Heather Munson (217.244.6488; email: hmunson);
  Stephanie Turza (217.244.8870; email: sturza2);
  Journals Circulation Manager: Cheryl Jestis (866.244.0626; email: jestis)
  Journals Marketing and Advertising Manager: Jeff McArdle (217.244.0381;
  email: jmcardle)

Chief Financial Officer: Alice Ennis (217.244.0091; email: atennis)
  Network Administrator: Louis W. Mesker (217.244.8025; email: lmesker)

Full Member

Established: 1918	Admitted to AAUP: 1937
Title output 2012: 93	Title output 2013: 82
Titles currently in print: 2,116	Journals published: 32

Editorial Program

Scholarly books and serious nonfiction, with special interests in American history; Literary biography and science fiction, critical theory; American music; African American history and literature; sport history; religious studies; cultural studies; communications; cinema studies; law and society; regional photography and art; philosophy; architectural history; environmental studies; sociology; women's history; women's studies; working-class history

Journals: *American Journal of Psychology; American Journal of Theology & Philosophy; American Literary Realism; American Music; American Philosophical Quarterly; Black Music Research Journal; Bulletin of the Council for Research in Music Education; Ethnomusicology; Feminist Teacher; History of Philosophy Quarterly; History of the Present; Illinois Classical Studies; Illinois Heritage; Journal of the Abraham Lincoln Association; Journal of Aesthetic Education; Journal of American Ethnic History; Journal of American Folklore; Journal of Animal Ethics; Journal for the Anthropological Study of Human Movement; Journal of Education Finance; Journal of English and Germanic Philology; Journal of Film & Video; Journal of the Illinois State Historical Society; Music and Moving Image; Perspectives on Work; The Pluralist; Polish American Studies; The Polish Review; Public Affairs Quarterly; Scandinavian Studies; Visual Arts Research; Women, Gender and Families of Color; World History Connected*

Special series, joint imprints, and/or copublishing programs: African American Music in Global Perspective; American Composers; The Asian American Experience; Bach Perspectives; The Beauvoir Series; Beethoven Sketchbook Series; Contemporary Film Directors; Critical Public Policy Issues; Democracy, Free Enterprise, and the Role of Law; Dissident Feminisms; Feminist Media Studies; Folklore Studies In a Multicultural World; The Geopolitics of Information; Heartland Foodways; Hispanisms; The History of Communication; The History of Emotions; Interpretations of Culture in the New Millennium; The Knox College Lincoln Studies Center; Latinos in Chicago and the Midwest; Lemann Institute for Brazilian Studies Series; Modern Masters of Science Fiction; Music in American Life; The New Black Studies Series; New Perspectives on Gender in Music; Popular Culture and Politics In Asia Pacific; Race and Gender In Science Studies; Sport and Society; Studies in the History of Music Theory and Literature; Studies in Sensory History; Studies of World Migrations; Topics in the Digital Humanities; Traditions; The Urban Agenda; Women in American History; Working Class in American History; Women Composers; Women and Film History International; Women, Gender and Technology

IMF Publications (International Monetary Fund)

Street Address:
700 19th Street, NW
Washington, DC 20431

Mailing Address:
Publications Services
P.O. Box 92780
Washington, DC 20090

Phone: 202.623.7430
Fax: 202.623.7201
Email: publications@imf.org

Orders:
202.623.7430
202.623.7201
Online: www.imfbookstore.org

Website and Social Media:
Websites: www.imfbookstore.org; www.elibrary.imf.org
Blog: blog-iMFdirect.imf.org
Twitter: IMFNews

Canadian Representative:
Renouf Publishing Co. Ltd.

UK/European Representative:
Eurospan Group

Staff

Publisher: Jeremy Clift (202.623.9464; email: jclift@imf.org)
Associate Publisher: Linda Griffin Kean (202.623.4124; email: lkean@imf.org)
Rights Manager/Acquisitions Editor/Conference Manager: Patricia Loo (202.623.8296;
    email: ploo@imf.org)
   Administrative Assistant: Suzanne Alavi (202.623.5348; email: salavi@imf.org)
   Staff Assistant: Akshay Modi (202.623.8964; email: amodi@imf.org)
Electronic Publishing Officer: Jim Beardow (202.623.7899; email: jbeardow@imf.org)
Web Publishing Officer: François Gouahinga (202.623.4121; email: fgouahinga@imf.org)
Digital Publishing Officer: S.M. Hassan Zaidi (202.623.8102; email: szaidi@imf.org)
Editors: Joanne Blake (202.623.8807; email: jblake@imf.org); Michael Harrup
    (202.623.7504; email: mharrup@imf.org); Joseph Procopio (202.623.9258; email:
    jprocopio@imf.org); Cathy Gagnet (202.623.6037; email: cgagnet@imf.org)
Marketing Manager: Cathy Willis (202.623.7426; email: cwillis@imf.org)
Licensing and Contracts Agent: Alexa Smith (952.944.5729; email: asmith2@imf.org)
Finance Administrator: Cristina Pagan (202.623.4824; email: cpagan@imf.org)
Process Management Consultant: John Brenneman (202.623.7092;
    email: jbrenneman@imf.org)

Associate Member

Established: 1948	Admitted to AAUP: 2011
Title output 2012: 31	Title output 2013: 39
Titles currently in print: 721	Journals published: 2

Editorial Program

The International Monetary Fund publishes a wide variety of books, periodicals, and
electronic products covering economics, international finance, monetary issues, statistics, and
exchange rates.

Journals: *Finance & Development; IMF Economic Review*
Special series: Departmental Papers; Occasional Papers; Staff Discussion Notes; Technical Notes and Manuals; World Economic and Financial Surveys (includes World Economic Outlook, Fiscal Monitor, Global Financial Stability Report, and Regional Economic Outlooks); Working Papers
Joint imprints and copublishing programs: Select titles copublished with John Wiley & Sons, MIT Press, Oxford University Press, Palgrave Macmillan, and Routledge.

Indiana University Press

Office of Scholarly Publishing
Herman B Wells Library 350
1320 E. 10th Street
Bloomington, IN 47405

Fulfillment Center:
C/O Ingram Publisher Services
1280 Ingram Drive
Chambersburg, PA 17202

Phone: 812.855.8817
Phone: 800.842.6796
Email: iupress@indiana.edu
Indiv: (user I.D.)@indiana.edu

Orders: 800.648.3013
Fax: 812.855.8507
Email (vendors): pubsupport@ingramcontent.com
Email (individuals): iuporder@indiana.edu

Canadian Representative:
Lexa Publishers' Representative

UK/European Representative:
Combined Academic Publishers

Website and Social Media:
Web: iupress.indiana.edu
Blog: iupress.typepad.com/blog
Twitter: iupress
Facebook: www.facebook.com/iupress
Google+: plus.google.com/115444288032700584669
YouTube: www.youtube.com/iupress

Staff

Executive Director, Office of Scholarly Publishing: Carolyn Walters (812.855.34037747; email: cwalters)
Interim Editor-in-Chief: Robert Sloan (812.855.7561; email: rjsloan)
Rights and Permissions Manager: Peter Froehlich (812.855.6314; email: pfroehli)
Acquisitions Editorial: Robert Sloan, Interim Editor-in-Chief (African American and Black Atlantic studies, bioethics, American history, military history, paleontology, philanthropy) (812.855.7561; email: rjsloan)
Senior Sponsoring Editor: Dee Mortensen (Africa, philosophy, religion) (812.855.0268; email: mortense)
Sponsoring Editors: Raina Polivka (music, film/media/cultural studies) (812.855.5261; email: rpolivka); Linda Oblack (regional, railroads) (812.855.2175; email: loblack); Rebecca Tolen (anthropology, Asia, Middle East, global studies) (812.855.2756; email: retolen)

Assistant Sponsoring Editors: Sarah Jacobi (assistant to Dee Mortensen, Linda Oblack, and Rebecca Tolen) (812.855.5262; email: sajacobi); Jenna Whittaker (assistant to Raina Polivka and Robert Sloan) (812.856.5810; email: jewhitta)

Editorial, Design, and Production (EDP): Bernadette Zoss, EDP Director (812.855.5563; email: bzoss)

Project Managers: June Silay (812.856.4645; email: jsilay); Nancy Lightfoot (812.855.1744; email: nlightfo); Darja Malcolm-Clarke (812.855.5428; email: dmalcolm); Michelle Sybert (812.855.5064; email: msybert)

Senior Artists and Book Designers: Pam Rude (812.855.0264; email: psrude); Jamison Cockerham (812.855.9640; email: jrc9)

Graphic Designer: Jennifer Witzke (812.855.4415; email: jwitzke)

Production Coordinator: Dan Pyle (812.856.5233; email: dapyle)

Publishing Services Coordinator: Tony Brewer (812.855.9444; email: tbrewer)

Production Assistant: Laura Hohman (812.855.6777; email: lhohman)

Project Managers: June Silay (812.856.4645; email: jsilay); Nancy Lightfoot (812.855.1744; email: nlightfo); Michelle Sybert (812.855.5064; email: msybert); Chandra Mevis (812.855.5031; email: cnmevis); Darja Malcolm-Clarke (812.855.5428; dmalcolm)

Marketing and Sales: Dave Hulsey, Marketing and Sales Director (812.855.6553; email: hulseyd)

Trade Marketing and Publicity Manager: Mandy Clarke (812.855.5429; email: mlclarke)

Electronic Marketing Manager: Laura Baich (812.855.8287; email: lbaich)

Advertising and Exhibit Manager: Mollie Ables (812.855.5429; email: mables)

Publicity Coordinator: Theresa Halter (812.855.8054; email: thalter)

Marketing Designer: Jennifer Witzke (812.855.4415; email: jwitzke)

Sales: Mary Beth Haas, Sales Manager (812.855.9440; email: mbhaas)

Sales and Marketing Assistant: Rhonda Van Der Dussen (812.855.6657; email: rdussen)

Journals, Electronic, and Serials Publishing: Kathryn Caras, Director of Electronic and Serials Publishing (812.855.3830; email: kcaras)

Electronic and Serials Manager: Joy Andreakis (812.856.5218; email: jandreak)

Journals Marketing Manager: Linda Bannister (812.855.9449; email: llbannis)

Journals Production Manager: Judith Caldwell (812.856.0582; email: jucaldwe)

Business and Operations: Michael Noth, Interim Fiscal Officer (812.855.3403; email: mnoth)

Interim Human Resources Officer: Jennifer Chaffin (812.855.5988; email: jlchaffi)

Senior Accounting Coordinator: Kathy Stout (812.855.2726; email: kwhaley)

Assistant Business Manager for Network Systems and Order Processing: Janie Pearson (812.855.1588; email: cjfender)

Assistant Business Manager for Accounts Receivable & Customer Service: Kim Childers (812.855.4134; email: kchilder)

Information Technology: Ted Boardman, Technology Director of Publishing Operations (812.855.6468; email: tboardma)

Systems Analyst/Programmer: Rich Pierce (812.856.0210; email: ripierce)

Full Member

Established: 1950

Title output 2012: 133

Titles currently in print: 2,570

Admitted to AAUP: 1952

Title output 2013: 140

Journals published: 27

Editorial Program

African studies; African American and African Diaspora studies; anthropology; Asian and South Asian studies; bioethics; cultural studies; ethnomusicology; film and media studies; folklore; history; international studies; Jewish and Holocaust studies; Latin American studies; Middle East studies; military history; music; paleontology; philanthropy; philosophy; railroad history; religion; Russian and East European studies; state and regional studies; women's and gender studies.

Journals: *Africa Today; ACPR: African Conflict and Peacebuilding Review; Aleph: Historical Studies in Science & Judaism; Black Camera; Chiricú: A Journal of Latino Literature, Art, and Culture; e-Service Journal; Ethics & the Environment; Film History; The Global South; History & Memory; Indiana Journal of Global Legal Studies; IJFAB: International Journal of Feminist Approaches to Bioethics; Israel Studies; Jewish Social Studies; Journal of Feminist Studies in Religion; JFR: Journal of Folklore Research; Journal of Modern Literature; Meridians: feminism, race, transnationalism; Nashim: A Journal of Jewish Women's & Gender Issues; PMER: Philosophy of Music Education Review; Prooftexts: A Journal of Jewish Literary History; Research in African Literatures; Spectrum: The Journal of Black Men; Teaching and Learning Inquiry; Transactions of the Charles S. Peirce Society: A Quarterly Journal in American Philosophy; Transition; Victorian Studies*

Special series: 21st Century Studies; African Epic; African Expressive Cultures; African Systems of Thought; American Philosophy; Bioethics and the Humanities; Blacks in the Diaspora; Chinese in Context Language Learning Series; Cinematheque Ontario Monographs; Counterpoints: Music and Education; Digital Game Studies; Ethnomusicology Multimedia; Excavations at Ancient Halieis; Excavations at Franchthi Cave, Greece; Global African Voices; The Helen and Martin Schwartz Lectures in Jewish Studies; A History of the Trans-Appalachian Frontier; Indiana Natural Science; Indiana Repertoire Guides; Indiana Series in Middle East Studies; Indiana Series in the Philosophy of Religion; Indiana Series in Sephardi and Mizrahi Studies; Indiana Studies in Biblical Literature; Indiana-Michigan Series in Russian and East European Studies; Jewish Literature and Culture; KINtop Studies in Early Cinema; Library of Indiana Classics; Life of the Past; The Modern Jewish Experience; Music and the Early Modern Imagination; Musical Meaning and Interpretation; New Anthropologies of Europe; New Directions in National Cinema; Philanthropic and Nonprofit Studies; Polis Center Series on Religion and Urban Culture; Profiles in Popular Music; Public Cultures of the Middle East and North Africa; Publications of the Early Music Institute; Railroads Past and Present; Readings in African Studies; Religion in North America; Russian Music Studies; Scholarship of Teaching and Learning; Selections from the Writing of Charles S. Peirce; South Asian Cinema; Spatial Humanities; Special Publications of the Folklore Institute, Indiana University; Studies in Continental Thought; Textual Cultures; Tracking Globalization; Twentieth-Century Battles; United Nations Intellectual History Project; The Variorum Edition of the Poetry of John Donne; World Philosophies; The Year's Work: Studies in Fan Culture and Cultural Theory

University of Iowa Press

Editorial Office:
119 West Park Road
100 Kuhl House
Iowa City, IA 52242-1000

Phone: 319.335.2000
Fax: 319.335.2055
Email: (user I.D.)@uiowa.edu

Website and Social Media:
Website: www.uiowapress.org
Blog: buroakblog.blogspot.com/
Facebook: www.facebook.com/UIowaPress

Order Fulfillment:
University of Iowa Press
c/o Chicago Distribution Center
11030 South Langley Avenue
Chicago, IL 60628
Phone: 800.621.2736
Fax: 800.621.8476

UK/European Representative:
Eurospan

Staff

Director: Jim McCoy (319.335.2013; email: james-mccoy)
   Assistant to the Director: Faye Schillig (319.335.3424; email: faye-schillig)
   Rights and Permissions: Lydia Crowe (319.384.2008; email: lydia-crowe)
Editorial:
   Acquisitions Editors: Elisabeth Chretien (literary criticism, poetics, creative nonfiction, humanities) (319.335.2015; email: elisabeth-chretien); Catherine Cocks (natural history, regional history, anthropology/archaeology, fan studies, food studies, performance studies) (319.384.1910; email: cath-campbell); Jim McCoy (poetry, short fiction, general trade) (319.335.2013; email: james-mccoy)
Managing Editor: Charlotte Wright (319.335.2011; email: charlotte-wright)
Design and Production: Karen Copp, Associate Director and Design and Production Manager (319.335.2014; email: karen-copp)
Marketing: Allison Thomas Means, Marketing Manager (319.335.3440; email: allison-means)

Full Member

Established: 1969
Title output 2012: 39
Titles currently in print: 850

Admitted to AAUP: 1982
Title output 2013: NR

Editorial Program

American literary criticism and history, particularly children's literature, biography, and women's studies, contemporary American literature; memoirs; short fiction (award winners only); poetry (single-author titles and anthologies); creative nonfiction; regional studies; regional natural history; archaeology/anthropology; theatre history; American studies; food studies; fan studies; public humanities.

Special series: American Land and Life Series; Bur Oak Books and Bur Oak Guides; Contemporary North American Poetry; Iowa Poetry Prize; Iowa Short Fiction Award and John Simmons Short Fiction Award; Iowa and the Midwest Experience; Iowa Whitman Series; Kuhl House Poets; Muse Books; New American Canon; Sightline Books: The Iowa Series in Literary Nonfiction; Studies in Theatre History and Culture; Writers in Their Own Time

Island Press

Editorial/Administration:
2000 M St NW, Suite 650
Washington, DC 20036

Phone: 202.232.7933
Fax: 202.234.1328
Email: firstinitiallastname@islandpress.org

Website and Social Media:
Website: www.islandpress.org
Blog: blog.islandpress.org
Facebook: www.facebook.com/IslandPress
Twitter: IslandPress

Order Fulfillment:
Chicago Distribution Center
11030 South Langley Avenue
Chicago, IL 60628
Phone: 800.621.2736
Fax: 800.621.8476

UK/European Representative:
Oxford Publicity Partners

Canadian Representative:
University of British Columbia Press

Staff
President: Charles C. Savitt
Assistant to the President: Ajay Abraham (ext. 27)
Senior VP & Publisher: David Miller (ext.14)
VP & Chief Financial Officer: Ken Hartzell (301.576.6221)
VP for Strategic Advancement: Denise Schlener (ext. 25)
Permissions: Amy Bridges (ext. 10)
Acquisitions/Editorial: Barbara Dean, Executive Editor (ecosystems, natural environment) (ext. 55); Heather Boyer, Executive Editor (built environment) (303.641.5344); Courtney Lix, Associate Editor (urban ecology); Emily Davis, Editor (health, freshwater, and food) (202.271.7399)
Design and Production: Maureen Gately, Director of Production and Design (ext. 49)
Marketing/Sales/Advertising/Publicity: Julie Marshall, VP of Marketing and Sales (ext. 32)
IT: Craig Elie, IT Manager (ext. 45)

Associate Member
Established: 1984

Admitted to AAUP: 1999

Title output 2012: 42

Title output 2013: 35

Titles currently in print: 831

Editorial Program
Scholarly and professional titles in environmental studies and natural resource management; nonfiction trade titles on nature and the environment; electronic publishing on environmental topics and news. Subject areas include ecosystems management, sustainable communities, protection of biodiversity and human health, environmentally responsible land use planning, sustainable design, marine science and policy, climate and energy, and economics and policy.
The Press's full name is Island Press—Center for Resource Economics.

Special series, joint imprints, and/or copublishing programs: Case Studies in Land and Community Design (with the Landscape Architecture Foundation); Ecoregions of the World: A Conservation Assessment (with The World Wildlife Fund); Foundations of Contemporary Environmental Studies; The Millennium Ecosystem Assessment; The Science and Practice of Ecological Restoration (with the Society for Ecological Restoration International); State of the Wild (with Wildlife Conservation Society); The World's Water (with The Pacific Institute for Studies in Development, Environment, and Security); International Assessment of Agricultural Knowledge, Science and Technology for Development; State of the World and Vital Signs (with the Worldwatch Institute), Metropolitan Planning + Design Series (with the University of Utah).

The Johns Hopkins University Press

2715 N. Charles Street
Baltimore, MD 21218-4363

Phone: 410.516.6900
Fax: 410.516.6998/6968
Email: (user I.D.)@press.jhu.edu

Distribution Center:
C/O Maple Logistics Solutions
Lebanon Distribution Center
704 Legionaire Drive
Fredericksburg, PA 17026

Orders and Customer Service:
Phone: 800.537.5487 (HFS)
Phone: 800.548.1784 (Journals)
Phone: 410.516.6989 (MUSE)

Website and Social Media:
Website: www.press.jhu.edu
Facebook: www.facebook.com/JohnsHopkinsUniversityPress
Twitter: JHUPress

UK Representative:
Yale Representation, Ltd.

Staff
Director: Kathleen Keane (410.516.6971; email: kk)
  Assistant to the Director: Jane Barchichat (410.516.6971; email: jeb)
  Rights and Permissions Manager: Kelly Rogers (410.516.6063; email: klr)
  Office and Facilities Coordinator: Nora Reedy (410.516.7035; email: ncr)
  Director, Finance and Administration: Erik Smist (410.516.6941; email: eas)
  Chief Information Officer: Timothy Fuller (410.516.3844; email: tdf)
Acquisitions Editorial: Gregory M. Britton, Editorial Director (Higher Education) (410.516.6919; email: gb)
  Executive Editors: Vincent J. Burke (science & math) (410.516.6999; email: vjb); Jacqueline C. Wehmueller (consumer health, history of medicine, psychology and psychiatry) (410.516.6904; email: jcw)
  Senior Editor: Robert J. Brugger (American history, history of science) (410.516.6909; email: rjb)

Editors: Matt McAdam (humanities and classics) (410.516.6903; email: mxm); Kelley Squazzo (public health) (410.516.6997; email: kas)

Associate Editor: Suzanne Flinchbaugh (political science, international relations, public policy, and WWCP) (410.516.6917; email: skf)

Assistant Editor: Sara Cleary (Anabaptist and Pietist studies) (410.516.6902; email: sjc)

Project MUSE: Dean J. Smith, Director (410.516.6981; email: djs)

Financial Manager: Nicole Kendzejeski (410.516.6969; email: nak)

Director, Marketing and Sales: Melanie B. Schaffner (410.516.3846; email: mbs)

Manager, International Sales: Ann Snoeyenbos (410.516.6992; email: aps)

Customer Service Coordinator: Lora Czarnowsky (410.516.2890; email: llc)

Associate Director, Publishing Technology: Wendy Queen (410.516.3845; email: wjq)

Associate Director, ContentAcquisitions and Publisher Relations: Teresa A. Ehling (410.516.6966; email tae)

MUSE Production Manager: Elizabeth R. Windsor (410.516.6510; email: brw)

Manuscript Editorial: Juliana M. McCarthy, Managing Editor (410.516.6912; email: jmm)

Assistant Managing Editor: Linda E. Forlifer (410.516.6911; email: lef)

Senior Manuscript Editors: Michele Callaghan (410.516.6910; email: mtc); Anne M. Whitmore (410.516.6916; email: amw)

Senior Production Editors: Andre M. Barnett (410.516.6995; email: amb); Courtney Bond (410.516.6905; email: cmb); Debby Bors (410.516.6914; email: dlb); Kimberly F. Johnson (410.516.6915; email: kfj); Mary Lou Kenney (410.516.6897; email: mk)

Assistant Manuscript Editor: Hilary Jacqmin (410.516.6901; email: hsj)

Design and Production: John Cronin, Design & Production Manager (410.516.6922; email: jgc)

Art Director: Martha Sewall (410.516.6921; email: mds)

Senior Book Designer: Glen Burris (410.516.6924; email: gmb)

Production Controller, Electronic Prepress: Robert Schreur (410.516.3855; email: rjs)

Production Controller, Electronic Media: Carol Eckhart (410.516.3862; email: cle)

Production Coordinator, Print Production: Linda West (410.516.6920; email: lmw)

Production Coordinator, Digital Archive: Patricia Bolgiano (410.516.7872; email: prb)

Marketing: Becky Brasington Clark, Director Marketing and Online Book Publishing (410.516.6931; email: rbc)

Sales Director: Tom Lovett (410.516.6936; email: tjl)

Promotion Manager: Karen Willmes (410.516.6932; email: klw)

Publicity Manager: Kathy Alexander (410.516.4162; email: ka)

Associate Sales Director: Brendan Coyne (410.516.6937; email: bcc)

Publicity & Community Relations Officer: Jack Holmes (410.516.6928; email: jmh)

Electronic Books: Claire McCabe Tamberino, Electronic Promotion Manager (410.516.6935; email: cmt)

Journals: William M. Breichner, Publisher (410.516.6985; email: wmb)

Journals Fulfillment Systems Project Manager: Matt Brook (410.516.6899; email: mb)

Journals Marketing Manager: Lisa Klose (410.516.6689; email: llk)

Journals Production Manager: Carol Hamblen (410.516.6986; email: crh)

Journals Subscription Manager: Alta Anthony (410.516.6938; email: aha)

Journals Publicist: Brian Shea (410.516.7096; email: bjs)

Business: Tony Jacobson, Accounting Manager (410.516.6974; email: tlj)

Fulfillment: Davida G. Breier, Manager, Fulfillment Operations (410.516.6961; email: dgb)

Fulfillment: Melinda Kelly, Assistant Manager, Fulfillment Operations (410.516.4449; email: mrk)

Credit & Collections: Keith Brock, Accounts Receivable Coordinator (410.516.3854; email: klb)

Full Member

Established: 1878   Admitted to AAUP: 1937

Title output 2012: 175   Title output 2013: 179

Titles currently in print: 3,351   Journals published: 70

Editorial Program

History (American, ancient, history of science, technology, and medicine); humanities (literary and cultural studies, ancient studies); medicine and health (consumer health, public health, psychology and psychiatry); science (biology, physics, and natural history); mathematics; political science; higher education; reference books; and regional books.

The Press is copublisher with the Woodrow Wilson Center Press.

The Press through Hopkins Fulfillment Service (HFS) handles book order processing and distribution for: Baylor University Press, Brookings Institution Press, Catholic University of America Press, Center for Talented Youth, Georgetown University Press, Johns Hopkins University Press, University of Kentucky Press, Maryland Historical Society, University of Massachusetts Press, University of Pennsylvania Press, University of Pennsylvania Museum Publications, University of Washington Press, and Urban Institute Press.

The Press, in cooperation with the Johns Hopkins University's Milton S. Eisenhower Library and the participating publishers, manages Project MUSE® (http://muse.jhu.edu). Project MUSE provides electronic subscription access to full-text content from 550 periodicals published by more than 125 not-for-profit publishers in the humanities and the social sciences. University Press Content Consortium (UPCC) e-book collections on Project MUSE, fully integrated with the existing journal collections, include 25,000 scholarly books from 95 publishers.

Other online publishing initiatives include electronic versions of *The Early Republic*; *The Johns Hopkins Guide to Literary Theory and Criticism*; *The Papers of Dwight David Eisenhower*; *the Encyclopedia of American Studies*; and *the World Shakespeare Bibliography*

Journals: *African American Review*; *American Imago*; *American Jewish History*; *American Journal of Mathematics*; *American Journal of Philology*; *American Quarterly*; *Arethusa*; *Book History*; *ariel, Bookbird*; *The Bulletin of the Center for Children's Books*; *Bulletin of the History of Medicine*; *Callaloo*; *The CEA Critic*; *Children's Literature*; *Children's Literature Association Quarterly*; *Classical World*; *Configurations*; *diacritics*; *Eighteenth-Century Studies*; *Encyclopedia of American Studies*; *The Emily Dickinson Journal*; *ELH: English Literary History*; *Feminist Formations*; *German Studies Review*; *The Henry James Review*; *Historically Speaking: The Bulletin of Historical Society*; *The Hopkins Review*; *Human Rights Quarterly*; *Journal of Asian American Studies*; *Journal of College Student Development*; *Journal of Colonialism and Colonial History*; *Journal of Democracy*; *Journal of Early Christian Studies*; *Journal of Health Care for the Poor and Underserved*; *Journal of Late Antiquity Journal of Modern Greek Studies*; *Journal of the History of Childhood and Youth*; *Journal of the History of Philosophy*; *Journal of Women's History*; *Kennedy Institute of Ethics Journal*; *Late Imperial China*; *L'Esprit Créateur*; *Leviathan*; *Library Trends*; *The Lion and the Unicorn*; *Literature and Medicine*; *MLN*; *Modern Fiction Studies*; *Modernism/Modernity*; *Narrative Inquiry in Bioethics and Digital Philology*; *New Literary*

History; Partial Answers: Journal of Literature and the History of Ideas; Perspectives in Biology & Medicine; Philosophy and Literature; Philosophy, Psychiatry, and Psychology; Poe Studies; portal: Libraries and the Academy; Postmodern Culture; Reviews in American History; Progress In Community Health Partnerships: Research, Education, and Action; Reviews in Higher Education; SAIS Review; SEL: Studies in English Literature; Sewanee Review; Shakespeare Bulletin; Shakespeare Quarterly; South Central Review; Spiritus: A Journal of Christian Spirituality; Social Research; Studies in American Fiction; Studies in the Novel , Technology & Culture; Theatre Journal; Theatre Topics; Theory and Event; The Wallace Stevens Journal; Transactions of the American Philological Association; Victorian Periodical Review; World Shakespeare Bibliography Online

Online-only journals: *Journal of Colonialism and Colonial History; Postmodern Culture; Theory and Event*

The Press also handles subscription fulfillment for *Imagine*, a publication of the Center for Talented Youth of The Johns Hopkins University, Penn State University Press Journals, and Catholic University of America Press Journals.

Special series, joint imprints, and/or copublishing programs: The Complete Poetry of Percy Bysshe Shelley; Documentary History of the First Federal Congress; Johns Hopkins: Poetry and Fiction; The Johns Hopkins Studies in the History of Technology; The Johns Hopkins University Studies in History and Political Science; The Papers of Dwight David Eisenhower; The Papers of George Catlett Marshall; The Papers of Frederick Law Olmsted; The Papers of Thomas A. Edison; New Series in NASA History

University Press of Kansas

2502 Westbrooke Circle
Lawrence, KS 66045-4444

Phone: 785.864.4154
Fax: 785.864.4586
Email: upress@ku.edu
Indiv: (user I.D.)@ku.edu

Website and Social Media:
Website: www.kansaspress.ku.edu
Facebook: www.facebook.com/kansaspress

UK/European Representative:
Eurospan

Warehouse Address:
2445 Westbrooke Circle
Lawrence, KS 66045-4440
Phone: 785.864.4156

Orders:
Phone: 785.864.4155
Email: upkorders@ku.edu

Canadian Representative:
Scholarly Book Services

Staff
Director: Charles T. Myers (785.864.9160; email: ctmyers)
Assistant to the Director: Sara Henderson White (785.864.9125; email: shwhite)
Editorial: Michael Briggs, Editor-in-Chief (political science, military history, law)
(785.864.9162; email: mbriggs)
Acquisitions Editors: Fred Woodward, Senior Editor (political science, presidential studies, US political history, American political thought, regional studies) (785.864.4667; email: fwoodward); TBA (American history, American studies, Native American studies, women's studies) (785.864.9185)

Manuscript Editorial, Design and Production:
  Production Editors: Larisa Martin (785.864.9169; email: lmartin); Kelly Chrisman Jacques (785.864.9186; email: kjchrism)
Marketing: TBA, Assistant Director and Marketing Manager (785.864.9165)
  Publicity Manager: Rebecca Murray Schuler (785.864.9170; email: rmschuler)
  Direct Mail & Exhibits Manager: Debra Diehl (785.864.9166; email: ddiehl)
  Art Director & Advertising Manager: Karl Janssen (785.864.9164; email: kjanssen)
  Marketing Assistant: Suzanne Galle (785.864.9167; email: sgalle)
Business: Conrad Roberts, Business Manager (785.864.9158; email: ceroberts)
  Accounting Manager: Britt DeTienne (785.864.9159; email: bdetienne)

Full Member

Established: 1946   Admitted to AAUP: 1946
Title output 2012: 57   Title output 2013: 54
Titles currently in print: 1,022

Editorial Program

American history; military and intelligence studies; Western history and Native American studies; American government and public policy; presidential studies; constitutional and legal studies; environmental studies; American studies and popular culture; women's studies; Kansas, the Great Plains, and the Midwest. The Press does not consider fiction, poetry, or festschriften for publication.

Special series, joint imprints, and/or copublishing programs: American Political Thought; American Presidential Elections; American Presidency; Constitutional Thinking; CultureAmerica; Kansas Nature Guides; Landmark Law Cases and American Society; Modern First Ladies; Modern War Studies; Studies in Government and Public Policy; US Army War College Guides to Civil War Battles

The Kent State University Press

Street Address:
1118 University Library
1125 Risman Drive
Kent, OH 44242-0001

Mailing Address:
1118 University Library
PO Box 5190
Kent, OH 44242-0001

Phone: 330.672.7913
Fax: 330.672.3104
Email: (user I.D.)@kent.edu

Orders:
Phone: 419.281.1802
Fax: 419.281.6883

Website and Social Media:
Website: www.kentstateuniversitypress.com
Facebook: www.facebook.com/kentstateuniversitypress
Twitter: KentStateUPress

UK/European Representative:
Eurospan

Canadian Representative:
Scholarly Book Services

Staff

Director: Will Underwood (330.672.8094; email: wunderwo)

Acquisitions: Joyce Harrison, Acquiring Editor (330.672.8099; email: jharri18)

Editorial: Mary D. Young, Managing Editor (330.672.8101; email: mdyoung)

Design and Production: Christine A. Brooks, Manager (330.672.8092; email: cbrooks)

Assistant Design and Production Manager: Darryl M. Crosby (330.672.8091; email: dcrosby)

Marketing: Susan L. Cash, Manager (330.672.8097; email: scash)

Journals Circulation/Administrative Assistant: Carol Heller (330.672.8090; email: cheller1)

Bookkeeper: Norma E. Hubbell (330.672.8096; email: nhubbell)

Full Member

Established: 1966

Title output 2012: 35

Titles currently in print: 687

Admitted to AAUP: 1970

Title output 2013: 37

Journals published: 2

Editorial Program

History: American Civil War era; US military, cultural/social, diplomatic, true crime; Ohio/Midwestern studies; fashion/costume; material culture. Literature: US (to ca. 1970); regional/Midwestern; British (Inklings). Ethnomusicology. Regional literary nonfiction; poetry only through Wick Poetry Center; no fiction.

Journals: *Civil War History; Ohio History*

Special series: American Abolitionism and Antislavery; Civil War in the North; Civil War Soldiers and Strategies; Cleveland Theater; Interpreting American History; Literature and Medicine; New Studies in US Foreign Relations; Reading Hemingway; Sacred Landmarks; Symposia on Democracy; Teaching Hemingway; Translation Studies; True Crime History; Wick Poetry

The University Press of Kentucky

663 South Limestone Street
Lexington, KY 40508-4008

Phone: 859.257.8400
Fax: 859.257.7975
Email: (user I.D.)@uky.edu

Website and Social Media:
Website: www.kentuckypress.com
Blog: kentuckypress.wordpress.com
Facebook: www.facebook.com/
   KentuckyPress
Twitter: KentuckyPress
YouTube: YouTube.com/univpressofky

Warehouse Address:
Maple Press Lebanon Distribution Center
704 Legionaire Drive
Fredericksburg, PA 17026

Orders:
c/o Hopkins Fulfillment Services
PO Box 50370
Baltimore, MD 21211
Phone: 800.537.5487 or 410.516.6956
Fax: 410.516.6998
Email: hfscustserv@ press.jhu.edu

UK/European Representative:
Eurospan

Canadian Representative:
Scholarly Book Services

Staff

Director: Stephen M. Wrinn (859.257.8432; email: smwrin2)
   Executive Assistant to the Director: Allison Webster (email: allison.webster2)
Acquisitions Editors: Stephen M. Wrinn (American history, American studies, world history, Civil War, military history, political science, political theory, public policy, international studies, African American studies); Anne Dean Watkins (film studies, popular culture, American and southern history) (859.257.8434; email: annedean.watkins); Ashley Runyon (Kentuckiana, regional studies, Appalachian studies, folklore) (859.257.8150; email: ashley.runyon)
   Editorial Assistant: Bailey Johnson (859.257.9492; email: bailey.johnson)
Editing, Design and Production: David Cobb, Director of Editing, Design and Production (859.257.4252; email: dlcobb2)
   Production Manager: Pat Gonzales (859.257.4669; email: pagonz0)
   Senior Supervising Editor: Ila McEntire (859.257.8433; email: ila.mcentire)
   Assistant Editor: Iris Law (859.257.8438; email: iala224)
Marketing: Amy Harris, Director of Marketing and Sales (859.257.4249; email: ae.harris)
   Publicity, Exhibits, and Rights Manager: Mack McCormick (859.257.5200; email: permissions)
   Publicity and Direct Promotions Manager: Cameron Ludwick (859.257.2817; email: cameron.ludwick)
   Marketing and Electronic Publishing Assistant: Blair Thomas (859.257.6855; email: blair.thomas)
Assistant Director/Director of Finance & Administration: Craig R. Wilkie (859.257.8436; email: crwilk00)
   Information Technology Manager: Tim Elam (859.257.8761; email: taelam2)

Assistant Director of Finance and Administration: Teresa W. Collins (859.257.8405; email: twell1)
Administrative Assistant: Robert Brandon (859.257.8400, 800.839.6855; email: rbrandon)

Full Member

Established: 1943	Admitted to AAUP: 1947
Title output 2012: 82	Title output 2013: 60
Titles currently in print: 1,360	

Editorial Program

Scholarly books in the fields of American history; military history; film studies; political science; international studies; folklore and material culture; African American studies; serious nonfiction of general interest. Regionally, the Press maintains an interest in Kentucky and the Ohio Valley, Appalachia, and the upper South. Submissions are not invited in fiction, drama, or poetry.

Special series: American Warriors; Asia in the New Millennium; Battles and Campaigns; Civil Rights and the Struggle for Black Equality in the Twentieth Century; Culture of the Land: A Series in the New Agrarianism; Essential Readers in Contemporary Media; Foreign Military Studies: Kentucky Remembered: An Oral History Series; Kentucky Voices; Material Worlds; New Books for New Readers; New Directions in Southern History; The Ohio River Valley; The Philosophy of Popular Culture; Place Matters: New Directions in Appalachian and Regional Studies; Political Companions to Great American Authors; Provocations: Political Thought and Contemporary Issues; Public Papers of the Governors of Kentucky; Religion in the South; Screen Classics; Studies in Conflict, Diplomacy, and Peace; Thomas D. Clark Studies in Education, Public Policy, and Social Change; Topics in Kentucky History; Virginia at War

Leuven University Press/Universitaire Pers Leuven

Minderbroedersstraat 4 - bus 5602
B-3000 Leuven
Belgium

Phone: +32 16 32 53 45
Fax: +32 16 32 53 52
Email: info@upers.kuleuven.be
Indiv. (user I.D.)@upers.kuleuven.be

US Representative:
Cornell University Press Services
P.O. Box 6525
750 Cascadilla Street
Ithaca, NY 14851-6525 USA
Phone: 607.277.2211
Email: orderbook@cupserv.org

Website and Social Media:
Website: www.lup.be
Facebook: www.facebook.com/pages/Leuven-University-Press/130250583714129

UK and European Sales Representative:
University Presses Marketing

UK and European Orders:
NBN International

Staff
Director and Acquisitions Editorial: Marike Schipper (+32 16 32 53 47; email: marike.schipper)
Acquisitions Editorial: Veerle De Laet (+32 16 32 81 26; email: veerle.delaet)
Manuscript Editorial: Beatrice Van Eeghem (+32 16 32 53 40; email: beatrice.vaneeghem)
Production: Patricia di Costanzo (+32 16 32 53 53; email: patricia.dicostanzo)
Marketing: Annemie Vandezande (+32 16 32 53 51; email: annemie.vandezande)
Customer Service and Order Processing: Margreet Meijer (+32 16 32 53 50; email: margreet.meijer)

International Member
Established: 1971   Admitted to AAUP: 2005
Title output 2012: 36   Title output 2013: 40
Titles currently in print: 900   Journals published: 2

Editorial Program
Scholarly publications with emphasis on music, art & theory, text & literature, history & archaeology, philosophy & religion, and society, law & economics
Journals: *Humanistica Lovaniensia: Journal of Neo-Latin Studies; HEROM, Journal on Hellenistic and Roman Material Culture*
Special series: Ancient and Medieval Philosophy Series 1; Ancient and Medieval Philosophy Series 2: Henrici de Gandavo Opera Omnia; Ancient and Medieval Philosophy - Series 3 Francisci de Marchia Opera Philosophica et Theologica; Avisos de Flandes; Orpheus Institute Series; Dynamics of Religious Reform; Egyptian Prehistory Monographs; Figures of the Unconscious; ICAG Studies; Jean François Lyotard Writings on Contemporary Art and Artists; Kadoc-Artes; Kadoc-Studies on Religion, Culture and Society; Lieven Gevaert Series; Mediaevalia Lovaniensia-Series 1/Studia; Plutarchea Hypomnemata; Sagalassos; Society, Crime & Criminal Justice; Studia Paedagogica; Studies in Archaeological Sciences; Studies in Musical Form; Supplementa Humanistica Lovaniensia.

Lincoln Institute of Land Policy

113 Brattle Street
Cambridge, MA 02138

Phone: 617.661.3016
Fax: 617.661.7235
Email: help@lincolninst.edu

Orders:
Publishers Storage and Shipping Company (PSSC)
Phone: 978.345.2121 ext. 282;
877.526.3257
Email: ewilson@pssc.com
Website: www.pssc.com

Website and Social Media:
Website: www.lincolninst.edu
Facebook: www.facebook.com/lincolninstituteoflandpolicy
Twitter: landpolicy
YouTube: www.youtube.com/user/LincolnLandPolicy
Blog: www.lincolninst.edu/news-events/at-lincoln-house-blog

Staff

Director of Publications and Senior Editor: Maureen Clarke (617.503.2143; email: mclarke@lincolninst.edu)
Managing Editor: Emily McKeigue (617.503.2115; email: emckeigue@lincolninst.edu)
Publications Coordinator: Susan Pace (617.503.2177; email: space@lincolninst.edu)
Marketing Consultant: Marissa Benson (617.309.9792; email: mbenson@lincolninst.edu)

Introductory Member

Established: 1974
Title output 2012: 15
Titles currently in print: 138

Admitted to AAUP: 2011
Title output 2013: 9
Journals published: 1

Editorial Program

The Lincoln Institute of Land Policy's publishing mission is to improve the quality of information, debate, and decisions in the areas of land policy and land-related taxation. Lincoln publishes books, eBooks, Policy Focus Reports; Working Papers; and Multimedia Resources (CDs and DVDs; short online videos).

Topics include land valuation; property taxation; urban and regional planning; urban economics; legal land use issues; housing and urban development; smart growth; land conservation; climate change; planning, architecture, and urban design; and international land policy focusing on Latin America and China.

Journal: *Land Lines*

Liverpool University Press

4 Cambridge Street
Liverpool L69 7ZU, UK

US Orders:
Oxford University Press
Phone: 800.445.9714

Phone: (+44) 151 7942233
Email: lup@liv.ac.uk
Indiv.: (user I.D.)@liv.ac.uk

UK Representative:
Turpin Distribution

Website and Social Media:
Website: www.liverpooluniversitypress.co.uk
Twitter: LivUniPress

Staff

Managing Director: Anthony Cond (+44151 7942237; email: a.cond)
Editorial Director: Alison Welsby (+44 151 7942231; email: a.welsby)
Design and Production: Patrick Brereton, Production Manager (+44 151 7943133; email: p.brereton)
Marketing: Jenny Howard, Sales & Marketing Director (+44 151 7942234; email: j.howard)
Journals: Clare Hooper, Journals Manager (+44151 7943135; email: c.hooper)
Business: Justine Greig, Finance Director (+44151 7942232; email: j.greig)

International Member

Established: 1899
Title output 2012: 48
Titles currently in print: 500

Admitted to AAUP: 2013
Title output 2013: 60
Journals published: 22

Editorial Program
Scholarly books in ancient, medieval, Irish, slavery and labour history. The modern languages, notably French and Francophone and Hispanic and Lusophone Studies. Science Fiction criticism, contemporary poetry criticism and sculpture. Occasional Liverpool trade titles, building on the city's significance in global migration and popular culture.

Journals: *Australian Journal of French Studies; British Journal of Canadian Studies; Bulletin of Hispanic Studies; Byron Journal; Catalan Review; Comma, Contemporary French Civilization; Essays in Romanticism; European Journal of Language Policy; Extrapolation; Francosphères; Historical Studies in Industrial Relations; International Development Planning Review; Journal of Literary and Cultural Disability Studies; Labour History Review; Modern Believing; Music, Sound, and the Moving Image; Québec Studies; Romani Studies; Science Fiction Film and Television; Sculpture Journal; Town Planning Review*

Special series: Contemporary French and Francophone Cultures; Contemporary Hispanic and Lusophone Cultures; Exeter Medieval Texts and Studies; Liverpool Science Fiction Texts and Studies; Reappraisals in Irish History; Liverpool English Texts and Studies; Liverpool Studies in International Slavery; Migrations and Identities; Public Sculpture of Britain; Poetry &….; Postcolonialism Across the Disciplines; Studies in Labour History; Translated Texts for Historians

Louisiana State University Press

3990 W. Lakeshore Drive
Baton Rouge, LA 70808

Phone: 225.578.6294
Indiv: (user I.D.)@lsu.edu

Website and Social Media:
Website: www.lsupress.org
Blog: lsupress.typepad.com/lsu_press_blog
Facebook: www.facebook.com/pages/LSU-Press/38236386996
Twitter: lsupress

Canadian Distributor:
Scholarly Book Services

Warehouse, Orders and Cust. Service:
Longleaf Services
PO Box 8895
Chapel Hill, NC 27515-8895
Phone: 800.848.6224
Fax: 800.272.6817
Email: longleaf@unc.edu

Staff
Director: MaryKatherine Callaway (225.578.6144; email: mkc)
   Assistant to the Director, Subrights and Permissions: Erica Bossier (email: ebossie)
Acquisitions Editorial: Rand Dotson (southern history, music and fiction) (225.578.6412; email: pdotso1); Margaret Lovecraft (general interest and regional books, literary studies, landscape architecture) (225.578.6319; email: lovecraft); Alisa Plant (European history, media studies, environmental studies, foodways) (225.578.6433; email: aplant)
Manuscript Editorial: Lee Sioles, Managing Editor (225.578.6467; email: lsioles)
   Senior Editor: Catherine Kadair (email: clkadair)

Design and Production: Laura Gleason, Assistant Director and Production Manager
(225.578.6469; email: lgleasn)
  Assistant Production Manager: Amanda Scallan (email: amandas)
Marketing: Erin Rolfs, Manager (225.578.8282; email: erolfs)
  Digital Initiatives and Database Manager: Robert Keane (email: rkeane)
  Assistant Marketing Manager Exhibits and Advertising Coordinator: Kate Barton (email:
  kbart04)
Financial Operations Manager: Rebekah Brown (225.578.6415; email: rbrown1)
Subsidiary Rights: McIntosh & Otis, Inc., 353 Lexington Ave., New York, NY 10016
(212.687.7400)
The Southern Review
  Fiction and Nonfiction Editor: Emily Nemens (225.578.5159; email: enemens)
  Poetry Editor: Jessica Faust (225.578.0896; email: jfaust1)

Full Member

Established: 1935   Admitted to AAUP: unknown
Title output 2012: 71   Title output 2013: 72
Titles currently in print: 2,056

Editorial Program

Humanities and social sciences, with special emphasis on Southern history and literature;
regional studies; European history in the Atlantic world; environmental studies; poetry; and
Louisiana roots music.

Special series, joint imprints and/or copublishing programs: Antislavery, Abolition,
and the Atlantic World; Conflicting Worlds; Making the Modern South; Media and Public
Affairs; Papers of Jefferson Davis; Southern Biography Southern Literary Studies; Southern
Messenger Poets; W.L. Fleming Lectures in Southern History; Walt Whitman Award of the
Academy of American Poets; Yellow Shoe Fiction

  The Press also distributes the Lena-Miles Weaver Todd Poetry Series.

The University of Manitoba Press

Street Address:
301 St. John's College
University of Manitoba
Winnipeg Manitoba R3T 2M5
Canada

Phone: 204.474.9495
Fax: 204.474.7556
Email: uofmpress@umanitoba.ca

Website and Social Media:
Website: uofmpress.ca
Blog: uofmpress.ca/blog
Facebook: www.facebook.com/UofMPress

Canadian Orders:
University of Toronto Press
Phone: 800.565.9523
Email: utpbooks@utpress.utoronto.ca

US Orders:
Michigan State University Press
Phone: 800.678.2120

Canadian Representative:
Ampersand and Company

Staff

Director: David Carr (204.474.9242; email: carr@cc.umanitoba.ca)
Senior Acquisitions Editor: Jean L. Wilson (email: jeanl.Wilson@shaw.ca)
Managing Editor: Glenn Bergen (204.474.7338; email: glenn_bergen@umanitoba.ca)
Marketing: Cheryl Miki, Sales and Marketing Supervisor (204.474.9998; email:
  miki@cc.umanitoba.ca)
Promotion/Editorial Assistant: Ariel Gordon (204.474.8048; email:
  gordojd@cc.umanitoba.ca)

Full Member

Established: 1967   Admitted to AAUP: 2011
Title output 2012: 9   Title output 2013: 9
Titles currently in print: 135

Editorial Program

Native studies; Native history; Canadian history; the Arctic and the North; ethnic studies;
Aboriginal languages; Canadian literary studies, especially Aboriginal literature; political
studies; regional trade titles.
Special series: Contemporary Studies on the North; Critical Studies in Aboriginal History
(formerly Manitoba Studies in Native History); First Voices, First Texts (Aboriginal literary
reprints), Publications of the Algonquian Text Society; Studies in Immigration and Culture

Marquette University Press

1415 West Wisconsin Avenue   Warehouse Address:
Box 3141   30 Amberwood Parkway, PO Box 388
Milwaukee, WI 53201-3141   Ashland, OH 44805

Phone: 414.288.1564   Orders and Customer Service:
Fax: 414.288.7813   Phone: 800.247.6553; 419.281.1802
Email: (user I.D.)@marquette.edu   Fax: 419.281.6883

Website and Social Media:
Website: marquette.edu/mupress

UK/European Distributor: Canadian Representative:
Eurospan   Scholarly Book Services

Staff

Director: Andrew Tallon (414.288.1564; email: andrew.tallon)
Editorial, Marketing, Design and Production: Andrew Tallon
Business: Maureen Kondrick (414.288.1564; email: maureen.kondrick)
Journals: Andrew Tallon
Journals Marketing: Pamela K. Swope (800.444.2419; email: pkswope@pdcnet.org)

Full Member

Established: 1916

Title output 2012: 17

Titles currently in print: 438

Admitted to AAUP: 1998

Title output 2013: 16

Journals published: 1

Editorial Program

Philosophy; theology; history; urban studies; journalism; education; regional studies; and mediæval history.

Journal: *Philosophy & Theology*

Philosophy series: Aquinas Lecture; Marquette Studies in Philosophy; Mediæval Philosophical Texts in Translation

Theology series: Marquette Studies in Theology; Père Marquette Lecture; Reformation Texts with Translation: Series 1, Biblical Studies; Series 2, Women in the Reformation; Series 3, Late Reformation

History series: Klement Lecture (Civil War); Marquette Studies in History (Modern); Urban Studies Series

Communication series: Diederich Studies in Media and Communication

University of Massachusetts Press

East Experiment Station
671 North Pleasant Street
Amherst, MA 01003

Phone: 413.545.2217
Fax: 413.545.1226
Email: (user I.D.)@umpress.umass.edu
(unless otherwise indicated)

Website and Social Media:
Website: www.umass.edu/umpress
Facebook: www.facebook.com/umasspress
Twitter: umasspress

Canadian Representative:
Scholarly Book Services

Boston Office:
Brian Halley
Provost Office, Quinn Building
UMass Boston
100 Morrissey Boulevard
Boston, MA 02125

Orders:
c/o Hopkins Fulfillment Services
PO Box 50370
Baltimore, MD 21211
Phone: 800.537.5487
Fax: 410.516.6998
Email: hfscustserv@press.jhu.edu

UK/European Distributor:
Eurospan

Staff

Director: Bruce Wilcox (413.545.4990; email: wilcox)

Acquisitions Editorial: Clark Dougan, Senior Editor (413.545.4989; email: cdougan)
    Boston Editor: Brian Halley (617.287.5610; email: brian.halley@umb.edu)

Manuscript Editorial: Carol Betsch, Managing Editor (413.545.4991; email: betsch)

Design and Production: Jack Harrison, Manager (413.545.4998; email: harrison)
    Designer & Associate Production Manager: Sally Nichols (413.545.4997; email: snichols)

Business and Marketing: Yvonne Crevier, Business Manager (413.545.4994; email: ycrevier)
    Promotion Manager: Karen Fisk (413.545.2217; email: kfisk)

Full Member

Established: 1963

Title output 2012: 39

Titles currently in print: 1,000

Admitted to AAUP: 1966

Title output 2013: 40

Editorial Program

Scholarly books and serious nonfiction, with special interests in African American studies; American history; American studies; architecture and landscape design; disability studies; environmental studies; gender studies; history of the book; journalism and media studies; literary and cultural studies; Native American studies; science and technology studies; urban studies; and books of regional interest.

Special series, joint imprints and/or copublishing programs: American Popular Music; AWP Award Series in Short Fiction (Grace Paley Prize); Culture, Politics, and the Cold War; Environmental History of the Northeast; Juniper Prizes (poetry and fiction); Library of American Landscape History (Critical Perspectives in the History of Environmental Design; Designing the American Park); Massachusetts Studies in Early Modern Culture; Native Americans of the Northeast; Public History in Historical Perspective; Science/Technology/Culture; Studies in Print Culture and the History of the Book

The MIT Press

55 Hayward Street

Cambridge, MA 02142-1315

Phone: 617.253.5646 (main)

Fax: 617.258.6779

Email: (user I.D.)@mit.edu

Journals:

Phone: 617.253.2864 (main)

Fax: 617.258.6779

Book Orders/Customer Service:

Phone: 800.405.1619 (US/Can);

401.531.2800 (International)

Fax: 800.406.9145 (US/Can);

401.531.2801 (International)

Email: mitpress-orders@mit.edu

London Office:

The MIT Press, Ltd.

Suite 2, 1 Duchess Street

London, W1W 6AN, UK

United Kingdom

Website and Social Media:

Website: mitpress.mit.edu

Journals Website: www.mitpressjournals.org

Blog: mitpress.mit.edu/blog

Facebook: www.facebook.com/mitpress

Twitter: mitpress

Phone: +44 (20) 7306 0603

Fax: +44 (20) 7306 0604

Email: info@hup-mitpress.co.uk

Staff

Director: Ellen Faran (617.253.4078; email: ewfaran)

   Assistant to the Director: Nia Lewis (617.253.5255; email: niav)

Associate Director and Director of Finance & Operations: Rebecca Schrader (617.253.5250; email: recs)

Director of Technology: Bill Trippe (617.452.3747; email: trippe)

Acquisitions Editorial: Gita Manaktala, Editorial Director (617.253.3172; email: manak)
   Editors: Marguerite Avery (science, technology & society (STS), information science & communication) (617.253.1653; email: mavery); Marie Lee (computer science, linguistics) (617.253.1588; email:marielee); Roger Conover (art, architecture, visual culture) (617.253.1677; email: conover); John S. Covell (economics, business, finance) (617.253.3757; email: jcovell); Philip Laughlin (cognitive science, philosophy) (617.252.1636; email: laughlin); Jane Macdonald (economics, business, finance) (617.253.1605; email: janem); Clay Morgan (environmental studies, bioethics, political science) (617.253.4113; email: claym); Robert Prior (life sciences, neuroscience, biology) (617.253.1584; email: prior); Doug Sery (new media, game studies, design) (617.253.5187; email: dsery)

Manuscript Editorial: Michael Sims, Managing Editor (617.253.2080; email: msims)

Digital Publishing Manager: Jake Furbush (617.258.0583; email: jfurbush)

Design: Yasuyo Iguchi, Design Manager (617.253.8034; email: iguchi)

Production: Janet Rossi, Production Manager (617.253.2882; email: janett)

Marketing and Promotions: Katie Hope, Marketing Director (617.258.0603; email: khope)
   Advertising Manager: Anar Badalov (617.258.7821; email: badalov)
   Exhibits Manager: John Costello (617.258.5764; email: jcostell)
   Promotions Manager & Direct Mail Manager: Astrid Baehrecke (617.253.7297; email: baehreck)
   Publicity Manager: Colleen Lanick (617.253.2874; email: colleenl)
   Subsidiary Rights Manager: Cristina Sanmartín (617.253.0629; email: csan)
   Permissions Manager: Pamela Quick (617.253.0080; email: quik)
   Textbook Manager: Michelle Pullano (617.253.3620; email: mpullano)

Sales: Anne Bunn, Sales Director (617.253.8838; email: annebunn)
   Sales Manager: Erika Valenti (617.258.0582; email: erikav)

Journals: Nick Lindsay, Journals Director (617.258.0594; email: nlindsay)
   Journals Business Manager: June McCaull (617.258.0593; email: jmccaull)
   Journals and Digital Products Customer Service Manager: Abbie Hiscox (617.452.3765; email: hiscox)
   Journals Editorial & Production Manager: Rachel Besen (617.258.0585; email: rbesen)
   Journals Marketing Manager: Jill Rodgers (617.258.0595; email: jillr)
   Journals Subsidiary Rights Manager: Pam Quick (617.253.0080; email: quik)

Warehouse: Robert O'Handley, Director of Operations (email: bob.ohandley@triliteral.org)
   Customer Service Manager: Cathy Morrone (401.531.2800; email: cathy.morrone@triliteral.org)

Full Member

Established: 1961   Admitted to AAUP: 1961
Title output 2012: 224   Title output 2013: 217
Titles currently in print: 3,850   Journals published: 30

Editorial Program

Architecture; artificial intelligence; bioethics; biology; business; cognitive sciences; communication; computer science; contemporary art; design; earth sciences; economics; environmental studies; finance; game studies; information science; life sciences; linguistics; natural history; nature; new media studies; neuroscience; philosophy; photography; political science; psychology; regional/MIT titles; science, technology, and society (STS); security studies.

Co-publishing and distribution programs: Afterall Books; Alphabet City; Boston Review Books; Perspecta; Semiotext(e); Whitechapel Documents of Contemporary Art; Zone Books.
Journals: *African Arts; Artificial Life; ARTMargins; Asian Economic Papers; Asian Development Review;The Baffler; Computational Linguistics; Computer Music Journal; Daedalus; Design Issues; Education Finance and Policy; Evolutionary Computation; Global Environmental Politics; Grey Room; Innovations; International Journal of Learning & Media, International Security; Journal of Cognitive Neuroscience; Journal of Cold War Studies; Journal of Interdisciplinary History; Leonardo; Leonardo Music Journal; Linguistic Inquiry; Neural Computation; The New England Quarterly; October; PAJ: A Journal of Performance and Art; Perspectives on Science; Presence: Teleoperators and Virtual Environments; The Review of Economics and Statistics; TDR: The Drama Review*
Special series: Acting with Technology; Adaptive Computation and Machine Learning; Afterall: One Work; Alvin Hansen Symposium Series on Public Policy; American Academy Studies in Global Security; American and Comparative Environmental Policy; Annotating Art's Histories; Arne Ryde Memorial Lectures; Basic Bioethics; BCSIA Studies in International Security; Boston Review Books; Bradford Books; Cairoli Lectures; Cellular and Molecular Neuroscience; Centre for European Policy Studies (CEPS); CESifo Book; CESifo Seminar; Cognitive Neuroscience; Computational Molecular Biology; Computational Neuroscience; Cooperative Information Systems; Current Studies in Linguistics; Dahlem Workshop Reports; Design Thinking, Design Theory Developmental Cognitive Neuroscience; Dibner Institute Studies in the History of Science and Technology; Digital Communication; Digital Libraries & Electronic Publishing; Documentary Sources in Contemporary Art; Documents Books; Documents of Contemporary Art; Earth System Governance; Economic Learning and Social Evolution; Electronic Culture; Engineering Studies; Engineering Systems; Essential Knowledge; Food, Health, and the Environment; Gaston Eyskens Lectures; George Santayana: Definitive Works; Global Environmental Accord: Strategies for Sustainability and Institutional Innovation; History and Foundation of Information Science; History of Computing; Information Revolution and Global Politics; Information Policy; Infrastructures; Inside Technology; Intelligent Robotics and Autonomous Agents; International Security Readers; Issues in Clinical and Cognitive Neuropsychology; Issues in the Biology of Language & Cognition; Jean Nicod Series; John D. & Catherine T. MacArthur Foundation Series on Digital Media and Learning; Lemelson Center Studies in Invention and Innovation; Leonardo Books; Life and Mind; Linguistic Inquiry Monographs; Lionel Robbins Lectures; Munich Lectures; Neural Information Processing; October Books; October Files; Ohlin Lectures; Perspecta: The Yale Architecture Journal; Philosophical Psychopathology: Disorders in Mind; Platform Studies; Playful Thinking; Politics, Science, and the Environment; Representation and Mind; Scientific and Engineering Computation; Semiotext(e); Short Circuits; Simplicity: Design, Technology, Business, Life; Social Neuroscience; Software Studies; Special Issues of Physica D; Structural Mechanics; Strüngmann Forum Reports; Studies in Contemporary German Social Thought; Studies in Neuropsychology & Neurolinguistics; Sustainable Metropolitan Communities Books; Tax Policy and the Economy; Technologies of Lived Abstraction; Topics in Contemporary Philosophy; Transformations: Studies in the History of Science and Technology; Urban and Industrial Environments; Vienna Series in Theoretical Biology; Walras-Pareto Lectures; Wicksell Lectures; Work Books; Writing Architecture; Writing Art; Yrjo Jahnsson Lectures Series; Zeuthen Lecture Series.

McGill-Queen's University Press

Montreal Office:
1010 Sherbrooke Street West
Suite 1720
Montreal, QC H3A 2R7
Canada

Phone: 514.398.3750
Fax: 514.398.4333
Email: mqup@mcgill.ca
Indiv: (user I.D.)@mcgill.ca

Website and Social Media:
Website: www.mqup.ca/
Blog: www.mqup.ca/blog/
Facebook: www.facebook.com/McGillQueens
Twitter: @scholarmqup

Kingston Office:
Douglas Library Building
93 University Avenue
Kingston, ON K7L 5C4
Canada

Phone: 613.533.2155
Email: mqup@queensu.ca

Canadian Distributor:
Georgetown Terminal Warehouses
34 Armstrong Avenue
Georgetown, ON L7G 4R9
Canada
Phone: 877.864.8477
Fax: 877.864.4272
Email: orders@gtwcanada.com

US Distributor:
CUP Services
PO Box 6525
750 Cascadilla Street
Ithaca, NY 14851-6525
Phone: 800.666.2211
Fax: 800.688.2877
Email: orderbook@cupserv.org

UK/European Distributor:
Marston Book Services Ltd

Staff

Executive Director: Philip J. Cercone (Montreal, 514.398.3750; email: philip.cercone)
  Business Manager: TBA
  Rights and Special Projects Manager: Adrian Galwin (514.398.2121; email: adrian.galwin)
  Information Systems Administrator: TBA
  Senior Administrative Coordinator: Margaret Merkourakis (514.398.2911; email: margaret.merkourakis)
  Accounts Payable: Carmie Vacca (514.398.2056; email: carmie.vacca)
Editor-in-Chief: Jonathan Crago (514.398.7480; email: jonathan.crago)
  Senior Editor: Kyla Madden (514.398.2056; email: kyla.madden)
  Editors: Mark Abley (514.398.6652; email: mark.abley); Jacqueline Mason (514.398.2250; email: jacqueline.mason); James MacNevin (613.533.2155; email: james.macnevin@queensu.ca)
  Editorial Assistants: Joanne Pisano (514.398.2068; email: joanne.pisano); Paloma Friedman (514.398.1343; email: editorial.mqup@mcgill.ca)
Managing Editor: Ryan Van Huijstee (514.398.3922; email: ryan.vanhuijstee)
  Assistant Managing Editor: Jessica Howarth (514.398.3279; email: jessica.howarth)

Production Manager: Elena Goranescu (514.398.7395; email: elena.goranescu)
  Assistant Production Manager: Rob Mackie (514.398.1342; email: robert.mackie)
  Production Assistant: Andrew Pinchefsky (514.398.6996; email: andrew.pinchefsky)
Marketing Director and Associate Director: Susan McIntosh (514.398.6306;
  email: susan.mcintosh)
  Sales Manager: Jack Hannan (514.398.5165; email: jack.hannan)
  Educational Sales Administrator: Roy Ward (514.398.7177; email: roy.ward)
  Direct Mail & Exhibits Coordinator: Filomena Falocco (514.398.2912; email: filomena.
  falocco)
  Online Marketing and Data Manager: Laurel Ovenden (514.398.6166; email:
  marketingweb.mqup@mcgill.ca)
  Marketing Assistant: Katie Heffring (514.398.2914; email: marketing.mqup)
  Publicist: Jacqueline Davis (514.398.2555; email: jacqueline.davis)

Full Member
Established: 1969 as a joint press
Admitted to AAUP: 1963 (as McGill University Press)
Title output 2012: 124   Title output 2013: 152
Titles currently in print: c. 3,100

Editorial Program
Scholarly books and well-researched studies of general interest in the humanities and social
sciences, including anthropology, especially North American native peoples; architecture;
Arctic and northern studies; art history; biography; Canadian studies; Canadian literature;
classics; communication and media studies; cultural studies; demography; economics;
education; environmental studies; ethnic studies; European studies; film studies; folklore and
material culture; gender studies; geography; health and society; history; history of medicine;
history of science; Irish and Gaelic studies; law; linguistics; literary criticism; medieval and
renaissance studies; military studies; music history and theory; native studies; philosophy;
poetry; photography; political economy; political science; public administration; public
affairs; public health; Quebec studies; religious studies; Slavic and Eastern European studies;
sociology; theatre; urban studies; and women's studies.
Special series: Art of Living; The Art of the State; Arts Insights; CHORA, Intervals in the
Philosophy of Architecture; Canada Among Nations; Canada: The State of the Federation;
Canadian Association of Geographers Series in Canadian Geography; Canadian Public
Administration; Carleton Library; Central Problems of Philosophy; Central Works of
Philosophy; Centre for Editing Early Canadian Texts; Comparative Charting of Social
Change; Continental European Philosophy; Critical Perspectives on Public Affairs;
Culture of Cities; Fontanus Monograph; Footprints; Foreign Policy, Security and Strategic
Studies; Fundamentals of Philosophy; Global Dialogue on Federalism; Global Dialogue
on Federalism Booklet; Governance and Public Management; Harbinger Poetry; Heretics;
How Ottawa Spends; Hugh MacLennan Poetry; Innovation, Science, Environment;
International Social Survey Programme; John Deutsch Institute; Key Concepts; Library
of Political Leadership; McGill-Queen's Native and Northern; McGill-Queen's Studies in
Ethnic History; McGill-Queen's Studies in the History of Ideas; McGill-Queen's Studies in

the History of Religion; McGill-Queen's/Associated Medical Services Studies in the History of Medicine, Health, and Society; McGill-Queen's/Beaverbrook Canadian Foundation Studies in Art History; McGill-Queen's Rural, Wildland, Resource Studies; Migration and Diversity: Comparative Issues and International Comparisons; Nordic Voices; Philosophy Now; Philosophy and Science; Public Policy; Queen's Policy Studies; Rupert's Land Record Society; Social Union; Studies in Nationalism and Ethnic Conflict; Studies on the History of Quebec/Études d'histoire du Québec; Thematic Issues in Federalism; Understanding Movements in Modern Thought; War and European Society.

Medieval Institute Publications

Street Address:
100 E Walwood Hall
Western Michigan University
Kalamazoo, MI 49008-5432

Mailing Address:
Western Michigan University
1903 W. Michigan Ave.
Kalamazoo, MI 49008-5432

Phone: 269.387.8754
Fax: 269.387.8750

Website and Social Media:
Website: www.wmich.edu/
medieval/mip/

Orders:
Phone: 269.387.8755

Staff
Managing Editor: Patricia Hollahan (email: patricia.hollahan@wmich.edu)
Editor and Exhibits Manager: Theresa M. Whitaker (email: theresa.m.whitaker@wmich.edu)
Production Editor: Thomas P. Krol (email: thomas.p.krol@wmich.edu)
Order Fulfillment Manager: Cynthia Seedorff (email: cynthia.seerdorff@wmich.edu)

Introductory Member
Established: 1978
Title output 2012: 9
Titles currently in print: 210

Admitted to AAUP: 2011
Title output 2013: 13
Journals published: 2

Editorial Program
Publications in archeology, art history, dance, drama, history, literature, music, philosophy, and theology of the European Middle Ages and early modern period, with very occasional publications on the history of science and technology.
Special series: Studies in Medieval Culture; Early Drama, Art, and Music; Publications of the Richard Rawlinson Center
Journals: *Medieval Prosopography*; *Studies in Iconography*

Mercer University Press

1400 Coleman Avenue
Macon, GA 31207

Orders:
Phone: 866.895.1472
Email: mupressorders@mercer.edu

Phone: 478.301.2880
Fax: 478.301.2585
Email: (user I.D.)@mercer.edu

Website and Social Media:
Website: www.mupress.org
Blog: merceruniversitypress.wordpress.com/
Facebook: www.facebook.com/MercerUniversityPress
Twitter: mupress

Staff
Director and Acquisitions: Marc A. Jolley (email: jolley_ma)
Production: Marsha Luttrell, Publishing Assistant (email: luttrell_mm)
Marketing: Mary Beth Kosowski, Director of Marketing and Sales (email: kosowski_mb)
Business: Regenia (Jenny) Toole, Business Office (email: toole_rw)
Customer Service: Candice Morris (email: morris_ce)

Full Member
Established: 1979
Title output 2012: 36
Titles currently in print: 550+

Admitted to AAUP: 2000
Title output 2013: 35

Editorial Program
Regional trade titles and serious works of nonfiction in history, particularly in the history
of the United States (with an emphasis on the American South), the history of religion, and
the history of literature; Southern regional studies; literature and literary criticism; Southern
literary fiction; poetry; African American studies; political science; natural history.
Special series: Baptists; Civil War Georgia; the International Kierkegaard Commentary;
Mercer Classics in Biblical Studies; the Mercer Commentary on the Bible; the Melungeons;
Mercer Paul Tillich Series; Mercer Flannery O'Connor Series; Music and the American
South; Sports and Religion; Voices of the African Diaspora.
Book Awards: The Ferrol Sams Award for Fiction; The Adrienne Bond Award for Poetry;
The Will D. Campbell Award for Creative Nonfiction

The University of Michigan Press

839 Greene Street
Ann Arbor, MI 48104-3209

Phone: 734.764.4388
Fax: 734.615.1540
Email: um.press@umich.edu
Indiv: (user I.D.)@umich.edu

Orders:
University of Michigan Press
c/o Perseus Distribution
210 American Drive
Jackson, TN 38301
Phone: 800.343.4499, ext. 1154
ESL Helpline: 877.364.2942
Fax: 877.364.7062
International Customers Fax: 731.935.7731

<u>Website and Social Media:</u>
Website: www.press.umich.edu
Blog: blog.press.umich.edu
Facebook: www.facebook.com/pages/University-of-Michigan-Press/37383103953
Twitter: UofMPress
YouTube: youtube.com/umichpress

<u>UK and European Representative:</u>
Eurospan

Staff

Acting Director: Paul Courant (734.764.8016; email: pnc)
  Assistant to the Director: Jennifer Purdy (734.764.8016; email: jlpurdy)
  Permissions: Debra Shafer (734.615.6478; email: dshafer)
Acquisitions Editorial:
Director of Editorial: Aaron McCollough, Cultural Studies, American Studies, Digital
  Humanities, Literary Studies, Communications and New Media, Jewish Studies, Medicine
  and Medical Humanities, History of Science and Technology, digitalculturebooks.org)
  (734.763.4134; email: amccollo)
  Editors: Ellen Bauerle, Executive Editor (music, writing, classical studies, German studies,
  early modern history) (734.615.6479; email: bauerle); LeAnn Fields (class studies,
  theater and performance studies) (734.647.2463; email: lfields); Melody Herr (political
  science, law, American history) (734.763.6419; email: mrherr); Scott Ham (regional)
  (734.764.4387; email: scottom); Chris Hebert, Editor-at-Large (popular music and
  jazz) (email: hebertc); Aaron McCollough, (cultural studies, American studies, digital
  humanities, literary studies, communications and new media, Jewish studies, medicine
  and medical humanities, history of science and technology, digitalculturebooks.org)
  (734.763.4134; email: amccollo); Kelly Sippell (ESL, applied linguistics) (734.764.4447;
  email: ksippell)
  Editorial Associates: Susan Cronin (734.936.2841; email: sjcronin); Christopher Dreyer
  (734.647.2463; email: mikage); Alexa Ducsay (734.936.8932; email: ducsaya)
English as a Second Language: Kelly Sippell, ELT Manager and Executive Acquisitions
  Editor (734.764.4447; email: ksippell)
  Assistant Marketing Manager: Jason Contrucci (734.936.0459; email: contrucc)
  ELT Market Analyst: Claudia Leo (734.936.0459; email: cvleo)
Digital Publishing Production: Kevin Hawkins, Director (734.763.6860; email: kshawkin)

Manuscript Editorial: Marcia LaBrenz, Lead Copyediting Coordinator(734.647.4480; email: mlabrenz)
 Senior Copyediting Coordinators: Mary Hashman (734.936.0461; email: mhashman); Andrea Olson (734.936.0394; email: ajolson); Kevin Rennells (734.763.1526; email: rennells)
 Copyediting Assistant: Rosemary Bush (734.763.0170; email: rabush)
Design and Production:
 Senior Production Coordinators: Jillian Downey (734.615.8114; email: jilliand); Paula Newcomb (734.763.6417; email: newcombp)
 Designer: Heidi Dailey (734.764.4128; email: hdailey)
 Digital Production Assistant, Editorial Assistant: Alix Keener (734.615.9335; email: alixkee)
 Digital Publishing Project Managers: Jason Coleman (734.647.6017; email: taftman); Jonathan McGlone (734.763.4260; email: jmcglone)
 Digital Publishing Assistant: Kelly Witchen (734.763.6860; email: kwitchen)
Marketing and Sales: Renee Tambeau Director of Marketing and Outreach (734.936.0388; email: rtambeau)
 Marketing Manager: Shaun Manning (734.763.0163; email: shaunman)
Publishing Technology Group: Jeremy Morse, Director (734.615.5739; email: jgmorse)
 Web Designer: Melissa Baker-Young (734.764.6802; email: mbakeryo)
 Programmer: Seth Johnson (734.764.3417; email: sethajoh)
 Systems Administrator: James Vanderwill (734.936.3636; email: jvanderw)
Business: Gabriela Beres, Business Manager (734.936.2227; email: gsberes)
 Accounts Payable: Linda Rowley (734.647.9083; email: lrowley)

Full Member

Established: 1930   Admitted to AAUP: 1963
Title output 2012: 121   Title output 2013: 106
Titles currently in print: 3,004

Editorial Program

Scholarly and trade works in African American studies; American studies; American history; cultural studies; disability studies; English as a second language; environmental studies; gay and lesbian studies; German studies; law; literature; media studies and film; Michigan and Great Lakes; music; Native American studies; political science; theater and performance; women and gender studies; sports; English language teaching textbooks.

The Press distributes works of the Center for Chinese Studies and the Center for South and Southeast Asian Studies, the American Academy in Rome.

Special series: Analytical Perspectives on Politics; The CAWP Series in Gender and American Politics; the Bard Graduate Center Cultural Histories of the Material World; Class: Culture; Contemporary Political and Social Issues; Configurations: Critical Studies of World Politics; Corporealities: Discourses of Disability; Critical Performances; Culture of Knowledge In the Early Modern World; Digital Humanities; Editorial Theory and Literary Criticism;; Great Lakes Environment; ; International Series on the Research of Learning and Instruction of Writing; Jazz Perspectives; Kelsey Museum Studies; Landmark Video Games; Law and Society in the Ancient World; Law, Meaning, and Violence; The Memoirs of the American Academy in Rome; The Michigan American Music Series; Michigan Series in English for Academic and Professional Purposes; The Michigan Series on Teaching Multilingual Writers; Michigan Modern Dramatists; Michigan Studies in Comparative Jewish Culture; Michigan Studies in International Political Economy; Michigan Studies in Political Analysis; New Comparative Politics; The New Media World; The Papers and Monographs of the American Academy in Rome; Perspectives on Contemporary Korea; Poets on Poetry; The Politics of Race and Ethnicity; Social History, Popular Culture, and Politics in Germany; Societas: Historical Studies In Classical Culture; Practices in Digital Humanities; Studies in Literature and Science; Technologies of the Imagination: New Media in Everyday Life; Theater: Theory/Text/Performance; Thomas Spencer Jerome Lectures; Tracking Pop; Triangulations: Lesbian/Gay/Queer/Theater/Drama/Performance; Under Discussion; Writers on Writing

Michigan State University Press

1405 South Harrison Road, Suite 25
East Lansing, MI 48823-5245

Phone: 517.355.9543
Director's Office Fax: 517.432.2611
Email: msupress@msu.edu
Indiv: (user I.D.)@msu.edu

<u>Website and Social Media:</u>
Website: msupress.org
Facebook: facebook.com/MSUPress
Twitter: msupress

<u>UK/European Distributor:</u>
Eurospan

<u>Orders:</u>
Chicago Distribution Center
11030 S. Langley Ave.
Chicago, IL 60628
Phone: 800.621.2736; 773.702.7000
Fax: 800.621.8476; 773.702.7212

<u>Canadian Distributor:</u>
Chicago Distribution Center

Staff
Director: Gabriel Dotto (517.884.6900; email: dotto)
Editor-in-Chief/Assistant Director: Julie L. Loehr (Great Lakes studies and regional history; environmental and natural sciences; agricultural sciences; ethnohistory) (517.884.6905; email: loehr)
　Senior Acquisitions Editor: J. Alex Schwartz (US history; sociology; criminology; political science; African studies and African fiction) (517.884.6906; email: as)
Managing Editor: Kristine Blakeslee (517.884.6912; email: blakes17)
　Digital Production Specialist: Annette Tanner, Manager (517.884.6910; email: tanneran)
　Editorial Assistant: Elise Jajunga (517.884.6913; email: jajugael)
Marketing & Sales Manager: Julie Reaume (517.884.6920; email: reaumej)
　Marketing and Sales Coordinator: Travis E. Kimbel (517.884.6918; email: kimbel)
　Website Coordinator: Dawn Martin (517.884.6919; email: marti778)
Journals:
　Production Editor: Natalie Eidenier (517.884.6915; email: eidenie1)

Finance/Business Officer: Julie Wrzesinski (517.884.6922; email: wrzesin2)
   Logistics: Brett Robinson (517.884.6909; email: whpress)
Information Systems: Jesse Howard, Manager (517.884.6908; email: howard10)

Full Member

Established: 1947	Admitted to AAUP: 1992
	(Previous membership, 1951-1972)
Title output 2012: 38	Title output 2013: 40
Titles currently in print: 870	Journals published: 10

Editorial Program

Scholarly books and general nonfiction with areas of special interest in African studies; African American studies; Agricultural Science; American studies; American Indian studies; creative nonfiction and poetry; environmental science and natural history; Great Lakes studies; immigration studies; Latino/a studies; politics and the global economy; mimetic theory;sociology ; US history; urban studies; women's studies.

   The Press distributes publications for University of Calgary Press; University of Manitoba Press; the Michigan State University Museum

Journals: *Contagion: Journal of Violence, Mimesis, and Culture*; *CR: The New Centennial Review*; *Fourth Genre: Explorations In Nonfiction; French Colonial History*; *Journal for the Study of Radicalism*; *Northeast African Studies*; *QED: A Journal in GLBTQ Worldmaking*; *Real Analysis Exchange*; *Red Cedar Review*; *Rhetoric & Public Affairs*

Special series: American Food In History Series; American Indian Studies Series (related imprint: Makwa Enewed); The Animal Turn Series; Breakthroughs in Mimetic Theory Series; Courageous Conversations Series; Environmental Research Series; Discovering the Peoples of Michigan Series; Latinos in the United States Series; Rhetoric and Public Affairs Series; Rhetorical History of the United States Series; Ruth Simms Hamilton African Diaspora Series; Studies in Violence, Mimesis, and Culture Series; Transformations in Higher Education: The Scholarship of Engagement Series

Minnesota Historical Society Press

345 Kellogg Blvd. West
Saint Paul, MN 55102

Phone: 651.259.3200
Fax: 651.297.1345
Email: (user I.D.)@mnhs.org

Orders:
Chicago Distribution Center
11030 South Langley Ave.
Chicago, IL 60628
Phone: 800.621.2736; 773.568.1550
Fax: 800.621.8476; 773.660.2235

Website and Social Media:
Website: www.mhspress.org
Blog: discussions.mnhs.org/10000books
Facebook: www.facebook.com/home.php?#!/
    pages/Minnesota-Historical-Society-Press-and-Borealis-Books/44328618980
Twitter: mhspress

UK/European Distributor:
Gazelle Book Services

Canadian Distributor:
Scholarly Book Service

Staff

Director: Pamela McClanahan (651.259.3210; email: pamela.mcclanahan;
    Twitter: @mcclan)
Acquisitions: Pamela McClanahan, Ann Regan, Shannon Pennefeather
Editor-in-Chief, Rights and Permissions: Ann Regan (651.259.3206; email: ann.regan)
Manuscript Editorial: Shannon Pennefeather (651.259.3212; email: shannon.pennefeather)
Design and Production: Dan Leary (651.259.3209; email: daniel.leary)
Digital Production: Robin Moir (651.259.3211; email: robin.moir)
Publicity and Promotions: Alison Aten (651.259.3203; email: alison.aten)
Sales and Marketing Director: Mary Poggione (651.259.3204; email: mary.poggione)
Sales Manager: Nan Fulle (651.259.3202; email: nan.fulle)
Journals: Anne Kaplan (651.259.3207; email: anne.kaplan)
MNopedia (online Minnesota encyclopedia) Editor: Molly Huber (651.259.3216;
    email: molly.huber)

Associate Member

Established: 1859
Title output 2012: 21
Titles currently in print: 433

Admitted to AAUP: 2001
Title output 2013: 20
Journals published: 1

Editorial Program

The Minnesota Historical Society Press publishes books and digital products on the history and culture of the Upper Midwest. Specific list strengths include history, regional studies, Native American studies, nature and conservation, travel and tourism, food and cookery, the immigration experience, Scandinavian studies, regional children's picture books, and teaching Minnesota history.

Journal: *Minnesota History*
Special series: Minnesota Byways; Native Voices; People of Minnesota; the Northern Plate
Imprints: MHS Press; Borealis Books

University of Minnesota Press

111 Third Avenue South
Suite 290
Minneapolis, MN 55401-2552

Phone: 612.627.1970
Fax: 612.627.1980
Email: (user I.D.)@umn.edu

<u>Orders:</u>
University of Minnesota Press
Chicago Distribution Center
11030 South Langley Avenue
Chicago, IL 60628
Phone: 800.621.2736; 773.568.1550
Fax: 800.621.8476; 773.660.2235

<u>Website and Social Media:</u>
Website: www.upress.umn.edu
Blog: www.uminnpressblog.com
Facebook: www.facebook.com/pages/Minneapolis-MN/
University-of-Minnesota-Press/40070783448
Twitter: UMinnPress

<u>UK Distributor:</u>
NBN Plymbridge

<u>UK Representative:</u>
University Presses Marketing

Staff

Director: Douglas Armato (612.627.1972; email: armat001)
  Associate Director and Test Division Manager: Beverly Kaemmer (612.627.1963; email: kaemm002)
  Rights and Permissions: Jeff Moen (612.627.1978; email: moenx017)
Acquisitions Editorial: Richard Morrison, Editorial Director (literary and cultural studies, art and visual studies, anthropology) (612.627.1974; email: morri094)
  Senior Editor: Jason Weidemann (geography, sociology) (612.627.1975; email: weide007)
  Editors: Pieter Martin (architecture, political science, urban studies) (612.627.1976; email: marti190); Erik Anderson (regional, Scandinavian studies) (612.627.1973; email: and00900)
  Associate Editor: Danielle Kasprzak (cinema, media) (612.627.0122; email: kasp0079)
Managing Editor: Laura Westlund (612.627.1985; email: westl003)
  Assistant Managing Editor: Michael Stoffel (612.627.1977; email: stoff004)
Design and Production: Daniel Ochsner, Manager (612.627.1981; email: ochsn013)
  Assistant Design and Production Manager: Rachel Moeller (612.627.1984; email: moel0067)
Marketing: Emily Hamilton, Assistant Director of the Book Division (612.627.1936; email: eph)
  Sales Manager: Matt Smiley (612.627.1931; email: mwsmiley)
  Publicist: Heather Skinner (612.627.1932; email: skinn077)
  Advertising and Promotions Coordinator: Anne Wrenn (612.627.1938; email: awrenn)
  Direct Marketing Coordinator: Maggie Sattler (612.627.1934; email: sattl014)
Business: Susan Doerr, Manager (612.627.1967; email: doer0012)
Journals: Susan Doerr, Business; Jason Weidemann, Acquisitions
IT Systems: John Henderson (612.627.1944; email: hende291)

Full Member

Established: 1925
Title output 2012: 120
Titles currently in print: 3,050

Admitted to AAUP: 1937
Title output 2013: 123
Journals published: 9

Editorial Program

Literary and cultural studies; social and political theory; cinema and media studies; art and visual studies; digital culture; feminist studies; gay and lesbian studies; anthropology; architecture; geography; international relations; Native American studies; personality assessment, clinical psychology and psychiatry; philosophy; and Upper Midwest studies.

Journals: *Buildings & Landscapes; Cultural Critique; Culture/Clinic: Applied Lacanian Psychoanalysis; Future Anterior; Mechademia; The Moving Image; Native and Indigenous Studies Journal; Verge; Wicazo Sa Review*

Special series, joint imprints, and/or copublishing programs: Borderlines; Contradictions; Critical American Studies; Cultural Studies of the Americas; difference incorporated; Electronic Mediations; Fesler-Lampert Minnesota Heritage Book Series; First Peoples: New Directions in Indigenous Studies; Globalization and Community; Indigenous Americas; Minnesota Studies in the Philosophy of Science; MMPI-2 Monographs; MMPI-A Monographs; Posthumanities; Public Worlds; Quadrant; Social Movements, Protest, and Contention; Theory and History of Literature

University Press of Mississippi

3825 Ridgewood Road
Jackson, MS 39211-6492

Phone: 601.432.6205
Fax: 601.432.6217
Email: press@mississippi.edu
Indiv: (user I.D)@mississippi.edu

Website and Social Media:
Website: www.upress.state.ms.us
Blog: upmississippi.blogspot.com
Facebook: www.facebook.com/UPMiss
Twitter: UPMiss

Canadian Representative:
Scholarly Book Services

Warehouse Address:
Maple Logistics Solutions
Lebanon Distribution Center
704 Legionaire Drive
Fredericksburg, PA 17026

Orders:
Phone: 800.737.7788; 601.432.6205

UK Representative:
Roundhouse Publishing

Staff

Director: Leila W. Salisbury (601.432.6275; email: lsalisbury) (film studies, popular culture, regional trade)
   Administrative Assistant/Rights and Permissions Manager: Cynthia Foster (601.432.6205; email: cfoster)
   Development Assistant: Tracey Curtis (601.432.6205; email: bookfriends)
Acquisitions Editorial: Craig Gill, Assistant Director/Editor-in-Chief (601.432.6371; email: cgill) (history, music, folklore, ethnomusicology, regional trade)

Acquisitions Editor: Vijay Shah (601.432.6102; email: vshah) (literature, Caribbean studies, American studies, African American studies, ethnic studies, comics studies)
Electronic Publishing: Steve Yates, Assistant Director/Marketing Director (601.432.6695; email: syates)
　Electronic Projects Manager: Todd Lape (601.432.6274; email: tlape)
Manuscript Editorial: Anne Stascavage, Managing Editor (601.432.6249; email: astascavage)
　Editorial Associate: Valerie Jones (601.432.6272; email: vjones)
　Editorial Assistant: Katie Keene (601.432.6206; email: kkeene)
Design and Production: John A. Langston, Assistant Director/Art Director (601.432.6554; email: jlangston)
　Assistant Production Manager/Designer/Electronic Projects Manager: Todd Lape (601.432.6274; email: tlape)
　Senior Production Editor: Shane Gong Stewart (601.432.6795; email: sgong)
　Designer: Pete Halverson (601.432.6274; email: phalverson)
Marketing and Sales: Steve Yates, Assistant Director/Marketing Director (601.432.6695; email: syates)
　Data Services and Course Adoptions Manager: Kathy Burgess (601.432.6105; email: kburgess)
　Publicity and Advertising Manager: Clint Kimberling (601.432.6424; email: ckimberling)
　Electronic and Direct-to-Consumer Marketing Specialist: Kristin Kirkpatrick (601.432.6459; email: kkirkpatrick)
　Marketing Assistant: Courtney McCreary (601.432.6516; email: cmccreary)
Business: Isabel Metz, Assistant Director/Business Manager (601.432-6551; email: imetz)
　Customer Service and Order Supervisor: Sandy Alexander (601/432-6704; email: salexander)

Full Member

Established: 1970　　　　　　　　　　Admitted to AAUP: 1976
Title output 2012: 144　　　　　　　　Title output 2013: 137
Titles currently in print: 1,203

Editorial Program

Scholarly and trade titles in African American studies; African Diaspora studies; American studies, literature, history, and culture; art and architecture; Caribbean studies; children's literature studies, comic studies; ethnic studies; folklore; film studies; media studies; music; ethnomusicology; natural sciences; photography; popular culture; regional studies; serious nonfiction of general interest; Southern studies; women's studies; other liberal arts.
Special series: African American Material Culture; American Made Music; Caribbean Studies; Chancellor Porter L. Fortune Symposium in Southern History; Children's Literature Association Series; Conversations with Comics Artists; Conversations with Filmmakers; Faulkner and Yoknapatawpha; Folklore Studies in a Multicultural World; Great Comic Artists; Hollywood Legends; Literary Conversations; Margaret Walker Alexander Series in African American Studies; Race, Rhetoric, and Media; Television Conversations Series; Willie Morris Books in Memoir and Biography

University of Missouri Press

2910 LeMone Boulevard
Columbia, MO 65201

Phone: 573.882.7641
Fax: 573.884.4498
Email: upress@missouri.edu
Indiv: (user ID)@missouri.edu

Website and Social Media:
Website: press.umsystem.edu
Facebook: www.facebook.com/pages/
    University-of-Missouri-Press/177293766515
Twitter: umissouripress
Blog: umissouripress.blogspot.com/

Orders:
University of Missouri Press
c/o Chicago Distribution Center
11030 South Langley Avenue
Chicago, IL 60628-3830
Phone: 800.621.2736; 773.702.7000
Fax: 800.621.8476
Email: orders@press.uchicago.edu

UK Representative:
Eurospan

Canadian Representative:
Scholarly Book Services

Staff

Director: David Rosenbaum (573.882.9478; email: rosenbaumd)
Acquisitions: Clair Willcox, Associate Director and Editor-in-Chief (573.882.9997; email: willcoxc)
    Acquisitions Editor: Gary Kass (573.884.1277; email: kassg)
Editorial: Sara Davis, Managing Editor (573.882.8714; email: davissd)
    Editorial Assistant: Greg Haefner (573.882.3044; email: gjhz7b)
Production: Nikki Waltz, Assistant Production Manager (573.882.0184; email: waltzn)
Marketing: Kristi Henson, Marketing and Sales Manager (573.882.9672; email: hensonk)
    Electronic Marketing Assistant: Kirk Hinkelman (573.882.8735; email: hinkelmank)
    Publicity and Sales Assistant: Lyn Smith (573.882.3000; email: smithls)
Business: Tracy Tritschler, Business Manager (573.882.9459; email: tritschlert)
    Business Assistant: Brittany Brown (573.882.7641; email: brownbritt)

Full Member

Established: 1958
Title output 2012: 29
Title currently in print: 1,100

Admitted to AAUP: 1960
Title output 2013: 18

Editorial Program

American and European history, including intellectual history and biography; African American studies; women's studies; American and British literary criticism; journalism; political science, including foreign relations; political philosophy and ethics; regional studies of Missouri, and the Midwest; and creative non-fiction.

Special series: American Military Experience; Give 'Em Hell Harry; Mark Twain and His Circle; Missouri Biography; Missouri Heritage Readers; Shades of Blue and Gray; Sports and American Culture

Modern Language Association of America

26 Broadway, 3rd floor
New York, NY 10004-1789

Phone: 646.576.5000
Fax: 646.458.0030
Email: info@mla.org
Indiv: firstinitiallastname@mla.org

Book Orders:
Phone: 646.576.5161
Fax: 646.576.5160
Email: bookorders@mla.org

Website and Social Media:
Website: www.mla.org
Twitter: MLAnews

Staff
Executive Director: Rosemary G. Feal (646.576.5102)
Director of Scholarly Communication: Kathleen Fitzpatrick (646.576.5110)
 Associate Director of Scholarly Communication: Anna Chang (646.576.5029)
 Senior Acquisitions Editor: Margit Longbrake (646.576.5022)
 Senior Acquisitions Editor: James C. Hatch (646.576.5044)
Managing Editor, *MLA Commons*: Katina Rogers (646.576.5114)
 Permissions and Contracts Manager: Marcia E. Henry (646.576.5042)
Manuscript Editorial (includes journals): Judy Goulding, Associate Executive Director and
 Director of Publishing Operations: (646.576.5015)
 Associate Managing Editor, Book Publications: Angela Gibson (646.576.5016)
Director of Print and Electronic Production: Judith Altreuter (646.576.5010)
Marketing and Sales Director: Kathleen Hansen (646.576.5018)
Member and Customer Services Manager: Leonard J. Moreton (646.576.5146)
Information Technology Center Manager: Kinglen Wang (646.576.5200)

Associate Member
Established: 1883

Title output 2012: 7

Titles currently in print: 298

Admitted to AAUP: 1992

Title output 2013: 6

Journals published: 6

Editorial Program
Scholarly, pedagogical, and professional books on language and literature.
Journals: *ADE and ADFL Bulletins; MLA International Bibliography; MLA Newsletter; PMLA; Profession*
Book series: Approaches to Teaching World Literature; New Variorum Edition of
Shakespeare; Options for Teaching; Teaching Languages, Literatures, and Cultures; Texts and
Translations; World Literatures Reimagined

The Museum of Modern Art

11 West 53rd Street
New York, NY 10019

Orders:
Individuals: 800.447.6662
www.momastore.org
Trade: 212.627.9484 / www.artbook.com

Phone: 212.708.9443
Fax: 212.333.6575 or 212.708.9779
Email: moma_publications@moma.org
Indiv: firstname_lastname@moma.org

Website and Social Media:
Website: www.moma.org
Blog: www.moma.org/insideout
Facebook: www.facebook.com/MuseumofModernArt
Twitter: MuseumModernArt
YouTube: www.youtube.com/MoMAvideos
Flickr: www.flickr.com/themuseumofmodernart

UK Representative:
Thames & Hudson

Canadian Representative:
ARTBOOK | D.A.P.

Staff
Publisher: Christopher Hudson (212.708.9445)
Associate Publisher: Charles Kim (212.708.9456)
Assistant to the Publisher: Makiko Wholey (212.708.9512)
Editorial Director: David Frankel (212.708.9448)
Editor: Emily Hall (212.708.9511)
Associate Editor: Rebecca Roberts (212.708.9883)
Production Director: Marc Sapir (212.708.9745)
Production Manager: Matthew Pimm (212.708.9742)
Senior Designer: Amanda Washburn (212.708.6572)
Marketing and Production Coordinator: Hannah Kim (212.708.9449)
Associate Business Manager: Bryan Stauss (212.708.9743)

Associate Member
Established: 1929
Title output 2012: 17
Titles currently in print: 300

Admitted to AAUP: 2008
Title output 2013: 23

Editorial Program
Modern and contemporary art, including painting, sculpture, drawings, prints and illustrated books, photography, film, media, architecture and design
Special series: MoMA Artist Series, MoMA Design Series, MoMA Primary Documents, Studies in Modern Art

The National Academies Press

500 Fifth Street, N.W.
Washington, DC 20001

Bookstore phone: 202.334.2612
Fax: 202.334.2793
Email: (user I.D.)@nas.edu

<u>Website and Social Media:</u>
Website: www.nap.edu
Facebook: www.facebook.com/NationalAcademiesPress
Twitter: NAPress

<u>Orders (US and Canada):</u>
Phone: 800.624.6242; 202.334.3313
Fax: 202.334.2451
Email: zjones@nas.edu

<u>UK Distributor:</u>
Marston Book Services

Staff
Executive Director: Barbara Kline Pope (202.334.3328; email: bkline)
Executive Assistant to the Director: Shelly Wolfe (202.334.3038; email: sewolfe)
Director of Operations: Sandy Adams (202.334.3157; email: sadams)
Executive Editor: Stephen M. Mautner (202.334.3336; email: smautner)
Production Manager: Dorothy Lewis (202.334.2409; email: dlewis)
Director, Composition, Graphics and Design: Jim Gormley (202.334.3325; email: jgormley)
Director, Marketing and Technology: Alphonse MacDonald (202.334.3625;
   email: amacdonald)
Permissions Editor: Barbara Murphy (202.334.1902; email: bmurphy)
Business Manager: Rachel Levy (202.334.3329; email: rlevy)
Customer Service Manager: Zina Jones (202.334.3116; email: zjones)

Associate Member
Established: 1864
Title output 2012: 150
Titles currently in print: 3,853

Admitted to AAUP: 1988
Title output 2013: 140
Titles currently in print: 4,172

Editorial Program
Primarily professional-level, policy-oriented titles in agricultural sciences; behavioral and social sciences; biology; chemistry; computer sciences; earth sciences; economics; education; energy; engineering; environmental issues; industry; international issues; materials science; medicine; natural resources; nutrition; physical sciences; public policy issues; statistics; transportation; and urban and rural development.

National Gallery of Art

Street Address:
Sixth Street and Constitution Avenue NW
Washington, DC

Mailing Address:
2000B South Club Drive
Landover, MD 20785

Phone: 202.842.6200
Fax: 202.408.8530
Email: (initial-last name)@nga.gov

Online shop:
shop.nga.gov
Customer Service / Order Fulfillment:
800.697.9350

Website and Social Media:
Website: www.nga.gov
Facebook: www.facebook.com/NationalGalleryofArt
Twitter: ngadc

Staff
Editor-in-Chief: Judy Metro (202.842.6205; email: j-metro)
Deputy Publisher and Production Manager: Chris Vogel (202.842.6209; email: c-vogel)
  Senior Editor for the Permanent Collections: Sally Bourrie (202.842.6208; email: s-bourrie)
  Senior Editors: Tam Bryfogle (202.842.6498; email: t-bryfogle); Julie Warnement (202.842.6136; email: j-warnement); Ulrike Mills (202.842.6613; email: u-mills)
  Editor: Caroline Weaver (202.842.6032; email: c-weaver)
  Assistant Editor: Lisa Wainwright (202.842.6669; email: l-wainwright)
Managing Editor of CASVA Publications: Cynthia Ware (202.842.6204; email: c-ware)
Design Manager: Wendy Schleicher (202.789.4601; email: w-schleicher)
  Designers: Brad Ireland (202.789.3082; b-ireland); Rio DeNaro (202.842.6697; email: r-denaro)
  Assistant Production Manager: John Long (202.842.6423; email: j-long)
  Production Assistant: Mariah Shay (202.842.6758; email: m-shay)
Permissions Coordinator: Sara Sanders-Buell (202.842.6719; email: s-sanders-buell)
Rothko Resarch Associates: Laili Nasr (202.842-6779; email: l-nasr); Mary Lee Corlett (202.842.6603; email: m-corlett)
Program Assistant: Mari Pappas (202.842.6200; email: m-pappas)

Associate Member
Established: 1941
Title output 2012: 9
Titles currently in print: 160

Admitted to AAUP: 1992
Title output 2013: 10

Editorial Program
The National Gallery publishes exhibition catalogues on all subjects and permanent collection catalogues (including Western art of the early Renaissance through the contemporary era); a symposium series; Studies in the History of Art, in conjunction with the Center for Advanced Study in the Visual Arts; educational online programs and catalogues; exhibition brochures and wall texts; online features and apps for permanent collection and special exhibitions; scholarly and popular publications based on objects in

the museum's collections; scholarly publications on conservation; educational materials and guides for use by the public and by teachers and schools; and the calendar of events, film and music programs, bulletins, and all Gallery ephemera. Unsolicited manuscripts are not invited.

Naval Institute Press

291 Wood Road
Annapolis MD 21402-5034

Orders:
Phone: 800.233.8764

Phone: 410.268.6110
Fax: 410.295.1084/5
Email: firstinitiallastname@usni.org

Website and Social Media:
Website: www.nip.org
Facebook: www.facebook.com/NavalInstitute
Twitter: USNIBooks

UK/European Representatives
Eurospan Group

Canadian Representatives
Scholarly Book Service

Staff
Director: Richard A. Russell (410.295.1031)
  Business Manager: Prospero Hernandez (410.295.1046)
Senior Acquisitions Editor/Subsidiary Rights Manager/Imports: Susan Todd Brook (410.295.1037)
Senior Acquisitions Editor/Director, Professional Publishing: Thomas J. Cutler (410.295.1038)
Senior Acquisitions Editor/Electronic Publications Manager: Adam Kane (410.295.1080)
  Assistant Editors: Taylor Skord (410.295.1030); Adam Nettina (410.295.1089)
Managing Editor: Susan Corrado (410.295.1032)
  Production Editors: Emily Bakely (410.295.1020); Marlena Montagna (410.295.1040)
  Editorial Assistant: Nicholas Lyle (410.295.1062)
Director of Sales and Marketing: George Keating (410.295.1025)
  Marketing Manager: Claire Noble (410.295.1039)
  Publicist: Judy Heise (410.295.1028)
  Exhibits and Special Sales Manager: Brian Walker (410.295.1082)
Journals, U.S. Naval Institute:
  Proceedings, Editor-in-Chief: Paul Merzlak (410.295.1072)
  Naval History, Editor-in-Chief: Richard Latture (410.295.1076)
  Publisher, U.S. Naval Institute: William M. Miller (410.295.1068)
  Chief Financial Officer, U.S. Naval Institute: Robert Johnson (410.295.1707)

Full Member

Established: 1898
Title output 2012: 76
Titles currently in print: 900

Admitted to AAUP: 1949
Title output 2013: 81
Journals published: 2

Editorial Program

General military subjects; military biography; naval history and literature; naval and military reference; ; navigation; military law; naval science; sea power; shipbuilding; professional guides; nautical arts and lore; technical guides; veterans affairs; fiction.

Journals: *Naval History*; *Proceedings*

Special series: Anatomy of the Ship Series; Bluejacket Books (paperback); Blue and Gold Professional Library; Leatherneck Classics; New Perspectives on Maritime History and Nautical Archaeology; Scarlet & Gold Professional Library

University of Nebraska Press

1111 Lincoln Mall
Lincoln, NE 68588-0630

Phone: 402.472.3581
Fax 402.472.6214
Email: (user I.D.)@unl.edu

Website and Social Media:
Website: www.nebraskapress.unl.edu;
bisonbooks.com
Blog: nebraskapress.typepad.com
Facebook: www.facebook.com/NebraskaPress

UK Distributor:
Combined Academic Publishers

Orders:
University of Nebraska Press
Longleaf Services
116 S. Boundary Street
Chapel Hill, NC 27514-3808

Phone: 800.848.6224
Fax: 800.272.6817
Email:
customerservice@longleafservices.org

Canadian Distributor:
Codasat Canada Ltd.

Staff

Director: Donna A. Shear (402.472.2861; email: dshear2)
Assistant Director for Business/CFO: Tera Beermann (402.472.0011; email: tbeermann2)
   Rights and Permissions: Leif Milliken (402.472.7702; email: lmilliken2)
Acquisitions Editorial: Derek Krissoff, Editor-in-Chief (402.472.4311; email: dkrissoff2)
   Sports Editor: Rob Taylor (402.472.0325; email: rtaylor6)
   Indigenous Studies Editor: Matthew Bokovoy (402.472.4452; email: mbokovoy2)
   History and Potomac Books Editor: Bridget Barry (402.472.0645; email: bbarry2)
   Cultural Criticism and Creative Works Editor: Kristen Elias Rowley (402.472.5949; email: keliasrowley2)
   American Studies and Potomac Books Editor: Alicia Christensen (402.472.0317; email achristensen6)
Editorial, Design, and Production: Ann Baker, Manager, EDP (402.472.0095; email: abaker2)
   Assistant Manager, EDP: Sabrina Stellrecht (402.472.7712; email: sstellrecht2)
   Project Editors: Joeth Zucco (402.472.0199; email: jzucco2); Sara Springsteen

(402.472.4008; email: sspringsteen1); Kathryn Owens (402.472.1565; email: kowens3); Kyle Simonsen (402.472.5333; email: ksimonsen2)
Assistant Production Manager: Alison Rold (402.472.7706; email: arold1)
Book Production Associate: Terry Boldan (402.472.0890; email: tboldan2)
Designers: Andrea Shahan (402.472.7718; email: ashahan1); Roger Buchholz (402.472.7713; email: rbuchholz1); Nathan Putens (402.472.5943; email: nputens2)
Marketing and Sales: Rob Buchanan, Sales Coordinator (402.472.0160; email: rbuchanan1)
  Publicity Manager: Acacia Gentrup (402.472.5938; email: agentrup3)
  Publicity and Social Media: Rosemary Vestal (402.472.9658; email: rvestal2)
  Direct Mail Manager: Tish Fobben (402.472.4627; email: pfobben2)
  Author Events and Exhibits Coordinator: Emily Giller (402.472.2759; email: egiller2)
  Regional and Special Sales Manager: Tom Swanson (402.472.5945; email: tswanson3)
Electronic Marketing Coordinator: Erica Corwin (402.472.9313; email: ecorwin1)
Accelerated Publishing and Management: Manjit Kaur, Manager (402.472.7703; email: mkaur2)
  Project Supervisor: Terence Smyre (402.472.2292; email: tsmyre2)
  Marketing and Fulfillment Manager: Joyce Gettman (402.472.8330; email: jgettman2)
  Fulfillment Coordinator: Odessa Anderson (402.472.8536; email: oanderson2)
  Project Coordinator: Joel Puchalla (402.472.3572; email: jpuchalla2)
  Desktop Compositor: Shirley Thornton (402.472.5028; email: sthorton3)
Business Services:
Accountant and Analyst: Mark Francis (402.472.5804; email: mfrancis2)
Royalty Accountant & Accounts Receivable: Odessa Anderson (402-472-8536; email: oanderson2)
  Accounts Payable: Claire Schwinck (402.472.7711; email: cschwinck2)
Digital Assets and IT: Jana Faust, Manager, Digital Assets and IT (402.472.0171; email: jfaust2)
  Coordinator: Amy Lage (402.472.3663; email: alage2)

Full Member

Established: 1941	Admitted to AAUP: Unknown
Title output 2012: 150	Title output 2013: 179
Titles currently in print3,200	Journals published: 26

Editorial Program

Native American and indigenous studies; history; Western Americana; sports; anthropology; geography; studies of food and environment; American studies; cultural criticism; creative works; JPS imprint: Judaica, bible, and bible commentary; Potomac imprint: military studies, current affairs, and intelligence.

The Press distributes for the Buros Institute of Mental Measurement, Caxton Press, Open Letter, the Society for American Baseball Research, and Whale & Star Press.

Journals: *American Indian Quarterly; Anthropological Linguistics; Collaborative Anthropologies; French Forum; Frontiers: A Journal of Women's Studies; Great Plains Quarterly; Great Plains Research; Journal of Austrian Studies; Journal of Literature and Trauma Studies; Journal of Sports Media; Legacy: A Journal of American Women Writers; Native South; NINE: A Journal of Baseball History & Culture; Nineteenth-Century French Studies; Nouvelles Etudes Francophones; Qui Parle: Critical Humanities and Social Sciences; Resilience: A Journal of the Environmental*

Humanities; *Storyworlds: A Journal of Narrative Studies*; *Studies in American Indian Literatures*; *Studies in American Naturalism*; *symploke: A Journal for the Intermingling of Literary, Cultural, and Theoretical Scholarship*; *Theoretical and Applied Ethics*; *The Undecidable Unconscious: A Journal of Deconstruction and Psychoanalysis*; *Western American Literature*; *Women and Music: A Journal of Gender and Culture*; and *Women in German Yearbook: Feminist Studies in German Literature and Culture*

Imprints: Bison Books; JPS (The Jewish Publication Society); Potomac Books

Book series: African Poetry; American Lives; American Indian Lives; At Table; Beyond Armageddon; Bison Frontiers of Imagination; Cather Studies; Complete Letters of Henry James; Critical Environments; Critical Studies in the History of Anthropology; Early American Places; Engendering Latin America; European Women Writers; Expanding Frontiers; Extraordinary Worlds; France Overseas; Frontiers of Narrative; Great Campaigns of the Civil War; History of the American West; Indians of the Southeast; Indigenous Education; Iroquoians and Their World; Journals of the Lewis and Clark Expedition; Key Issues of the Civil War Era; Latin American Women Writers; Law in the American West; North American Indian Prose Award; Our Sustainable Future; Politics and Governments of the American States; Post-Western Horizons; Sources of American Indian Oral Literature; Stages; Studies in Jewish Civilization (for Creighton University Press); Studies in the Anthropology of North American Indians; Studies in the Native Languages of the Americas; Studies in War, Society, and the Military; Teaching and Learning in Higher Education; Texts and Contexts; This Hallowed Ground: Guides to Civil War Battlefields; Willa Cather Scholarly Edition; Women in German Yearbook; Women in the West

University of Nevada Press

Morrill Hall, Mail Stop 0166
Reno, NV 89557-0166

Phone: 775.784.6573
Fax: 775.784.6200
Email: (user I.D.)@unpress.nevada.edu

Order Fulfillment:
Chicago Distribution Center
11030 South Langley Ave.
Chicago, IL 60628
Phone: 800.621.2736
Fax: 800.621.8476

Website and Social Media:
Website: www.unpress.nevada.edu
Facebook: www.facebook.com/pages/University-of-Nevada-Press/

Canadian Representative:
Scholarly Book Services

UK Representative:
Eurospan

Staff

Director: Joanne O'Hare (775.682.7389; email: johare)
Acquisitions Editors: Matt Becker, Senior Acquisitions Editor (775.882.7390; email: mbecker); Joanne O'Hare
Marketing & Sales Manager: Michael O. Campbell (775.682.7395; email: mcampbell) Marketing and Editorial Associate: Mayanne Coyne (775.682.7394; email: mcoyne)
Editing, Design & Production Manager: Kathleen Szawiola (775.682.7391; email: kszawiola)
Business Manager: JoAnne Banducci (775.682.7387; email: jbanducci)

Full Member

Established: 1961

Title output 2012: 16

Titles currently in print: 408

Admitted to AAUP: 1982

Title output 2013: 13

Editorial Program

Scholarly and general interest books about the history, literature, anthropology, archaeology, and natural history of the American West, Nevada, and the Great Basin. Additional interests include books dealing with the Basque peoples of Europe and the Americas; Native American Studies; mining; environmental studies; and gaming and gambling.

Special series: Basque Studies; Gambling Studies; The Urban West; Western Literature; West Word Fiction; Wilbur S. Shepperson Series in Nevada History

University Press of New England

1 Court Street, Suite 250

Lebanon, NH 03766-1358

Customer Service/Order Fulfillment:

Phone: 800.421.1561

Fax: 603.448.9429

Phone: 603.448.1533

Fax: 603.448.7006

Email: university.press@dartmouth.edu

Indiv: firstname.lastname@dartmouth.edu

Warehouse:

UPNE Fulfillment Center

c/o Maple Press Company

Lebanon Distribution Center

704 Legionaire Drive

Fredricksburg, PA 17026

Website and Social Media:

Website: www.upne.com

Facebook: www.facebook.com/

   UniversityPressOfNewEngland

Canadian Representative:

University of British Columbia Press

European Representative:

Eurospan

Staff

Director: Michael Burton (ext. 241)

   Assistant to the Director, Permissions Manager: Deborah J. Gray (ext. 201)

   Associate Director, Operations: Thomas Johnson (ext. 251)

   Systems Administrator/Webmaster: David Bellows (ext. 257)

Editor-in-Chief: Phyllis Deutsch (603.448.1533, ext. 222)

   Acquisitions Editors: Stephen P. Hull (781.736.4605); Richard Pult (ext. 226)

Manuscript Editorial: Amanda Dupuis, Managing Editor (ext. 243)

   Production Editors: Susan A. Abel (ext. 244); Lauren D. Seidman (ext. 235)

   Production Assistant: Michaela R. Weglinski (ext. 217)

Design and Production: Eric M. Brooks, Assistant Director of Design and Production (ext. 211)

   Designer: Mindy B. Hill (ext. 246)

   Production Coordinator: Douglas Tifft (ext. 245)

Marketing: David Corey, Assistant Director Marketing & Sales (ext. 234)
  Sales & Trade Exhibits Manager: Sherri Strickland (ext. 238)
  Publicity and Subsidiary Rights Manager: Barbara Briggs (ext. 233)
  New Media Marketing Coordinator: Catherine A. (Katy) Grabill (ext. 237)
  Sales & Exhibit Coordinator: Susan Sylvia (ext. 236)
Business: Thomas Johnson, Associate Director, Operations (ext. 251)
  Accounting Supervisor: Donna Youngman (ext. 252)
  Accounting Associate: Timothy Semple (ext. 253)
  Order Fulfillment Supervisor: Barbara Benson (ext. 255)
  Senior Customer Service Clerk: Barbara McBeth (ext. 256)

Full Member

Established: 1970   Admitted to AAUP: 1975
Title output 2012: 65   Title output 2013: 69
Titles currently in print: 898
Publishes books under the consortium member imprints of Brandeis University Press, Dartmouth College Press, University of New Hampshire Press, Northeastern University Press, and University Press of New England.

<u>**Editorial Program**</u>

General trade, scholarly, instructional, and reference works for scholars, teachers, students, and the public. The Press concentrates in American studies, literature, history, religion, and cultural studies; art, architecture, photography, and material culture; ethics; ethnic studies (including African American, Jewish, Native American, and Shaker studies); interdisciplinary studies; folklore, music, and popular culture; languages; nature and the environment; natural sciences; marine ecology; maritime culture; New England studies; social issues/social sciences; and Trans-Atlantic and cross-cultural studies. Special series feature such topics as criminology, modernism, visual culture, and sustainability.

The Press, through UPNE Book Partners handles book order processing and distribution for: Acdemia Press; Bauhan Publishing; Cadent Publishing; Carnegie Mellon University Press; Cavankerry Press; Chaucer Press Books; Chipstone Foundation; Four Way Books; Gordian Knot Books; International Polar Institute Press; Nightboat Books; Oberlin College Press; Saturnalia Books; Sheep Meadow Press; Tagus Press; Vermont Folklife Center; and Wesleyan University Press.

Special series: Becoming Modern: New Nineteenth-Century Studies; Brandeis Series in American Jewish History, Culture and Life; HBI Series on Gender, Culture, Religion, and Law; HBI Series on Jewish Women; Civil Society: Historical and Contemporary Perspectives; Collected Writings of Rousseau; Interfaces: Studies in Visual Culture; Menahem Stern Jerusalem Lectures: Brandeis University/Historical Society of Israel; The Northeastern Library of Black Literature; The Northeastern Series on Gender, Crime, and Law; Revisiting New England: The New Regionalism; Re-Mapping the Transnational: A Dartmouth Series in American Studies; Tauber Institute for the Study of European Jewry Series.

University of New Mexico Press

Mailing Address:
MSCO5 3185
1 University of New Mexico
Albuquerque NM 87131-0001

Phone: 505.277.3495
Fax: 505.277.3343
Email: unmpress@unm.edu
Indiv: (user I.D.)@unm.edu
(unless otherwise indicated)

Website and Social Media:
Website: www.unmpress.com
Facebook: www.facebook.com/pages
   /University-of-New-Mexico-Press/109620976711
Twitter: UNMPress

Street Address:
1717 Roma NE
NE Albuquerque NM 87106-4509

Business and Order Fulfillment:
1312 Basehart Road SE
Albuquerque NM 87106-4363

Orders:
Phone: 800.249.7737; 505.272.7777
Fax: 505.272.7778

UK/European Representative:
Eurospan

Canadian Representative:
Codasat Canada

Staff

Director: John Byram (505.277.3280; email: jbyram; Twitter: @jwbyram) (anthropology, archaeology, linguistics, sciences)

Rights and Royalties Coordinator: Briony Jones (505.925.9512; email: briony)

Editor-in-Chief: Clark Whitehorn (505.277.2293; email: clarkw) (Chicano/a studies, history, Latin American studies, Native studies, natural history)

Senior Acquisitions Editor: Elise McHugh (505.277.3327; email: elisemc) (American literature and criticism, poetry, fiction, art, photography)

Editorial, Design, and Production Manager: Maya Allen-Gallegos (505.277.3324; email: mayag)

Art Director: Lisa Tremaine (505.277.3333; email: ltremaine)

Production Editors: James Ayers (505.277.3436; email: ayers); Felicia Cedillos (505.277.3322; email: fcedillo)

Production Coordinator: Trish Kanavy (505.277.2153; email: trishk)

Designers: Catherine Leonardo (505.277.3299; email: davinci); Lila Sanchez (505.277.3256; email: lilamar)

Sales and Marketing Manager: Katherine White (505.277.3294; email: kwhite03)

Publicist: Lauren Consuelo Tussing (505.277.3291; email: laurenconsuelo)

Marketing Associate: Zoya Lozoya (505.277.3289; email: zoya)

Sales Representatives: Kay Marcotte (505.272.7544; email: kaym); Sheri Hozier (email: sherih)

Associate Director for Business Operations: Richard Schuetz (505.277.3284; email: rschuetz)

Fiscal Services: Lyudmila Markova (505.272.7774; email: milam)

Accounts Receivable/Payable: Tiffany Rawls (505.272.7775; email: trawls)

Customer Service and Credit Manager: Stewart Marshall (505.925.9506; email: stewartm)

Customer Service Associates: Susan Hoffman (505.925.9508; email: soozjh); Judy Kepler

(505.925.9508; email: jkepler)
Warehouse Manager: Susan Coatney (505.272.7770; email: susanc)
IT Support Manager: Darrell Banward (505.277.0978; email: dbanward)

Full Member

Established: 1929 | Admitted to AAUP: 1937
Title output 2012: 68 | Title output 2013: 73
Titles currently in print: 1,100

Editorial Program

Scholarly books, fiction, poetry, and literary nonfiction, with special interests in social and cultural anthropology; archaeology of the Americas; art, architecture, and photography; Chicano/a studies; frontier history; legal studies, especially water issues; American literature; Latin American studies; Native studies; and books that deal with important aspects of Southwest or Rocky Mountain states, including natural history and land grant studies

Special series, joint imprints and/or copublishing programs: Barbara Guth Worlds of Wonder Science Series for Young Readers; Diálogos Series; Histories of the American Frontier; Mary Burritt Christiansen Poetry Series; Pasó por Aquí Series on the Nuevomexicano Literary Heritage; Recencies Series on Twentieth-Century American Poetics; Archaeologies of Landscapes in the Americas Series; Cambio Series on Business, Economics, and Society in Latin America; Querencias Series on Transnational Culture of the U.S./Mexico Borderlands; Contextos Series on Latino/a Contemporary Issues; Religions of the Americas

New York University Press

838 Broadway, 3rd Floor
New York, NY 10003-4812

Phone: 212.998.2575
Fax: 212.995.3833
Email: orders@nyupress.edu
Indiv: firstname.lastname@nyu.edu

Website and Social Media:
Website: www.nyupress.org
Blog: www.fromthesquare.org
Facebook: www.facebook.com/fromthesquare
Twitter: NYUpress

UK/European Representative:
Combined Academic Publishers

Orders and Customer Service:
Phone: 800.996.6987
Fax: 212.995.4798

Warehouse:
The Maple Press
Lebanon Distribution Center
704 Legionnaire Drive
Fredricksburg, PA 17026

Staff

Director: Steve Maikowski (212.998.2573)
   Assistant to the Director/Subsidiary Rights Administrator: Margie Guerra (212.998.2540)
Acquisitions Editorial: Eric Zinner, Assistant Director and Editor-in-Chief (cultural and media studies, literary studies, American studies, twentieth-century American history) (212.998.2544)

Executive Editor: Ilene Kalish (sociology, criminology, politics) (212.998.2556)
Editor: Clara Platter (American history, military history, law) (212.998.2570)
Senior Editor: Jennifer Hammer (religion, Jewish studies, psychology, anthropology) (212.998.2491)
Managing Editor, Library of Arabic Literature: Chip Rossetti (212.998.2433)
Assistant Editors: Alicia Nadkarni (film and media studies) (212.998.2426); Caelyn Cobb (212.992.9013)
Editorial Assistants: Constance Grady (212.998.4252); Gemma Juan-Simo (212.998.2575)
Program Officer for Digital Scholarly Publishing: Monica McCormick (212.998.2528)
Production and Design Manager: Charles Hames (212.998.2628)
  Managing Editor: Dorothea Halliday (212.998.2575)
  Assistant Production Manager: Adam Bohanan (212.998.2578)
  Production Editor: Alexia Traganas (212.992.9998)
  Editing and Production Specialist: Edith Alston (212.992.7303)
Marketing and Sales: Mary Beth Jarrad, Marketing and Sales Director (212.998.2588)
  Advertising and Direct Mail Specialist: Patricia Palao (212.998.2558)
  Senior Publicist: Betsy Steve (212.992.9991)
  Exhibits Coordinator: Tom Sullivan (212.998.2547)
  E-marketing Coordinator: Jodi Narde (212.998.2591)
  Sales Assistant: Sam Peterson (212.992.7312)
Business: Tom Helleberg, Business and Budget Manager (212.998.2569)
  Accounts Receivable Supervisor: Lakisha Williams (212.992.9987)
  Accounts Payable and Royalties Coordinator: Susan Hamilton (212.998.2524)
  Customer Service and Print on Demand Coordinator: Kevin Cooper (212.998.2546)
Computer and Information Systems: Miguel Sandoval, Information Systems Manager (212.998.2536)

Full Member

Established: 1916   Admitted to AAUP: 1937
Title output 2012: 125   Title output 2013: 139
Titles currently in print: 2,809

Editorial Program

American history; law; sociology; Asian American studies; African American studies; Latino/a studies, political science; criminology; psychology; gender studies; cultural and literary studies; media, film, and communications; urban studies; Jewish studies; anthropology; religion; environmental studies; New York regional interest.

NYU Press is the exclusive North American distributor for Monthly Review Press.
Special series: Alternative Criminology; America and the Long Nineteenth Century; American History and Culture; Biopolitics; American Literatures Initiative; Children and Youth in America; Citizenship and Migration in the Americas; Clay Sanskrit Library; Critical Cultural Communications; Cultural Front; Culture, Labor, History; Early American Places; Families, Law, and Society; Gender and Political Violence; The History of Disability; Intersections: Transdisciplinary Perspectives on Genders and Sexualities; Library of Arabic Literature; Modern and Contemporary Catholicism; Nation of Newcomers; New and Alternative Religions; New Perspectives on Crime, Deviance, and Law; NOMOS;

North American Religions; NYU Series in Social & Cultural Analysis; Postmillenial Pop; Psychology and Crime; Psychology of Law; Qualitative Studies in Psychology; Religion and Social Transformation; Religion, Race, and Ethnicity; Re-imagining North American Religions; Qualitative Studies in Psychology; Qualitative Studies in Religion; Sexual Cultures; Warfare and Culture

The University of North Carolina Press

116 South Boundary Street
Chapel Hill, NC 27514-3808

Phone: 919.966.3561
Fax: 919.966.3829
Email: uncpress@unc.edu
Indiv: first name_last name@unc.edu

<u>Website and Social Media:</u>
Website: www.uncpress.unc.edu
Blog: uncpressblog.com
Facebook: www.facebook.com/UNCPress
Twitter: uncpressblog

<u>UK/European Representative:</u>
Eurospan

<u>Warehouse:</u>
Maple Press Company
Lebanon Distribution Center
704 Legionnaire Drive
Fredericksburg, PA 17026

<u>Orders:</u>
Longleaf Services
Phone: (800) 848.6224
Fax: (800) 272.6817
Email: customerservice@longleafservices.org

<u>Canadian Representative:</u>
Scholarly Book Services

Staff

Director: John Sherer (919.962.3748)
  Assistant to the Director and Advancement Coordinator: Laura Gribbin (919.962.0358)
  Director of Development: Joanna Ruth Marsland (919.962.0924)
Acquisitions Editorial: Mark Simpson-Vos, Editorial Director (American studies, gender and sexuality, literary studies, Native American and Indigenous studies, Civil War history) (919.962.0535)
  Assistant Editor and Assistant to the Editorial Director: Caitlin Bell-Butterfield (919.962.0538)
  Assistant Director and Senior Editor: Charles Grench (history, craft studies) (919.962.0481)
  Senior Executive Editor: Elaine Maisner (religious studies, Latin American and Caribbean studies, cooking and foodways, regional trade) (919.962.0810)
  Senior Editor: Joe Parsons (sociology, geography, politics, health and health policy, documentary studies, creative nonfiction, business and entrepreneurship) (919.962.0690)
  Editor: Brandon Proia (history, current affairs, African American studies, environmental history, military history, southern studies) (919.962.0482)
  Editorial Assistants: Lucas Church (919.962.0536); Alison Shay (919.962.0390)
Manuscript Editorial: Ron Maner, Assistant Director and Managing Editor (919.962.0540)
  Associate Managing Editor: Paula Wald (919.962.0544)
  Assistant Managing Editor: Paul Betz (919.962.0530)
  Manuscript Editors: Mary Caviness (919.962.0545); Stephanie Wenzel (919.962.0366); Jay Mazzocchi (919.962.0546)

Assistant Editor: Ian Oakes (919.962.0549)

Design and Production: Heidi Perov, Assistant Director and Design and Production Manager (919.962.0572)

Design Director and Assistant Production Manager: Kim Bryant (919.962.0571)

Reprints Controller: Jackie Johnson (919.962.0569)

Senior Compositor & Designer: Rebecca Evans (919.962.0575)

Journals Production Manager & Composition Controller: Michelle Wallen (919.962.0577)

Production Assistant: Sally Scruggs (919.962.0690)

Marketing: Dino Battista, Assistant Director and Senior Director of Marketing and Digital Business Development (919.962.0579)

Sales Director: Michael Donatelli (919.962.0475)

Assistant Sales Manager: Susan Garrett (919.843.7897)

Director of Publicity: Gina Mahalek (919.962.0581)

Senior Publicist: Jennifer Hergenroeder (919.962.0585)

Director of Electronic Marketing: Ellen Bush (919.962.0582)

Direct Mail Manager: Matt Hartman (919.962.0583)

Exhibits Manager and Awards Coordinator: Ivis Bohlen (919.962.0594)

Marketing Designer: Joanne Thomas (919.962.0590)

Journals: Suzi Waters, Journals Manager (919.962.4201)

Business: Robbie Dircks, Associate Director & CFO (919.962.1400)

Office Manager: Laura Gribbin (919.962-0358)

Director of Contracts and Subsidiary Rights: Vicky Wells (919.962.0369)

Rights and Contracts Assistant: Rachel Mazzara (919.962.4200)

Accounting Manager: Jami Clay (919.962.4203)

Accounts Payable Manager and Accounting Assistant: Deborah Strickland (919.962.4204)

Operations Manager for Longleaf Services: BJ Smith (919.962.1230)

Customer Service Manager: Teresa Thomas (919.962.1231)

Credit Manager: Terry Miles (919.962.1263)

Information Systems: Tom Franklin, Information Technology Manager (919.962.4196)

Network Support Specialist: Juancarlos Aponte (919.962.0486)

Network Manager: Jim Dawson (919.962.0331)

Digital Assets Coordinator: Marjorie Fowler (919.962.0471)

Digital Production Specialist: Thomas Elrod (919.843.8644)

Full Member

Established: 1922	Admitted to AAUP: 1937
Title output 2012: 102	Title output 2013: 114
Titles currently in print: 3,100	Journals published: 9

Editorial Program

African American studies; American and European history; American literature; American studies; ancient history and classics; business and entrepreneurship; cooking and foodways; craft and craft history; diplomatic history; geography; Latin American studies; legal history; military history; Native American and Indigenous studies; nature and environmental studies; politics; popular culture; public policy; regional trade and North Caroliniana; religious studies; sexuality and gender studies; social medicine; sociology; Southern studies; Women's studies. Submissions are not invited in fiction, poetry, or drama.

Journals: *Appalachian Heritage*; *The Comparatist*; *Early American Literature*; *The High School Journal*; *Journal of the Civil War Era*; *Southern Cultures*; *Southern Literary Journal*; *Studies in Philology*; *Southeastern Geographer*

Special series: Civil War America; Documentary Arts and Culture; Envisioning Cuba; Gender and American Culture; Islamic Civilization and Muslim Networks; The John Hope Franklin Series in African American History and Culture; Justice, Power, and Politics; Latin America in Translation/en Traducción/em Traducão;The Luther H. Hodges, Jr. and Luther H. Hodges, Sr. Series in Business and Entrepreneurship; The New Cold War History; New Directions in Southern Studies; Richard Hampton Jenrette Series in Architecture and the Decorative Arts; The Steven and Janice Brose Lectures in the Civil War Era; Studies in Social Medicine; Studies in the History of Greece and Rome; Studies in the Romance Languages and Literatures

Joint imprints: Omohundro Institute of Early American History and Culture, sponsored by Colonial Williamsburg and the College of William and Mary

University of North Texas Press

1155 Union Circle #311336
Denton, TX 76203

<u>Orders:</u>
Phone: 800.826.8911

Phone: 940.565.2142
Fax: 940.565.4590
Email: firstname.lastname@unt.edu

<u>UK Representative:</u>
Eurospan

<u>Canadian Representative:</u>
Scholarly Book Services

<u>Website and Social Media:</u>
Website: untpress.unt.edu
Facebook: www.facebook.com/pages/University-of-North-Texas-Press/
   365891204624

Staff
Director: Ronald Chrisman
   Assistant to the Director: Lori Belew
Assistant Director/Managing Editor: Karen DeVinney
Marketing Manager: Paula Oates

Full Member
Established: 1988
Title output 2012: 21
Titles currently in print: 453

Admitted to AAUP: 2003
Title output 2013: 26
Journals published: 2

Editorial Program
Humanities and social sciences, with special emphasis on Texas history and culture, military history, western history, music, criminal justice, folklore, multicultural topics, nature writing, natural and environmental history, culinary history, and women's studies. Submissions in poetry and fiction are invited only through the Vassar Miller and Katherine Anne Porter Prize competition.

Journals: *Theoria*; *Journal of Schenkerian Studies*

Special series: A. C. Greene; Al Filo: Mexican American Studies; Evelyn Oppenheimer;

Frances B. Vick; Great American Cooking; Katherine Anne Porter Prize in Short Fiction; North Texas Crime and Criminal Justice; North Texas Lives of Musicians; North Texas Military Biography and Memoir; Philosophy and the Environment; Practical Guide; Publications of the Texas Folklore Society; Southwestern Nature Writing Series; Temple Big Thicket; Texas Poets; Texas Writers; Vassar Miller Prize in Poetry; War and the Southwest; Western Life

Northern Illinois University Press

2280 Bethany Road
DeKalb, IL 60115

Phone: 815.753.1075
Fax: 815.753.1845
Email: (user I.D.)@niu.edu

Website and Social Media:
Website: www.niupress.niu.edu
www.switchgrass.niu.edu
Facebook: www.facebook.com/NIUPress
www.facebook.com/SwitchgrassBooks
Twitter: NIUPress

UK Distributor:
John Wiley Distribution Center

Orders:
Chicago Distribution Center
11030 S. Langley Ave.
Chicago, IL 60628
Phone: 800.621.2736
Fax: 800.621.8476
Email: orders@press.uchicago.edu

Staff
Director: Linda Manning (815.753.9899; email lmanning2) (U.S. history, regional studies, Southeast Asian studies, and fiction)
Assistant to the Director: Pat Yenerich (815.753.1075; email: pyenerich)
Acquisitions Editor: Amy Farranto (815.753.9946; email: afarranto) (Russian studies, European history, religion, history of religion, and philosophy)
Managing Editor: Susan Bean (815.753.9908; email: sbean)
Production Manager: Shaun Allshouse (815.753.9904; email: sallshou)
    Production Assistant: Yuni Dorr (815.753.9906; email: ydorr)
Marketing/Sales: Eric Miller, Marketing Manager (815.753.9905; email: emiller4)
Business: Cara Carlson, Business Manager (815.753.1826; email: ccarlso2)

Full Member
Established: 1964
Title output 2012: 33
Titles currently in print: 509

Admitted to AAUP: 1972
Title output 2013: 25

Editorial Program
U.S. history; U.S. Civil War; European history; Russian history and culture; history of religion; Southeast Asian studies; urban studies; women's studies; studies on alcohol and

substance abuse, regional studies on Chicago and the Midwest; Midwest literary fiction.
Special series: Drugs and Alcohol: Contested Histories; Orthodox Christian Studies; Railroads in America; Russian Studies
Imprint: Switchgrass Books

Northwestern University Press

629 Noyes Street
Evanston, IL 60208-4210

Phone: 847.491.2046
Fax: 847.491.8150
Email: nupress@northwestern.edu
Indiv: (user I.D.)@northwestern.edu

Orders:
Northwestern University Press
Chicago Distribution Center
11030 South Langley Avenue
Chicago, IL 60628
Phone: 800.621.2736; 773.568.1550
Fax: 800.621.8476; 773.660.2235

Website and Social Media:
Website: www.nupress.northwestern.edu
Facebook: www.facebook.com/pages/Northwestern-University-Press/116644703843
Twitter: NorthwesternUP

UK Distributor:
Eurospan

Canadian Distributor:
Scholarly Book Service

Staff

Director: Jane Bunker (847.491.8111; email: j-bunker)
Assistant Director, Foreign Rights Manager, and Senior Editor: Henry Carrigan
  (847.491.8112; email: h-carrigan)
Acquisitions Editor: Mike Levine (847.491.7384; email: mike-levine)
  Assistant Acquisitions Editor: Gianna Mosser (847.467.1279; email: g-barbera)
Managing Editor and Manager of Design and Production: Anne Gendler (847.491.3844;
  email: a-gendler)
  Special Projects Editor: Nathan MacBrien (847.467.7362; email nathan.macbrien)
Art Director: Marianne Jankowski (847.467.5368; email: ma-jankowski)
Production Manager: A. C. Racette (847.491.8113; email: a-racette)
  Production Coordinator: Morris (Dino) Robinson (847.467.3392; email: morris-robinson)
Sales and Subsidiary Rights Manager: Parneshia Jones (847.491.7420; email: p-jones3)
  Marketing and Publicity Manager: Rudy Faust (847.467.0319; email: r-faust)
  Sales and Marketing Coordinator: Greta Bennion (847.491.5315; email g-bennion)
  Sales Representatives: Blake Delodder (301.322.4509; email: bdelodder@press.uchicago.
  edu); Gary Hart (323.663.3529; email: ghart@press.uchicago.edu); Bailey Walsh
  (608.218.1669; email: bwalsh@press.uchicago.edu); George Carroll (425.922.1045; email:
  george@redsides.com); Don Morrison, Barbara Arendall, Amy Willis (336.775.0226;
  email: msgbooks@aol.com)
Business Manager: Kirstie Felland (847.491.8310; email: kfelland)
  Administrative Assistant: Liz Hamilton (847.491.2458; email: emhamilton)

Full Member

Established: 1959
Title output 2012: 60
Titles currently in print: 1,216

Admitted to AAUP: 1988
Title output 2013: 60
Journals published: 1

Editorial Program

The Press publishes in drama/performance studies; Chicago regional; fiction; German studies; poetry; literary criticism; literature in translation; law; philosophy; Slavic studies; Jewish studies, African American studies.

Distributed presses: Lake Forest College Press; Tia Chucha Press

Imprints: Curbstone; The Marlboro Press; TriQuarterly Books

Journal: *Islamic Africa*

Special series: Comparative and Continental Philosophy; Cultural Expressions of World War II; Flashpoints; IDIOM; Jewish Lives; Medill School of Journalism's Visions of the American Press; Northwestern World Classics; the Northwestern-Newberry Edition of the Writings of Herman Melville; Rereading Ancient Philosophy; Rethinking the Early Modern; Studies in Phenomenology and Existential Philosophy; Studies in Russian Literature and Theory; Topics in Historical Philosophy

University of Notre Dame Press

310 Flanner Hall
Notre Dame, IN 46556

Phone: 574.631.6346
Fax: 574.631.8148
Email: undpress.1@nd.edu
Indiv: (user I.D.)@nd.edu

Orders:
University of Notre Dame Press
Chicago Distribution Center
11030 South Langley Avenue
Chicago, IL 60628
Phone: 800.621.2736
Fax: 800.621.8476

Website and Social Media:
Website: www.undpress.nd.edu
Facebook: www.facebook.com/pages/
    University-of-Notre-Dame-Press/296947140331384
Twitter: UNDPress
YouTube: www.youtube.com/user/UofNotreDamePress?feature=watch

UK/European Representative:
Eurospan

Staff

Interim Managing Director: Harv Humphrey (574.631.3265; email: hjhumphrey.undpress)
Senior Acquisitions Editor: Charles Van Hof (574.631.4912; email: cvanhof)
    Acquisitions Editor: Stephen Little (574.631.4906; email: slittle2)
    Acquisitions Coordinator: Robyn Karkiewicz (574.631.4913; email: karkiewicz.2)
Manuscript Editorial: Rebecca DeBoer, Managing Editor (574.631.4908; email: rdeboer)
    Manuscript Editor: Matthew Dowd (574.631.4914; email: mdowd1)

Assistant Editor: Elizabeth Sain (574.631.4911; email: sain.6)
Design and Production: Wendy McMillen, Manager (574.631.4907; email: mcmillen.3)
 Assistant Production Manager: Jennifer Bernal (574.631.3266; email: bernal.7)
Marketing: Kathryn Pitts, Manager (574.631.3267; email: pitts.5)
 Electronic Marketing Manager: Emily McKnight (574.631.4909; email: mcknight.3)
 Assistant Manager: Ann Bromley (574.631.4910; email: bromley.1)
 Exhibits Coordinator: Susan Berger (574.631.4905; email: susan.m.berger)
Business: Diane Schaut, Manager (574.631.4904; email: schaut.1)
 Coordinator of Office Services: Gina Bixler (574.631.6346; email: bixler.1)
IT: Stephen Little, IT Consultant (574.631.4906; email: slittle2)

Full Member

Established: 1949	Admitted to AAUP: 1959
Title output 2012: 51	Title output 2013: 45
Titles currently in print: 1,000	

Editorial Program

Religion; theology; philosophy; ethics; political science; medieval and early modern studies; classics; Catholic studies; business ethics; American history; European history; European Studies, Latin American studies; religion and literature; Irish studies; history and philosophy of science; international relations; literary criticism; peace studies; patristics; political science, political theory. Submissions are not invited in the hard sciences, mathematics, psychology, or novel-length fiction.

Special series, joint imprints, and/or copublishing programs: Andrés Montoya Poetry Prize; The African American Intellectual Heritage; Catholic Social Tradition; Christianity and Judaism in Antiquity; The Collected Works of Jacques Maritain; Contemporary European Politics and Society; The Conway Lectures in Medieval Studies; Ernest Sandeen Prize in Poetry; From the Helen Kellogg Institute for International Studies; From the Joan B. Kroc Institute for International Peace Studies / Kroc Institute Series on Religion, Conflict, and Peacebuilding; John W. Houck Notre Dame Series in Business Ethics; Latino Perspectives; Liturgical Studies; Michael Psellos in Translation; Notre Dame Conferences in Medieval Studies; Notre Dame Review Book Prize; Notre Dame Studies in Ethics and Culture; Notre Dame Studies in Medical Ethics; Notre Dame Texts in Medieval Culture; Poetics of Orality and Literacy; Reading the Scriptures; ReFormations: Medieval and Early Modern; The Review of Politics Series; Richard Sullivan Prize in Short Fiction; Studies in Judaism and Christianity; Studies in Science and the Humanities from the Reilly Center for Science, Technology, and Values; Thresholds in Philosophy and Theology; The Ward-Phillips Lectures in English Language and Literature; The William and Katherine Devers Series in Dante and Medieval Italian Literature; The Works of Cardinal Newman: Birmingham Oratory Millennium Edition

Ohio University Press

215 Columbus Road, Suite 101
Athens, OH 45701-2979

Phone: 740.593.1154
Fax: 740.593.4536
Email: (user I.D.)@ohio.edu

Orders:
Ohio University Press
Chicago Distribution Center
11030 South Langley Avenue
Chicago, IL 60628
Phone: 800.621.2736
Fax: 800.621.8476

<u>Website and Social Media:</u>
Website: www.ohioswallow.com
Facebook: www.facebook.com/pages/Ohio-University-Press-Swallow-Press/317964522187

<u>UK/European Representative:</u>
Combined Academic Publishers

Staff

Director: Gillian Berchowitz (740.593.1159; email: berchowi)
Acquisitions Editor: Rick S. Huard (740.593.1157; email: huard)
Managing Editor: Nancy Basmajian (740.593.1161; email: basmajia)
Production Manager: Beth Pratt (740.593.1162; email: prattb)
  Marketing Designer: Sebastian Biot (740.597.2998; email: biot)
Marketing and Sales: Sarah Welsch, Sales and Marketing Director (740.593.1160;
  email: welsch)
  Publicity Manager: Jeff Kallet (740.593.1158; email: kallet)
Business Manager: Kristi Goldsberry (740.593.1156; email: goldsbek)
  Customer Service and Permissions Specialist: Rebecca Welch (740.593.1154;
  email: welchs)

Full Member

Established: 1964
Title output 2012: 43
Titles currently in print: 1,042

Admitted to AAUP: 1966
Title output 2013: 45

Editorial Program

Imprints: Swallow Press
Special series, joint imprints, and/or copublishing programs: Africa in World History;
Cambridge Centre of African Studies Series; The Civil War in the Great Interior; The
Collected Letters of George Gissing; The Collected Works of William Howard Taft; The
Complete Works of Robert Browning; Eastern African Studies; Hollis Summers Poetry Prize;
Indian Ocean Studies Series; Law, Society, and Politics in the Midwest; Modern African
Writing; New African Histories; Ohio Bicentennial; Ohio Quilt Series; Ohio Short Histories
of Africa; The Papers of Clarence Mitchell, Jr.; Perspectives on the History of Congress and
Perspectives on the Art and Architecture of the United States Capitol (for the US Capitol
Historical Society); Perspectives on Global Health; Polish and Polish-American Studies
Series; Research in International Studies: Southeast Asia, Africa, Latin America, and Global
and Comparative Studies Series; Series in Race, Ethnicity and Gender in Appalachia; Series
in Continental Thought; Series in Ecology and History; War and Society in the North
America; Western African Studies; White Coat Pocket Guide

University of Oklahoma Press

2800 Venture Drive
Norman, OK 73069

Phone: 405.325.2000
Faxes: 405.325.4000 (director/rights/acquisitions/marketing);
405.307.9048 (manuscript editing/production/finance)
Email: (user I.D.)@ou.edu

Orders:
Phone: 800.627.7377
Fax: 405.364.5798; 800.735.0476

Website and Social Media:
Website: www.oupress.com
Blog: www.oupressblog.com
Facebook: www.facebook.com/oupress
Twitter: OUPress

UK Representative:
Bay Foreign Language Books

Canadian Representative:
Hargreaves, Fuller & Co.

Staff

Director: B. Byron Price (405.325.5666; email: b_byron_price)
Editorial: Charles E. Rankin, Associate Director and Editor-in-Chief; Publisher, Arthur H.
   Clark imprint (405.325.2873; email: cerankin)
Acquisitions Editors: Jay Dew (contemporary American West, Texas history, political
   science, regional studies, natural history) (405.325.7991; email: jaydew); Alessandra
   Jacobi Tamulevich (native studies: North, Central, and South America, classical studies)
   (817.538.9802; email: jacobi); Kathleen Kelly (women's history, literature)(405.325.1216;
   email: kathleenkelly); Charles E. (Chuck) Rankin (American West, military history,
   Mormon studies, Borderlands) (405.325.2873; email: cerankin)
Manuscript Editing: Steven Baker, Managing Editor (405.325.1325; email: steven.b.baker)
Production: Emmy Ezzell, Assistant Director/Production Manager (405.325.3186; email:
   eezzell)
   Production Editor: Susan Garrett (405.325.2408; email: sgarrett)
Marketing and Sales: Dale Bennie, Associate Director/Sales and Marketing Manager
   (405.325.3207; email: dbennie)
   Electronic Publishing Manager: Brent Greyson (405.325.3202; email: bgreyson)
   Publicity Manager: Sandy See (405.325.3200; email: ssee)
   Designer: Tony Roberts (405.325.4283; email: tonyroberts)
Business: Diane Cotts, Assistant Director/Chief Financial Officer (405.325.3276;
   email: dcotts)
   Customer Service: Kathy Benson (405.325.2287; email: presscs)
   Operations & Accounts Receivable: Diane Cannon (405.325.2326; email: pressdist)

Full Member

Established: 1928
Title output 2012: 77
Titles currently in print: 1,664

Admitted to AAUP: 1937
Title output 2013: 66

Editorial Program

Scholarly books, general nonfiction, and some fiction with special interests in the American West, Military History, Classical Studies, Native Studies (North, Central, and South America), Natural History, Political Science, and Regional Studies.

Special series: After Gold (A.H. Clark); American Exploration and Travel; American Indian Law and Policy; American Indian Literature and Critical Studies; Animal Natural History; Campaigns and Commanders; Charles M. Russell Center Series on Art and Photography of the American West; Chicana & Chicano Visions of the Américas; Chinese Literature Today; The Civilization of the American Indian; Congressional Studies; Early California Commentaries (A.H. Clark); Gilcrease-Oklahoma Series on Western Art and Artists; International and Security Affairs; Julian J. Rothbaum Distinguished Lecture Series; Kingdom in the West - The Mormons and the American Frontier (A. H. Clark); Latin American and Caribbean Arts and Culture - Mellon Initiative; Motoring West (A. H. Clark); New Directions in Native American Studies; Oklahoma Series in Classical Culture; The Oklahoma Western Biographies; Race and Culture in the American West; Recovering Languages and Literacies In the Americas - Mellon Initiative; Sam Noble Oklahoma Museum of Natural History Publications; Variorum Chaucer; Western Frontier Library; The Western Legacies

Oregon State University Press

121 The Valley Library
Corvallis, OR 97331-4501

Phone: 541.737.3166
Fax: 541.737.3170
Email: osu.press@oregonstate.edu
Indiv: (user I.D.)@oregonstate.edu

Order Fulfillment & Distribution:
Chicago Distribution Center
11030 S. Langley Ave.
Chicago, IL 60628
Phone: 800.621.2736
Fax: 800.621.8476

Website and Social Media:
Website: osupress.oregonstate.edu
Facebook: www.facebook.com/OregonStateUniversityPress
Twitter: osupress

Canadian Distributor:
University of British Columbia Press

Staff

Director: Faye A. Chadwell (541.737.8528; email: faye.chadwell)
Associate Director: Tom Booth (503.796.0547; fax 503.796.0549; email: thomas.booth)
Acquisitions Editor: Mary Elizabeth Braun (541.737.3873; email: mary.braun)
Managing Editor & Production Manager: Jo Alexander (541.737.3864; email: jo.alexander)
Marketing Manager: Micki Reaman (541.737.4620; email: micki.reaman)
Editorial & Production Assistant: Judy Radovsky (541.737.3302; email: judy.radovsky)

Full Member

Established: 1961

Title output 2012: 18

Titles currently in print: 258

Admitted to AAUP: 1991

Title output 2013: 18

Editorial Program

The Oregon State University Press publishes scholarly and general interest books in the environmental humanities; forestry; natural resource management; environmental and natural history; Native American and Indigenous studies; and the history, culture, and arts of the Pacific Northwest.

University of Ottawa Press | Les Presses de l'Université d'Ottawa

542 King Edward Avenue
Ottawa, ON K1N 6N5 Canada

Phone: 613.562.5246
Fax: 613.562.5247
Email: puo-uop@uottawa.ca

Website and Social Media:
Website: www.press.uottawa.ca
Facebook: www.facebook.com/uOttawaPress
Twitter: www.twitter.com/uOttawaPress

Canadian Orders (English titles):
University of Toronto Press
Phone: 800.565.9523; 416.667.7791
Fax: 800.221.9985; 416.667.7832
Email: utpbooks@utpress.utoronto.ca

Canadian Orders (French titles):
Prologue Inc.
1650 Lionel-Bertrand Boulevard
Boisbriand, Quebec J7H 1N7 Canada
Phone: 800.363.2864; 450.434.0306
Fax: 800.361.8088; 450.434.4135
Email: prologue@prologue.ca

US Orders (English titles):
University of Toronto Press
Phone: 800.565.9523
Fax: 800.221.9985
Email: utpbooks@utpress.utoronto.ca

US Orders (French titles):
Exportlivre

France, Belgium, Luxembourg (French titles):
Distribution du Nouveau Monde

UK and European Orders (English titles):
Marston Book Services

Switzerland (French titles):
Servidis SA

Staff

Director: Lara Mainville (613.562.5663; email: lara.mainville@uottawa.ca)

Acquisitions Editor: Dominike Thomas (613.562.5800 ext.3065;
    email: dthomas@uottawa.ca)

Production Manager: Suzanne Cloutier (613.562.5800 ext. 2853;
    email: scloutier@uottawa.ca)

Digital Content Manager: Lisa Marie Smith (613.562.5800 ext. 2854;
    email: lisa.smith@uottawa.ca)

Full Member

Established: 1936

Title output 2012: 21

Titles currently in print: 455

Admitted to AAUP: 2005

Title output 2013: 23

Journals published: 3

Editorial Program

Translation; Canadian Literature; Education; French America; International Development and Globalization; Philosophy; Law; Canadian Archeology and Ethnography; Health and Society; Translation Studies

Journals: *Cahiers Charlevoix; Francophonies d'Amérique; Journal of Prisoners on Prisons*

Special series: Amérique française; Archives des lettres canadiennes; Canadian Literature Collection; Critical Issues in Risk Management; Cultural Transfers; Governance; Health and Society; Law, Technology and Society; Literary Translation; Mercury Series; Perspectives on Translation; Philosophica; Reappraisals: Canadian Writers; Studies in International Development and Globalization; Visual Arts

Imprints: Harvest House

Oxford University Press, Inc.

Editorial Offices:

198 Madison Avenue

New York, NY 10016

Phone: 212.726.6000

Fax: 212.726.6440

Email: firstname.lastname@oup.com

Website and Social Media:

Website: www.oup.com

Blog: blog.oup.com

Customer Service:

Orders/Prices: 800.451.7556

Inquiries: 800.445-9714

ELT: 800.441-5445

Journals: 800.852.7323

Music Retail: 800.292.0639

Fax: 919.677.1303

Distribution Center &

Journals Marketing Office:

2001 Evans Road

Cary, NC 27513

Phone: 919.677.0977

Dist. Fax: 919.677.8877

Journals Fax: 919.677.1714

Oxford University Press (UK):

Great Clarendon Street

Oxford OX2 6DP

United Kingdom

Phone: +44 1865 556767

Fax: +44 1865 556646

American English Language Teaching

(AMELT):

Phone: 212.726.6300

Fax: 212.726.6388

Staff

President: Niko Pfund

  Assistant to the President: Henry Singleton

  Senior Vice President Administration and CFO, Finance Distribution, Accounting: Kevin Allison

  Vice President, Legal, and General Counsel: Barbara Cohen

  Vice President and Publisher, Higher Education Group: John Challice

  Publisher, Reference and Online: Damon Zucca

  Publisher, Trade, Academic and Journals: Niko Pfund

  Vice President, Global Business Development and Rights, Academic & US Divisions: Casper Grathwohl

  Vice President, Global Marketing and US Sales: Colleen Scollans

  Vice President, Human Resources: Marilyn Okrent

  Vice President, Operations: Tom Shannon

  Vice President and Director, Content Operations: Catherine Pearce

  AMELT General Manager: Laura Pearson

<u>Trade and Academic</u>

Publisher: Niko Pfund

  Editorial: Scott Parris (economics and finance); Tim Bent (trade, history and politics); James Cook (sociology, criminology); Susan Ferber (history); Nancy Toff (history); Jeremy Lewis (chemistry); Brendan O'Neill (literature and film); Peter Ohlin (philosophy and linguistics; Cynthia Read (religion); Theo Calderara (religion); Suzanne Ryan (music); Norm Hirschy (music), Todd Waldman (music); Stefan Vranka (classics and ancient history); David McBride (politics, law); Angela Chnapko (politics); Donald Kraus (Bibles); Phyllis Cohen (math, physics)

<u>Law</u>

Publisher: John Louth

  Editorial: Andy Redman

<u>Medical</u>

Editorial Director, GAB: Catherine Barnes

  VP/Editorial Director: Joan Bossert (neuropsychology, cognitive psychology)

  Associate Editorial Director: Craig Panner (neurology, clinical neuroscience)

  Senior Editors: Dana Bliss (social work); Andrea Seils (Oxford American handbooks, pain medicine, anesthesia, critical care, palliative care & oncology, radiology); Sarah Harrington (clinical psychology, developmental psychology, forensic psychology)

  Editors: Abby Gross (social psychology, positive psychology, industrial & organizational psychology, educational psychology); Chad Zimmerman (public health/epidemiology, clinical genetics); Chris Reid (medicine journals, psychiatry)

  Associate Editor: David D'Addona (psychiatry); Agnes Bannigan (social work)

  Digital Develppment Editor/Medical Editorial: Nicholas Liu

<u>Reference and Online</u>

Publisher: Damon Zucca

  Reference Editorial: Alixandra Gould (Content Development); Tanya Laplante (Director of Digital Development); Anna-Lise Santella (Oxford/Grove Music); Alodie Larson (Oxford/Grove Art); Robert Repino (African American Studies); David Pervin (Economics, Business, Political Science); Julia Kostova (Humanities, Religion); Ada Brunstein (Psychology, Neuroscience); Adina Berk (History, Classics); Max Sinsheimer (Trade Reference); Katherine Martin (US Dictionaries)

Higher Education
Publisher: John Challice
  Editorial: Patrick Lynch (editorial director); Robert Miller (philosophy & religion); Carrie
  Brandon (English & Linguistics); Fred Speers (English & linguistics); Richard Carlin
  (art & music); Jennifer Carpenter (politics); Sherith Pankratz (sociology, anthropology,
  & archaeology); Sarah Calabi (criminology & criminal justice); Jane Potter (psychology);
  Jason Noe (life sciences & chemistry); Nancy Blaine (engineering & computer science);
  Valerie Ashton (economics, finance, & business); Dan Kaveney (earth and environmental
  sciences); Mark Haynes (communication & journalism); Brian Wheel (history of the
  Americas); Charles Cavaliere (world history and classics)
  Marketing: Frank Mortimer
  Sales: Bill Marting
Content Operations
Head of Content Operations: Deborah Shor
  Production Managers: Kate Hind, Diem Bloom, David Ford
  Demand Planning Manager: Nancy Wu
  Creative Director: Linda Secondari
Business Development and Rights
Vice President, Global Business Development and Rights: Casper Grathwohl
  Director, Global Business Development and Rights: Nancy Roberson
  Business Development Manager, Americas: Jessica Dosch
  Business Development Manager, GAB: Zach Haynes
  Business Development Coordinator: Charles Devilbiss
  Assistant to Vice President: Ime Oweka
Sales and Marketing
Global Chief Marketing Officer: Colleen Scollans
  US Marketing Director and Retail Sales: Kim Craven
  Global Marketing Director: Colleen Scollans
  Publicity Director: C. Purdy
  Director of Library Sales: Rebecca Seger
  Director of Direct and Content Marketing: Rose Pintaudi-Jones
  Director of Distribution Client Management: Kurt Hettler
  International Sales: Nick Parker
  Manager of E-Book Sales: Margaret Harrison
Operations
Operations: Tom Shannon
  Human Resources: Marilyn Okrent
  Office Services: Terese Dickerson
Finance
Senior Vice President and Chief Financial Officer: Kevin Allison
American English Language Teaching (AMELT) Group
General Manager: Laura Pearson
  US Publisher: Stephanie Karras
  US Sales Director: Myndee Males
  US Marketing Director: Karen Horton

ADP Director: Susan Sanguily
Executive Publishing Manager, AMELT International Adult: Erik Gundersen
Executive Publishing Manager, AMELT International Primary: Shelagh Speers
Journals (North Carolina)
US Editor-in-Chief: Alison Denby
  US Customer Services Manager: Carolyn Wilson
  Senior Marketing Manager: Tricia Hudson
  US Production Director: Cindy Brown
  US Director, Corporate Sales: Amy Luchsinger
Distribution Center (North Carolina)
  Inventory Planning/Control: Kenneth Guerin
  Credit and Collection: Dottie Warlick
  Customer Service: Cheryl Ammons-Longtin
  Warehouse Operations: Todd Hayes
  Accounting Services: Dottie Warlick
  Cary Facilities: Chris Vidourek
Technology
  Director of Business Technology: Erik Diaz

Full Member

Established: 1895	Admitted to AAUP: 1950
Title output 2012: 1,400	Title output 2013: 1,550
Titles currently in print: 21,000	Journals published (US only): 64

Editorial Program

Scholarly monographs; general nonfiction; Bibles; college textbooks; medical books; music; reference books; journals; children's books; English language teaching. Submissions are not invited in the area of fiction.

Journals published in the US: *Applied Economic Perspectives and Policy; American Historical Review; American Journal of Agricultural Economics; American Journal of Epidemiology; American Journal of Hypertension; American Literary History; Archives of Clinical Neuropsychology; BioScience; Cerebral Cortex; Christian Bioethics; Clinical Infectious Diseases; Children and Schools; Diplomatic History; Early Music; Enterprise and Society; Environmental History; Epidemiologic Reviews; The Gerontologist; Health Education Research; Health Promotion International; Health and Social Work; Holocaust and Genocide Studies; The ILAR Journal; ISLE: Interdisciplinary Studies in Literature and Environment; Journal of American History; Journal of Analytical Toxicology; Journal of Chromatographic Science; Journal of Church and State; Journal of Deaf Studies and Deaf Education; Journals of Gerontology Series A: Biomedical Sciences and Medical Sciences; Journals of Gerontology Series B: Psychological Sciences and Social Sciences; The Journal of Hindu Studies; The Journal of Infectious Diseases; Journal of Islamic Studies; Journal of Medicine and Philosophy; Journal of Public Administration Research And Theory; Journal of Pediatric Psychology; Journal of Social History; Journal of Survey Statistics and Methodology; Journal of the American Academy of Religion; Journal of the History of Medicine and Allied Sciences; Journal of the National Cancer Institute; Journal of the National Cancer Institute Monographs; Journal of the Pediatric Infectious Diseases Society; Journal of Theological Studies; Literary Imagination; Multi-Ethnic Literature of the United States; Medical Mycology; Modern Judaism: A Journal of Jewish Ideas and Experience; Music and Letters; Music Theory Spectrum; The Musical Quarterly; Nicotine & Tobacco Research; OAH Magazine of History;*

Open Forum Infectious Diseases; The Opera Quarterly; The Oral History Review; Political Analysis; Public Policy & Aging Report; Publius; Public Opinion Quarterly; The Quarterly Journal of Economics; Review of Asset Pricing Studies; Review of Environmental Economics and Policy; Review of Corporate Finance Studies; The Review of Financial Studies; Schizophrenia Bulletin; Social Forces; Sociology of Religion: A Quarterly Review; Social Work; Social Work Research; Toxicological Sciences; The World Bank Economic Review; The World Bank Research Observer

University of Pennsylvania Press

3905 Spruce Street
Philadelphia, PA 19104-4112

Phone: 215.898.6261
Fax: 215.898.0404
Email: (user I.D.)@upenn.edu

Website and Social Media:
Website: www.pennpress.org
Blog: pennpress.typepad.com
Facebook: www.facebook.com/PennPress
Twitter: PennPress

Order Department:
PO Box 50370
Baltimore, MD 21211-4370
Phone: 800.537.5487
Fax: 410.516.6998
Email (inquiries only):
custserv@pobox.upenn.edu

Warehouse & Returns:
Maple Press Company
Lebanon Distribution Center
704 Legionaire Drive
Fredericksburg, PA 17026

UK/European Distributor:
Marston Book Services

Canadian Representative:
Scholarly Book Services

Staff

Director: Eric Halpern (215.898.1672; email: ehalpern)
  Assistant to the Director and Rights Administrator: Jaime Estrada (215.898.6263; email: estradaj)
Acquisitions: Peter Agree, Editor-in-Chief (human rights, policy and politics, anthropology) (215.573.3816; email: agree)
  Senior Editors: Jerome E. Singerman (literary criticism and cultural studies; ancient, medieval, and Renaissance studies; landscape architecture; Jewish studies) (215.898.1681; email: singerma); Robert Lockhart (American history, regional books) (215.898.1677; email: rlockhar)
  Acquiring Editor: Bill Finan (peace and conflict studies, international relations) (215.573.7129; email: wfinan)
  Consulting Editors: Deborah Blake (ancient studies) (44-7867-540881; email: dcblake.pennpress@virginmedia.com); Damon Linker (current affairs, digital shorts) (610.613.4546; email: linkerpennpress@gmail.com)
  Assistant Editor: Caroline Hayes (215.898.3252; email: hayesca)

Acquisitions Assistant: Rachel Taube (215.898.6262; email: rtaube)
Manuscript Editing and Production: Elizabeth Glover, Editing & Production Manager (215.898.1675; email: gloverel)
  Assistant Production Manager: William Boehm (215.573.4059; email: boehmwj)
  Managing Editor: Alison Anderson (215.898.1678; email: anderaa)
  Associate Managing Editor: Erica Ginsburg (215.898.1679; email: eginsbur)
  Production Editor: Noreen O'Connor (215.898.1709; email: nmoconno)
  Production Coordinator: Susan Staggs (215.898.1676; email: sstaggs)
  Art Director: John Hubbard (215.573.6118; email: wmj)
Marketing: Laura Waldron, Marketing Director (215.898.1673; email: lwaldron)
  Publicity & Public Relations Manager: Gigi Lamm (215.898.1674; email: glamm)
  Electronic Promotion Coordinator: Stephanie Brown (215.898.8678; email: browns2)
  Direct Mail & Advertising Manager: Sara Davis (215.898.9184; email: saradav)
Journals: Paul Chase (circulation) (215.573.1295; email: paulbc); Dave Lievens (editing and production) (215.898.7588; email: lievens)
Business: Joseph Guttman, Business Manager (215.898.1670; email: josephgg)
  Financial Coordinator: Kathy Ranalli (215.898.1682; email: ranalli)
  Customer Service Representative: Marlene DeBella (215.898.1671; email: custserv@pobox.upenn.edu)

Full Member

Established: 1890	Admitted to AAUP: 1967
Title output 2012: 145	Title output 2013: 161
Titles currently in print: 1,725	Journals published: 13

Editorial Program

Scholarly and semipopular nonfiction, with special interests in American history and culture; ancient, medieval, and Renaissance studies; human rights; urban studies, political science; Jewish studies; anthropology; landscape architecture; corporate governance and business ethics; economics of poverty; and Pennsylvania regional studies.

Journals: *Change Over Time; Dissent; Early American Studies; The Eighteenth-Century: Theory and Interpretation; Hispanic Review; Humanity; Jewish Quarterly Review; Journal for Early Modern Cultural Studies; J19: The Journal of Nineteenth-Century Americanists; Magic, Ritual, and Witchcraft; Journal of the Early Republic; Journal of the History of Ideas; Revista Hispanica Moderna*

Special series: American Business, Politics, and Society; American Governance; Arts and Intellectual Life in Modern America; Contemporary Ethnography; City in the 21st Century; Democracy, Citizenship, and Constitutionalism; Divinations; Early American Studies; Early Modern Americas; Empire and After; Encounters with Asia; Ethnography of Political Violence; Jewish Culture and Contexts; Material Texts; Metropolitan Portraits; The Middle Ages; National and Ethnic Conflict in the 21st Century; Penn Studies in Landscape Architecture; Pennsylvania Studies in Human Rights; Personal Takes; Politics and Culture in Modern America

Copublishing programs: Ceramics Handbooks, International Food Policy Research Institute

Imprint: Pine Street Books, University of Pennsylvania Museum of Archaeology and Anthropology

Pennsylvania State University Press

820 North University Drive
USB-1, Suite C
University Park, PA 16802-1003

Orders:
Phone: 800.326.9180
Fax: 877.778.2665

Phone: 814.865.1327
Fax: 814.863.1408
Email: (user I.D.)@psu.edu

Website and Social Media:
Website: www.psupress.org
Twitter: PSUPress
Facebook: www.facebook.com/psupress

UK Representative:
NBN International (effective March 2014)

Canadian Distributor:
University of Toronto Press

Staff

Director: Patrick H. Alexander (814.867.2209; email: pha3)
  Assistant to the Director: Teresa Craig (814.865.1327; email: tac6)
Rights and Permissions Manager: Sheila S. Sager (814.867.2831; email: sss2)
Acquisitions Editorial: Kendra Boileau, Editor-in-Chief (814.867.2220; email: klb60)
  Executive Editor, Art History and Humanities: Eleanor Goodman (814.867.2212;
  email: ehg11)
  Acquisitions Editor: Kathryn Yahner (814.865.1327; email: kby3)
  Editorial Assistants: Charlee Redman (814.865.1592; email: cmr5291); Robert Turchick
  (814.865.1328; email: rst5043)
Managing Editor: Laura Reed-Morrisson (814.865.1606; email: lxr168)
  Manuscript Editors: John Morris (email: jpm42); Julie Schoelles (814.867.2214; email:
  jls1001)
Design and Production: Jennifer Norton, Associate Director/Design and Production
  Manager (814.863.8061; email: jsn4)
  Chief Designer: Steven Kress (814.867.2215; email: srk5)
  Book Production Coordinator: Patty Mitchell (814.867.2216; email: pam18)
  Production Assistant: Jon Gottshall (814.867.2213; email: jeg31)
Marketing/Sales: Tony Sanfilippo, Assistant Director/Marketing and Sales Director
  (814.863.5994; email: ajs23)
  Advertising Manager: Brian Beer (814.867.2210; email: bxb110)
  Publicity Manager: Daniel Bellet (814.865.1329; email: djb49)
  Sales Manager: Kathleen Scholz-Jaffe (814.867.2224; email: kxs56)
Journals Manager: Diana Pesek (814.867.2223; email: dlp28)
  Production Coordinator: Julie Lambert (814.863.5992; email: jas1035)
  Marketing Manager: Heather Smith (814.863.0524; email: hms7)
  Managing Editor: Astrid Meyer (814.863.3830; email: aum38)
  Production Assistant: Jessica Karp (email: jxk82)
Business Manager: Tina Laychur (814.863.5993; email: txs17)
  Assistant Business Manager: Kathy Vaughn (814.863.6771; email: kmv1)

Shipping Clerk: Dave Buchan (814.863.5496; email: dcb11)
Fulfillment Support Associate: Curtiss Smith (814.865.6056; email: ces36)
Information Systems Manager: Ed Spicer (814.867.2219; email: res122)
IT Support Specialist: Denis Tremblay (email: dyt3)

Full Member

Established: 1956   Admitted to AAUP: 1960
Title output 2012: 142   Title output 2013: 121
Titles currently in print: 1,340   Journals published: 29

<u>**Editorial Program**</u>
Scholarly books in the humanities and social sciences, with current emphasis on animal studies; architecture; art history; American, European, and Latin American history; communication studies and rhetoric; medieval studies; philosophy; religion. Submissions are not invited in fiction, poetry, or drama.

Journals: *Chaucer Review; Comparative Literature Studies; Critical Philosophy of Race; The Edgar Allan Poe Review; Eugene O'Neill Review; The F. Scott Fitzgerald Review; The Good Society; Interdisciplinary Literature Studies; Journal of Africana Religions; Journal of Assessment and Institutional Effectiveness; Journal of Ayn Rand Studies; Journal of Eastern Mediterranean Archaeology and Heritage Studies; Journal of General Education; Journal of Medieval Religious Cultures; Journal of Modern Periodical Studies; Journal of Moravian History Journal of Nietzsche Studies; Journal of Speculative Philosophy; The Mark Twain Annual; Mediterranean Studies; Pacific Coast Philology; Pennsylvania History; Philosophy and Rhetoric; Preternature; Soundings; Reception; SHAW: The Annual of Bernard Shaw Studies; Soundings; Steinbeck Review; Studies in American Jewish Literature; Transportation Journal; Utopian Studies*

Special series: Animalibus: Of Animals and Cultures; Buildings, Landscapes, and Societies; Edinburgh Edition of Thomas Reid; Graphic Medicine; Interdisciplinary Perspectives on Jewish Experience and Culture Latin American Originals; Magic in History; Max Kade Institute German-American Research Series; Penn State Series in the History of the Book; Pietist, Moravian, and Anabaptist Studies; Refiguring Modernism; Religion Around; Re-Reading the Canon; Rhetoric and Democratic Deliberation; Rome Perspectives; The Stone Art Theory Institutes; Signifying on Scriptures

Special imprints: Keystone Books®

PISA University Press

Lungarno Pacinotti, 43/44
56126 Pisa Italy

Phone: +39 050 2212056
Fax: + 39 050 2212945
Email: press@unipi.it

Website and Social Media:
Website: www.pisauniversitypress.It

Orders:
Phone: +39 050 2212055
Fax: +39 050 2212945

UK/North American Representatives:
Libro Co. Italia
Herder Editrice e Libreria, Casalini Libri

Board of Directors
President Scientific Committee: Ada Carlesi
Chief Executive: Riccardo Grasso

Staff
Marketing Manager and Acquisitions Editorial: Claudia Napolitano (+39 050 2212053;
  email: napolitano.press@unipi.it, press@unipi.it)
Central Administration/Order Processing: Ambra Seymons (+39 050 2212055;
  email: seymons.press@unipi.it, press@unipi.It)

International Member
Established: 2000
Title output 2012: 43
Titles currently in print: 820

Admitted to AAUP: 2005
Title output 2013: 80
Journals published: 9

Editorial Program
Pisa University Press supports the academic mission of Pisa University by publishing scholarly books and journals for a diverse, worldwide readership. These publications, written by authors representing a broad range of intellectual perspectives, reflect the academic and institutional strengths of the university. Pisa University Press publishes handbooks and peer-reviewed works of academic distinction, of very good editorial and production quality, in many subjects. These publications primarily service the scholarly community, and many also reach the general reading public.

Journals: *Agogè*; *Agrochimica*; *Archives Italiennes de Biologie*; *Cultura e Diritti*; *Egitto e Vicino Oriente*; *Frustula Entomologica*; *Polittico*; *Studi Classici e orientali*; *Rivista d Igiene*

Special series: Conversations at the "Sapienza"; Eco-history Notebooks; History and Sociology of Modernity; Greek, Arabic, Latin: Roads to Knowledge; Methexis Project; Peace Studies; Pisan Linguistics Studies; Russian Literature; Studies and Sources for the History of Sculpture; Teaching in a University Context

University of Pittsburgh Press

7500 Thomas Boulevard
Pittsburgh, PA 15260
info@upress.pitt.edu
Phone: 412.383.2456
Fax: 412.383.2466
Email: (user I.D.)@upress.pitt.edu

Order Fulfillment:
University of Pittsburgh Press
Chicago Distribution Center
11030 South Langley Avenue
Chicago, IL 60628
Phone: 773.568.1550; 800.621.2736
Fax: 773.660.2235

Website and Social Media:
Website: www.upress.pitt.edu
Facebook: www.facebook.com/pages/Pitt-Poetry-Series/123300654375394?
Twitter: UPittPress

UK Representative:
Eurospan

Canadian Representative:
Scholarly Book Services

Staff

Director: Peter Kracht (email:pkracht)
  Assistant to the Director: Kelley H. Johovic (email: kjohovic)
  Business Manager: Cindy Wessels (email: cwessels)
Editorial Director: Sandy Crooms (412.383.2582; email: scrooms)
Senior Acquisitions Editor: Joshua Shanholtzer (email: jshanholtzer)
  Acquisitions Editor: Abby Collier (email: acollier)
  Editorial Assistant: Amberle Sherman (email: editorial.assistant)
Production Director: TBA
  Managing Editor: Alex Wolfe (email: awolfe)
  Production Designer/Editor: Joel Coggins (email: jcoggins)
Marketing Director: Lowell Britson (email: lbritson)
  Direct Mail/Advertising Manager: David Baumann (email: dbaumann)
  Publicist: Maria Sticco (email: msticco)
  Subsidiary Rights Manager: Margie Bachman (email: mbachman)

Full Member

Established: 1936
Title output 2012: 50
Titles currently in print: 1,081

Admitted to AAUP: 1937
Title output 2013: 49

Editorial Program

History; Russian and East European studies; Central Eurasian studies; Latin American studies; composition and literacy studies; poetry; history and philosophy of science; history of architecture; urban studies; environmental history; Pittsburgh and western Pennsylvania. The Press does not invite submissions in the hard sciences, original fiction (except DHLP), festschriften, memoirs, symposia, or unrevised doctoral dissertations.

    The Press distributes and copublishes selected titles with the Carnegie Museum of Art, the Carnegie Museum of Natural History, the Frick Art and Historical Center, the Historical Society of Western Pennsylvania, the Mattress Factory, and the Westmoreland Museum of American Art.

Special series: Agnes Lynch Starrett Poetry Prize; Ayn Rand Society Philosophical Studies;

Central Eurasia In Context; Cuban Studies; Culture, Politics, and the Built Environment; Drue Heinz Literature Prize; History of the Urban Environment; Illuminations: Cultural Formations of the Americas; Pitt Latin American Series; Pitt Poetry Series; Pitt Series in Russian and East European Studies; Pittsburgh Series in Composition, Literacy, and Culture; Pittsburgh/Konstanz Series in Philosophy and History of Science

Princeton University Press

Executive Offices:
41 William Street
Princeton, NJ 08540-5237

Phone: 609.258.4900
Fax: 609.258.6305
Email:
firstname_lastname@press.princeton.edu

Website and Social Media:
Website: press.princeton.edu
Blog: press.princeton.edu/blog
Facebook: www.facebook.com/PrincetonUniversityPress
Twitter: PrincetonUPress

European Editorial Office:
6 Oxford St.
Woodstock, Oxfordshire OX20 1TW
United Kingdom
Phone: +44 1993 814500
Fax: +44 1993 814504
Email: firstinitiallastname@pupress.co.uk

Order Fulfillment (US and Canada):
California/Princeton Fulfillment Services
1445 Lower Ferry Road
Ewing, NJ 08618
Phone: 800.777.4726; 609.883.1759
Fax: 800.999.1958; 609.883.7413

UK/European Sales Representation:
The University Press Group Ltd.
California | Columbia | MITP | Princeton
1 Oldlands Way, Bognor Regis
West Sussex P022 9SA
United Kingdom
Phone: +44 1243 842165
Fax: +44 1243 842167

Staff

Director: Peter J. Dougherty (609.258.6778)
  Assistant to the Director: Martha Camp (609.258.4953)
  Associate Director and Controller: Patrick Carroll (609.258.2486)
  Assistant Director for Planning & International Development: Al Bertrand (609.258.5775)
  Human Resources Generalist: Carol Swoboda (609.258.7737)
  Contracts, Copyrights, and Permissions Supervisor: Mike Schwartz (609.258.1611)
Acquisitions Editorial (see also European Office): Brigitta van Rheinberg, Assistant Director, Editor-in-Chief and Executive Editor (history) (609.258.4935)
  Humanities: Rob Tempio, Group Publisher and Executive Editor (philosophy, ancient world, political theory) (609.258.0843); Al Bertrand, Assistant Director for Planning & International Development and Senior Editor (general humanities) (609.258.5775); Beth Clevenger, Associate Editor (609.258.2336); Eric Crahan, Senior Editor (political science, American history) (609.258.4922); Alison MacKeen, Senior Editor (art, literature)

(609.258.4569); Anne Savarese, Executive Editor and Reference & Backlist Editor (reference) (609.258.4937)

Field Guides and Natural History: Robert Kirk, Executive Editor and Publisher (609.258.4884)

Mathematics & Natural Sciences: Ingrid Gnerlich, Group Publisher and Executive Editor (physical sciences) (011.44.1517.09672); Alison Kalett, Senior Editor (biology, earth science) (609.258.9232); Vickie Kearn, Senior Editor (mathematics) (609.258.2321)

Social Sciences: Seth Ditchik, Group Publisher and Executive Editor (finance, economics) (609.258.9428); Fred Appel, Executive Editor (anthropology, religion) (609.258.2484); Peter Dougherty, Director (economic history & education) (609.258.6778); Eric Schwartz, Senior Editor (cognitive science & sociology) (609.248.4908)

Editorial Administrator: Linny Schenck (609.258.0183)

Manuscript Editorial: Neil Litt, Assistant Director; Director of Editing, Design, and Production (609.258.5066)

Managing Editor: Elizabeth Byrd (609.258.2589)

Manager of Digital Publications: Ken Reed (609.258.2485)

Assistant Manager of Digital Publications: Eileen Reilly (609.258.2719)

Director of Design: Maria Lindenfeldar (609.258.7557)

Production Manager: Betsy Litz (609.258.1253)

Marketing: Adam Fortgang, Assistant Director; Director of Marketing (609.258.4896)

Associate Director of Marketing; Martha Campketing Social Media Manager: Leslie Nangle (609.258.5881)

Director of Sales: Tim Wilkins (609.258.4898)

Director of Publicity: Andrew DeSio (609.258.5165)

Advertising Manager: Donna Liese (609.258.4924)

Director of Digital Sales: Priscilla Treadwell (609.258.9387)

Digital Information Manager: Avi Paradise (609.258.5745)

Domestic Subsidiary Rights Manager: Shaquona Crews (609.258.5799)

Exhibits Manager: Melissa Burton (609.258.4915)

Senior Text Promotion Manager: Julie Haenisch (609.258.6856)

Website Technology Manager: Ann Ambrose (609.258.7749)

Business: Patrick Carroll, Associate Director and Controller (609.258.2486)

Associate Controller: Debbie Greco (609.882.0550)

Information Systems: Mike Volk, Director of Information Technology (609.258.1681)

European Office:

Head of Office, Europe; European Director of Publicity: Caroline Priday (+44 1993 814503)

Editors: Ben Tate (humanities) (+44 1993 814502); Kimberley Williams (translations) (+44 1993 814509)

International Rights Manager: Kimberley Williams (+44 1993 814509)

Full Member

Established: 1905	Admitted to AAUP: 1937
Title output 2012: 322	Title output 2013: 304
Titles currently in print: 7,516	

Editorial Program
Humanities: American, European, World, Asian, Slavic, and Jewish history; ancient world; classics; art history; philosophy; political theory; literature; religion
Reference: humanities; social sciences; and science
Science:; biology; earth sciences; mathematics; natural history; ornithology; physical sciences
Social science: anthropology; cognitive science; economics; finance; law; political science; sociology. The Press does not publish drama or fiction.
Special imprints: The Bollingen Series, established in 1941 by the Bollingen Foundation, has been published by Princeton University Press since 1967. The Press is not accepting further contributions to the series.
Special monograph series: Advances in Financial Engineering; America in the World; A.W. Mellon Lectures in the Fine Arts; Annals of Mathematics Studies; The Bard Music Festival; Buddhism; Carl G. Hempel Lecture Series; CREI Lectures in Macroeconomics; The Econometric and Tingergen Institutes Lectures; Frontiers in Biology; Frontiers of Economic Research; The Gorman Lectures in Economics; Human Rights and Crimes against Humanity; In a Nutshell; In-Formation; The Isaac Newton Institute Lectures; James Madison Library in American Politics; Jews, Christians, and Muslims from the Ancient to the Modern World; Jung Seminars; The Kauffman Foundation Series on Innovation and Entrepreneurship; The Lawrence Stone Lectures; Lives of Great Religious Books; London Mathematical Society Monographs; Martin Classical Lectures; Mathematical Notes; Miriam S. Balmuth Lectures in Ancient History and Archaeology; Monographs in Behavior and Ecology; Monographs in Population Biology; Mythos; New Forum Books; Oddly Modern Fairy Tales; POINT: Essays on Architecture; Politics and Society in Twentieth-Century America; Porter Lectures; Primers in Complex Systems; Princeton-China Series; Princeton Classics; Princeton Computer Science Notes; Princeton Economic History of the Western World; Princeton Environmental Institute Series; Princeton Essays in Literature; Princeton Field Guides; Princeton Field Guides to Art; Princeton Foundations of Contemporary Philosophy; The Princeton Frontiers of Biology Lecture Series; Princeton Frontiers in Physics; Princeton History of the Ancient World; Princeton Illustrated Checklists; Princeton Landmarks in Biology; Princeton Landmarks in Mathematics and Physics; Princeton Lectures in Finance; Princeton Library of Asian Translations; Princeton Lectures In Politics and Public Affairs; Princeton Mathematical Series; Princeton Monographs in Philosophy; Princeton Pocket Guides; Princeton Primers in Climate; Princeton Readings in Religion; Princeton Science Library; Princeton Series in Applied Mathematics; Princeton Series in Astrophysics; Princeton Series in Computer Science; Princeton Series in Finance; Princeton Series in International Economics; Princeton Series in Modern Observational Astronomy; Princeton Series in Physics; Princeton Series in Theoretical and Computational Biology; Princeton Studies in American Politics; Princeton Studies in Business and Technology; Princeton Studies in Complexity; Princeton Studies in Cultural Sociology; Princeton Studies in Culture and Technology; Princeton Studies in International History and Politics; Princeton Studies in Muslim Politics; The Public Square; The Richard Ullman Lectures; The Roundtable Series in Behavioral Economics; The Russian Archives Project; Science Essentials; Soochow University Lectures in Philosophy; Studies in Church and State; The Toni Morrison Lecture Series; The Toulouse Lectures in Economics; Translation/Transnation; The University Center for Human Values Series; W. H. Auden: Critical Editions;

WILDGuides; Writers on Writers
Poetry series: Facing Pages; The Lockert Library of Poetry in Translation; Princeton Series of Contemporary Poets
Original source series: The Collected Papers of Albert Einstein; Collected Works of Spinoza; The Complete Works of W. H. Auden; Kierkegaard's Writings; Kierkegaard's Journals and Notebooks; The Papers of Thomas Jefferson (also Second Series; Retirement Series); The Papers of Woodrow Wilson; The Philosophical, Political and Literary Works of David Hume; Selected Writings of Wilhelm Dilthey; The Writings of Henry D. Thoreau

University of Puerto Rico Press

Street Address:
Edificio Editorial/Diálogo
Jardín Botánico Área Norte
Carretera No. 1, KM 12.0
Río Piedras, San Juan, PR 00931
Phone: 787.250.0435
Fax: 787.753.9116, 751.8785

Mailing Address:
PO Box 23322
U.P.R. Station
San Juan, PR 00931-3322

Website and Social Media:
Website: www.laeditorialupr.com

Staff
Executive Director: José Ortiz Valladares (email: jose.ortiz3@upr.edu)
Editor: Rosa V. Otero
Sales: José Burgos (email: jburgos@upr.edu)
Marketing and Promotion: Ruth Morales (email: ruth.morales2@upr.edu)
Exhibits and Special Projects: José Burgos (email: jburgos@upr.edu), Ruth Morales (email: ruth.morales2@upr.edu)
Shipping, Receiving and Inventory: Ernesto Pancorbo (email: ernesto.pancorbo@upr.edu)
Warehouse: Ángel Ortiz
Journals: *Revista La Torre*
Journals Marketing: Ruth Morales

Full Member
Established:1943
Title output 2012: NR
Titles currently in print: 989

Admitted to AAUP: 1971
Title output 2013: NR
Journals published: 1

Editorial Program
Scholarly studies on Puerto Rico, the Caribbean and Latin America; philosophy; history; architecture; law; social sciences; health; women's studies; economics; literary theory and criticism; creative poetry and prose; literary anthologies; nature studies; flora; fauna; ecosystems; children's books; reference; other general interest publications.
Journals: *Revista La Torre* (the humanities). In distribution: *Revista de Estudios Hispánicos* (Spanish language studies); and *Historia y Sociedad* (Puerto Rican and Caribbean history); *Diálogos* (philosophy)
Special series: literary anthologies; philosophy; creative literature; scholarly nonfiction; nature

Special imprints: Antología Personal (Selections by renowned hispanic writers); Clásicos no tan clásicos (Faithful re-edition of works written between 1890 and 1930 with annotations by 21st century scholars); Books on Puerto Rican Cooking; Colección Eugenio María de Hostos (complete works); San Pedrito (children's books); Colección Nueve Pececitos (young readers); Cuentos de un mundo perdido (middle school readers)

Purdue University Press

Stewart Center, Room 370
504 West State Street
West Lafayette, IN 47907-2058

Phone: 765.494.2038
Fax: 765.496.2442
Email: pupress@purdue.edu
Indiv: (user I.D.)@purdue.edu

Orders:
Purdue University Press
PO Box 388
Ashland, OH 44805
Phone: 800.247.6553
Fax: 419.281.6883
Email: order@bookmasters.com

Website and Social Media:
Website: www.press.purdue.edu; www.lib.purdue.edu/publishing
Facebook: www.facebook.com/purduepress
Twitter: publishpurdue

European Distributor:
Eurospan

Canadian Distributor:
Bookmasters

Staff
Director: Charles Watkinson (765.494.8251; email: ctwatkin)
Managing Editor: Katherine Purple (765.494.6259; email: kpurple)
Production Editors: Kelley Kimm (765.494.8024; email: kkimm); Dianna Gilroy
    (765.494.2035; email: dianna)
Administrative Assistant: Becki Corbin (765.494.8144; email: rlcorbin)
Editorial Assistant: Jennifer Lynch (765.494.4943; email: lynch23)
Sales & Marketing Manager: Bryan Shaffer (765.494.8428; email: bshaffer)

Full Member
Established: 1960
Title output 2012: 26
Titles currently in print: 500

Admitted to AAUP: 1993
Title output 2013: 27
Journals published: 14

Editorial Program
Dedicated to the dissemination of scholarly and professional information aligned with the strengths of its parent institution, the Press provides quality resources in technology and engineering, library and information science, public policy, aeronautics and astronautics, Indiana history, agriculture, health and human sciences, veterinary studies, European history, Jewish studies, and global languages and literatures.
Journals: *CLCWeb: Comparative Literature and Culture*; *Data Curation Profiles Directory*;

Education and Culture: The Journal of the John Dewey Society; First Opinions—Second Reactions; Global Business Languages; The Interdisciplinary Journal of Problem Based Learning; The Jewish Role in American Life: An Annual Review; Journal of Aviation Technology and Engineering; Journal of Human Performance in Extreme Environments; Journal of Pre-College Engineering Education Research; Journal of Problem Solving; Phillip Roth Studies; Shofar: An Interdisciplinary Journal of Jewish Studies; Studies in Jewish Civilization
Special series: Central European Studies; Comparative Cultural Studies; New Directions in the Human-Animal Bond; Purdue Studies in Romance Literatures; Shofar Supplements in Jewish Studies; Purdue Information Literacy Handbooks; Purdue Studies in Public Policy. Charleston Insights in Library, Archival, and Information Sciences with Against the Grain Press; Pets and People with the American Veterinary Medical Association.

RAND Corporation

Street Address:
1776 Main Street
Santa Monica, CA 90407

Mailing Address:
PO Box 2138
Santa Monica, CA 90407-2138

Phone: 310.393.0411
Fax: 310.451.7026

Customer Service:
Phone: 877.584.8642
Fax: 412.802.4981
Email: order@rand.org

Website and Social Media:
Website: www.rand.org/publications
Facebook: www.facebook.com/RANDCorporation
Twitter: RANDCorporation
YouTube: www.youtube.com/user/TheRANDCorporation
Blog: www.rand.org/blog.html

US Distributor:
National Book Network
Phone: 800.462.6420 or 717.794.3800
Fax: 800.338.4550

UK/European Distributor:
NBN International

Staff
Director: Jane Ryan (ext. 7260; email: ryan@rand.org)
Manager, Production, Printing, and Distribution: Paul Murphy (ext. 7806;
    email: murphy@rand.org)
Business Manager: Russell Nakamura (ext. 6722; email: nakamura@rand.org)
Managing Editor: Steve Kistler (ext. 6318; email: skistler@rand.org)
Computing Manager: Edward Finkelstein (ext. 7417; email: edwardf@rand.org)

Associate Member
Established: 1948
Title output 2012: 175
Titles currently in print: 20,000

Admitted to AAUP: 2000
Title output 2013: 160
Journals published: 2

Editorial Program
For more than 65 years, decision-makers in the public and private sectors have turned to the RAND Corporation for objective analysis and effective solutions that address the challenges facing the nation and the world. Publication topics include policy issues such as education;

environment and energy; health care; immigration, labor, and population; international affairs; national security; public safety and justice; science and technology; and terrorism and homeland security. Unsolicited manuscripts are not accepted.

Journals: *RAND Health Quarterly; RAND Journal of Economics*

RIT Press

90 Lomb Memorial Drive
Rochester, NY 14623-5604

Orders:
Phone: 585.475.6766

Phone: 585.475.6766
Fax: 585.475.4090
Email: lmdwml@rit.edu

Website and Social Media:
Website: ritpress.rit.edu
Facebook: www.facebook.com/pages/RIT-Press/172326337130?ref=hl
Twitter: RITPress

Staff
Director: Bruce A. Austin (585.475.2879; email: baagll@rit.edu)
Managing Editor: Molly Q. Cort (585.475.4088; email: mqcwml@rit.edu)
Business Manager: Laura DiPonzio Heise (585.475.5819; email: lmdwml@rit.edu)
Design & Marketing Specialist: Marnie Soom (585.475.4089; email: mxswml@rit.edu)

Introductory Member
Established: 2001
Title output 2012:
Titles currently in print: 70

Admitted to AAUP: 2009
Title output 2013: 9
Journals published: 1

Editorial Program
RIT Press is a scholarly publishing enterprise at Rochester Institute of Technology. Established in 2001 as RIT Cary Graphic Arts Press, the Press initially focused on publishing titles that documented graphic communication processes, printing history, and bookmaking. As its editorial policies evolved, the Press has broadened its reach to include content that supports all academic disciplines offered at RIT, our host institution.

RIT Press is dedicated to the innovative use of new publishing technology while upholding high standards in content quality, publication design, and print/digital production. The Press also offers trade editions for mass-market audiences and occasional limited edition books with unique aesthetic standards.

Special series: Digital Innovation Series; First Person Corporate History; Graphic Design Archives Chapbook; Philosophy and Ethics; Popular Culture Series (Comics Monograph Series); Printing Industry Center Series, Sports Studies

Journal: *HAYDN* an online journal of the Haydn Society of North America, peer-reviewed, bi-annual digital-only publication of musicological research.

The University of Rochester Press

668 Mount Hope Avenue
Rochester NY 14620-2731

Phone: 585.275.0419
Fax: 585.271.8778

Orders:
Phone: 585.275.0419
Email: boydell@boydellusa.net

Website and Social Media:
Website: www.urpress.com
Facebook: www.facebook.com/boydellandbrewerfans
Twitter: boydellbrewer
Pinterest: www.pinterest.com/boydellbrewer
Instagram: www.instagram.com/boydellandbrewer

UK Representative:
Boydell & Brewer, Ltd.

Canadian Representative:
Scholarly Book Services

Staff

Editorial Director: Sonia Kane (585.273.5778; email: sonia.kane@rochester.edu)
Managing Editor/Manuscript Editorial: Ryan Peterson (585.273.4429; email: peterson@boydellusa.net)
Assistant Editor: Julia Cook (585.273.4356; email: cook@boydellusa.net)
Production Manager: Sue Smith (585.273.2817; email: smith@boydellusa.net)
  Production Editor: Tracey Engel (585.273.2818; email: engel@boydellusa.net)
Marketing Executives: Kristin Stine (585.273.5779; email: stine@boydellusa.net); Leslie Ballard (585.275.0391; email: ballard@boydellusa.net)
Manager of Web and Online Media: Joan Simpson (585.273.5709; email: simpson@boydellusa.net)
  Customer Service: Jennifer Shannon (585.273.2959; email: shannon@boydellusa.net)
  Accounts Assistant: Olga Reshota (585.273.5777; email: reshota@boydellusa.net)

Full Member

Established: 1989

Title output 2012: 26
Titles currently in print: 581

Admitted to AAUP: 2008 (intro. member)
Admitted to AAUP: 2011 (full member)

Title output 2013: 26

Editorial Program

Musicology and music theory; ethnomusicology; African and diaspora studies with an emphasis on political and economic history; the history of medicine in the US and internationally; early modern European history; Central and Eastern European studies; gender and race in nineteenth and twentieth century America; political theory and philosophy.

Special series: Changing Perspectives on Early Modern Europe; Eastman Studies in Music; Eastman/Rochester Studies in Ethnomusicology; North American Kant Society Publications; Race and Gender in American History; Rochester Studies in African History and the Diaspora; Rochester Studies in East and Central Europe; Rochester Studies in Medical History

The Rockefeller University Press

1114 First Avenue, 3rd Floor
New York, NY 10065-8325

Phone: 212.327.7938
Fax: 212.327.8587
Email: (user I.D.)@rockefeller.edu

<u>Website and Social Media:</u>
Websites: www.rupress.org, jcb.rupress.org, jem.rupress.org, jgp.rupress.org
Blogs: news.rupress.org, jcb-biowrites.rupress.org
Facebook: www.facebook.com/JCellBiol, www.facebook.com/JExpMed, www.facebook.com/
JGenPhysiol
Twitter: JCellBiol, JExpMed, JGenPhysiol

Staff
Editor-in-Chief: Linda J. Miller (212.327.8881; email: lmiller)
  Assistant to the Editor-in-Chief: JoAnn Greene (212.327.8025; email: greenej)
Manuscript Editorial: Liz Williams, Executive Editor, *The Journal of Cell Biology*
  (212.327.8011; email: lwilliams); Marlowe Tessmer, Senior Editor, *The Journal of
  Experimental Medicine* (212.327.8393; email: mtessmer); Liz Adler, Executive Editor, *The
  Journal of General Physiology* (212.327.8651; email: eadler)
Advertising: Lorna Petersen, Sales Director (212.327.8880; email: petersl)
Journals: Robert O'Donnell, Electronic Publishing and Production Director (212.327.8545;
  email: odonner)
Business: Raymond T. Fastiggi, Finance Director (212.327.8567; email: fastigg)
  Business Development Director: Gregory Malar (212.327.7948; email: malarg)

Full Member
Established: 1958   Admitted to AAUP: 1982
Title output 2012: 1   Title output 2013: 0
Titles currently in print: 40   Journals published: 3

Editorial Program
The Rockefeller University Press publishes three biomedical research journals. *The Journal
of Cell Biology* provides a rigorous forum for publication of topics across the complete
spectrum of cell biology. *The Journal of Experimental Medicine* publishes seminal work in all
areas of experimental medicine, with a current emphasis on immunological, stem cell, and
disease research. Articles in *The Journal of General Physiology* elucidate important biological,
chemical, or physical mechanisms of broad physiological significance.

Russell Sage Foundation

112 East 64th Street
New York, NY 10065

Phone: 212.750.6000
Fax: 212.371.4761
Email: pubs@rsage.org
Indiv: firstname@rsage.org

<u>Website and Social Media:</u>
Website: www.russellsage.org/about/press-list
Blog: www.russellsage.org/blog
Facebook: www.facebook.com/russellsagefoundation
Twitter: RussellSageFdn

<u>UK/European Representative:</u>
University Presses Marketing

Orders:
Russell Sage Foundation
CUP Services
750 Cascadilla St.
PO Box 6525
Ithaca, NY 14851
Phone: 800.666.2211; 607.277.2211
Fax: 800.688.2877; 607.277.6292

Staff
Director of Publications: Suzanne Nichols (212.750.6026)
Publications Assistant: Nina Psoncak (212.750.6038)
Production Editor: April Rondeau (212.750.6034)
Director of Public Relations: David A. Haproff (212.750.6037)
Assistant Book Marketing Manager and Web Programmer: Bruce Thongsack (212.750.6021)
Web Editor and Staff Writer: Jennifer Pan (212.750.2024)
Exhibits/Permissions: Nina Psoncak (212.750.6038)
Foundation President: Sheldon Danziger

Associate Member
Established: 1907
Title output 2012: 33
Titles currently in print: 700

Admitted to AAUP: 1989
Title output 2013: 28

Editorial Program
Scholarly books on current research and policy issues in the social sciences. Recent research programs sponsored by the Russell Sage Foundation include the future of work, sustainable employment, current US immigration, the analysis of the 2010 US Census, the social psychology of cultural contact, the social dimensions of inequality, carework, and behavioral economics.

Rutgers University Press

106 Somerset Street, 3rd Floor
New Brunswick, NJ 08901

Warehouse, Fulfillment, & Cust. Service:
c/o Longleaf Services, Inc.
PO Box 8895
Chapel Hill, NC 27515-8895

Phone: 848.445.7762
Fax: 732.745.4935
Email: (user I.D.)@rutgers.edu

Phone: 800.848.6224
Fax: 800.272.6817
Email: longleaf@unc.edu

Website and Social Media:
Website: rutgerspress.rutgers.edu
Facebook: www.facebook.com/pages/Rutgers-University-Press/212072346925
Twitter Handle: RutgersUPress

UK/European Representative:
Eurospan

Canadian Representative:
Scholarly Book Services

Staff

Director: Marlie Wasserman (848.445.7784; email: marlie)
  Assistant to the Director/Rights Manager/E-book Manager: Allyson Fields (848.445.7785; email: amfields)
Acquisitions Editorial: Leslie Mitchner, Associate Director/Editor-in-Chief (American studies, humanities, Latino studies, popular culture, film, and media) (848.445.7787; email: lmitch)
  Executive Editor: Dana Dreibelbis (clinical medicine) (848.445.7792; email: dana. dreibelbis)
  Editors: Marlie Wasserman (anthropology and human rights) (848.445.7784; email: marlie); Peter Mickulas (health, sociology, environment, and criminology) (848.445.7752; email: mickulas); Katie Keeran (Asian American studies, Caribbean studies, higher education, and women's studies) (848.445.7786; email: ckeeran)
  Editorial Assistant: Lisa Boyajian (848.445.7791; email: lboyajian@rutgerspress.rutgers.edu)
Manuscript Editorial and Production: Marilyn Campbell, PrePress Director (848.445.7756; email: marilync)
  Senior Production Manager: Anne Hegeman (848.445.7761; email: hegeman)
  Production Coordinator: Bryce Schimanski (848.445.7764; email: brycesch)
  Production Editor: Carrie Hudak (848.445.7755; email: carrie.hudak)
Marketing: Elizabeth Scarpelli/Associate Director/Sales and Marketing Director (848.445.7781; email: escarpel)
  Marketing and Publicity Manager: Lisa Fortunato (848.445.7775; email: lisafort)
  Direct Response/Webmaster/E-Marketing Manager: Brice Hammack (848.445.7765; email: bhammack)
  Exhibit Coordinator/Marketing Assistant: Victoria Verhowsky (848.445.7782; email: victoria.verhowsky)
Business: David Flum, Manager (848.445.7763; email: dflum)
  Customer Service Liaison/IT: Penny Burke (848.445.7788; email: pborden)

Full Member

Established: 1936

Title output 2012: 88

Titles currently in print: 2708

Admitted to AAUP: 1937

Title output 2013: 90

Editorial Program

American Literatures Initiative; American studies; anthropology; Asian American studies; African American studies; Caribbean studies; film and media; higher education studies; history of science/technology; human rights; Jewish studies; Latino/a studies; popular culture; public policy; regional studies; sociology; women's studies

Special series: Asian American Studies Today; Behind the Silver Screen; Comics Culture; Critical Caribbean Studies; Critical Issues in Crime and Society; Critical Issues in Health and Medicine; Critical Issues In Sport and Society; Current Cardiology; Families in Focus; Genocide, Political Violence, Human Rights; Global Perspectives on Aging; Jewish Cultures of the World; Key Words In Jewish Studies; Latinidad: Transnational Cultures in the United States, Nature Society, and Culture; New Directions in International Studies; Neurointensive Care; Precision Oncology; Rivergate Regionals; Rutgers Series in Childhood Studies; Techniques of the Moving Image; Violence Against Women and Children; War Culture

Saint Joseph's University Press

5600 City Avenue

Philadelphia, PA 19131-1395

Phone: 610.660.3402

Fax: 610.660.3412

Email: sjupress@sju.edu

Indiv.: (user I.D.)@sju.edu

Website and Social Media:

Website: www.sjupress.com

Orders:

Phone: 610.660.3402

Email: orders@sjupress

Staff

Director: Carmen Robert Croce (610.660.3402; email: ccroce)

Editorial Director: Joseph F. Chorpenning (610.660.1214; email: jchorpen)

Introductory Member

Established: 1997

Title output 2012: 5

Titles currently in print: 55

Admitted to AAUP: 2011

Title output 2013: 3

Editorial Program

Jesuit studies (with an emphasis on history and the visual arts), regional studies (Philadelphia and environs)

Special series: Early Modern Catholicism and the Visual Arts (1500-French Revolution)

SAR Press

Street Address:
660 Garcia St.
Santa Fe, NM 87505

Mailing Address:
PO Box 2188
Santa Fe, NM 87504-2188

Phone: 505.954.7206
Fax: 505.954.7241
Email: Press@sarsf.org

US Orders:
Phone: 505.954.7206
Email: bkorders@sarsf.org

Website and Social Media:
Website: www.sarpress.org
Facebook: www.facebook.com/schoolforadvancedresearch.org

UK & European Distributor:
Eurospan Ltd.

Canadian Distributor:
Scholarly Book Services

Staff:
Director: Lynn Thompson Baca (505.954.7260; email: baca@sarsf.org)
Managing Editor: Lisa Pacheco (505.954.7261; email: pacheco@sarsf.org)
Editorial Assistant: Ellen Goldberg (505.954.7277; email: goldberg@sarsf.org)
Designer & Production Manager: Cynthia Dyer (505.488.2062; email: dyer@sarsf.org)
Bookkeeper: Cynthia Selene (505.954.7262; email: selene@sarsf.org)
Warehouse Manager: John Noonan (505.954.7210; email: noonan@sarsf.org)

Introductory Member
Established: 1908
Title output 2012: 8
Titles currently in print: 165

Admitted to AAUP: 2013
Title output 2013: 7

Editorial Program
Quality books in anthropology and related fields, the arts and aesthetics of Indigenous peoples, and the peoples and cultures of the American Southwest, past and present. We offer trenchant analysis and thought-provoking research at great prices.
Special series: Advanced Seminar; Global Indigenous Politics; Resident Scholar; Popular Archaeology

Society of Biblical Literature

The Luce Center
825 Houston Mill Road, Suite 350
Atlanta, GA 30329

Phone: 404.727.3100
Fax: 404.727.3101
Email: sblexec@sbl-site.org
Indiv: firstname.lastname@sbl-site.org

Orders:
Phone: 877.725.3334
Fax: 802.864.7626

Journal Subscriptions and Membership:
Phone: 866.727.9955
Fax: 404.727.2419

Website and Social Media:
Website: www.sbl-site.org
Facebook: www.facebook.com/group.php?gid=49602519254

Staff
Executive Director: John F. Kutsko (404.727.3038)
Editorial Director: Bob Buller (970.669.9900)
Managing Editor: Leigh Andersen (404.727.2327)
Acquisitions Editor: Billie Jean Collins (404.727.0807)
Publishing Marketing Manager: Kathie Klein (404.727.2325)
Sales Manager: Heather McMurray (404.727.3096)
Director of Finance and Administration: Susan Madara (404.727.3103)
Director of Administrative and Technology Services: Missy Colee (404.727.3124)
Manager of Technology: Chris O'Connor (404.727.2187)
Manager of Web Communications: Sharon Johnson (404.727.3102)
Development Officer: Sandra Stewart-Kruger (404.727.9484)
Manager of Programs: Charles Haws (404.727.3095)
Director of Global Conferences: Trista Krock (404.727.3137)
Manager of Membership & Subscriptions: Navar Steed (404.727.9494)
Public Initiatives Coordinator: Moira Bucciarelli (404.727.9484)

Associate Member
Established: 1880
Title output 2012: 30
Titles currently in print: 794

Admitted to AAUP: 2003
Title output 2013: 42
Journals published: 2

Editorial Program
The SBL publishes works in biblical and religious studies. Monographic publications include major reference works; commentaries; text editions and translations; collections of essays; doctoral dissertations; and tools for teaching and research fields; archaeological, sociological, and historical studies; volumes that use archaeological and historical data to illuminate Israelite religion or the culture of biblical peoples; scholarly works on the history, culture, and literature of early Judaism; scholarly works on various aspects of the Masorah; scholarly congress proceedings; critical texts of the Greek Fathers including evaluations of data; philological tools; studies employing the methods and perspectives of linguistics, folklore studies, literary criticism, structuralism, social anthropology, and postmodern studies; studies

of the Septuagint including textual criticism, manuscript witnesses and other versions, as well as its literature, historical milieu, and thought; studies related to the Jewish apocrypha and pseudepigrapha of the Hellenistic period, and the subsequent development of this literature in Judaism and early Christianity; studies in biblical literature and/or its cultural environment; text-critical works related to Hebrew Bible/Old Testament and New Testament including investigations of methodology, studies of individual manuscripts, critical texts of a selected book or passage, or examination of more general textual themes; translations of ancient Near Eastern texts; translations of ancient texts from the Greco.Roman world.

SBL is the exclusive North American distributor for Sheffield Phoenix Press (UK), and the sole producer and distributor of volumes in the Brown Judaic Studies series (Brown University). SBL also distributes the Manuscripts of the Greek New Testament Series by Reuben Swanson.

Journals: *Journal of Biblical Literature; Review of Biblical Literature*

Special series: Ancient Israel and Its Literature; Archaeology and Biblical Studies; Biblical Encyclopedia Translations; Biblical Scholarship in North America; Commentary on the Septuagint; Early Christianity and Its Literature; Early Judaism and Its Literature; Global Perspectives on Biblical Scholarship; History of Biblical Studies; Masoretic Studies; The New Testament in the Greek Fathers; Resources for Biblical Study; Semeia Studies; Septuagint and Cognate Studies; Studia Philonica Annual and Monographs; Text-Critical Studies; Wisdom Literature from the Ancient World; Writings from the Ancient World; Writings from the Ancient World Supplements; Writings from the Greco-Roman World; Writings from the Greco-Roman World Supplements

Joint imprints and co-publishing programs: SBL Handbook of Style for Ancient Near Eastern, Biblical, and Early Christian Studies with Hendrickson Publishers; HarperCollins Study Bible (NRSV), HarperCollins Bible Dictionary, Revised Edition, HarperCollins Bible Commentary, Revised Edition, and Harper's Bible Pronunciation Guide with HarperCollins; Hardback editions with Brill Academic Publishers of Leiden, The Netherlands; The Greek New Testament: SBL Edition with Logos Bible Software.

Online books: SBL, along with six participating partners, provides PDF files of academic books for free download to individuals and libraries in underresourced areas of the globe. Through software that recognizes the IP address of the web visitor, persons from countries whose GDP is considerably less than the average GDP of the US and the EU are given access to the files. The program, as of late 2012, includes almost 350 titles.

EBooks: SBL has entered the e-book market and partners with Bibliovault to make titles available in multiple formats.

The University of South Carolina Press

1600 Hampton Street
5th Floor
Columbia, SC 29208-3400

Phone: 803.777.5243
Fax: 803.777.0160
Email: (user I.D.)@sc.edu

Website and Social Media:
Website: www.sc.edu/uscpress
Facebook: www.facebook.com/USC.Press

Business Office and Warehouse:
718 Devine Street
Columbia, SC 29208-0001
Phone: 800.768.2500
Fax: 800.868.0740
Email: (user I.D.)@sc.edu

UK/European Distributor:
Eurospan

Canadian Distributor:
Scholarly Book Services

Staff

Director: Jonathan Haupt (803.777.2243; email: jhaupt)
  Assistant Director for Operations: Linda Haines Fogle (803.777.4848; email: lfogle)
  Assistant to the Director: Vicki Bates (803.777.5245; email: batesvc)
Acquisitions Editors: Linda Haines Fogle (regional, trade) (803.777.4848; email: lfogle);
  Alexander Moore (African American studies, history, Southern studies) (803.777.8070;
  email: alexm); Jim Denton (literature, religious studies, rhetoric/communication, social
  work) (803.777.4859; email: denton)
Manuscript Editorial: Bill Adams, Managing Editor (803.777.5075; email: adamswb)
  Editorial Assistant: Elizabeth Jones (803.777.9055; email: jonesem6)
Design and Production: Pat Callahan, Design and Production Manager (803.777.2449;
  email: mpcallah)
  Book Designer: Brandi Lariscy-Avant (803.777.9056; email: lariscyb)
  Design and Production Assistant: Ashley Mathias (803.777.2238; email: samathi)
Marketing: Suzanne Axland, Director (803.777.2021; email: axland)
  Promotions Manager: Carolyn Martin (803.777.5029; email: clmartin)
  Advertising and Direct Mail Manager: Lynne Parker (803.777.5231; email: parkerll)
Business/Warehouse: Vicki Sewell, Acting Business Manager and Permissions (803.777.7754;
  email: sewellv)
  Customer Service Representative: Libby Mack (803.777.1774; email: lmack)
  Warehouse Assistant: Eddie Hill (803.777.0184; email: jehill)

Full Member

Established: 1944
Title output 2012: 62
Titles currently in print: 1,120

Admitted to AAUP: 1948
Title output 2013: 67

Editorial Program

Scholarly works, mainly in the humanities and social sciences, and general interest titles,
particularly those of importance to the state and region. Subjects include African American
studies; history, especially American history, military history, maritime history, and Southern
history; literature and literary studies; religious studies, including comparative religion;

Southern studies; rhetoric/communication; and social work.

Special series, joint imprints, and/or copublishing programs: AccessAble Books; The Belle W. Baruch Library in Marine Science; The Carolina Lowcountry and the Atlantic World; Chief Justiceships of the United States Supreme Court; Historians in Conversation; Joseph M. Bruccoli Great War Series; Palmetto Poetry Series; The Papers of John C. Calhoun; The Papers of Henry Laurens; The Papers of Howard Thurman; Social Problems and Social Issues; South Carolina Encyclopedia Guides; South Carolina Poetry Book Prize; Southern Classics; Southern Revivals; Story River Books; Studies in Comparative Religion; Studies in Maritime History; Studies in Rhetoric / Communication; Studies on Personalities of the New Testament; Studies on Personalities of the Old Testament; Understanding Contemporary American Literature; Understanding Contemporary British Literature; Understanding Modern European and Latin American Literature; Women's Diaries and Letters of the South; Young Palmetto Books

Southern Illinois University Press

1915 University Press Drive
SIUC Mail Code 6806
Southern Illinois University
Carbondale, IL 62901-6806

Orders:
Southern Illinois University Press
c/o Chicago Distribution Center
11030 South Langley Avenue
Chicago, IL 60628-3830

Phone: 618.453.2281
Fax: 618.453.1221
Email: (user I.D.)@siu.edu

Phone: 800.621.2736
Fax: 800.621.8476
Email: custserv@press.uchicago.edu
EDI; PUBNET at 202-5280

Website and Social Media:
Website: www.siupress.com
Facebook: www.facebook.com/siupress
Twitter: SIUPress

UK/European Distributor:
Eurospan

Canadian Representative:
Scholarly Book Services

Staff
Interim Director: Barb Martin (618.453.6614; email: bbmartin)
Rights and Permissions: Angela Moore-Swafford (618.453.6617; email: angmoore) (Rights email: rights)
Acquisitions Editorial: Karl Kageff, Editor-in-Chief (Beat studies, regional studies, rhetoric and composition) (618.453.6629; email: kageff)
    Executive Editor: Sylvia Frank Rodrigue (Civil War, Lincoln, Reconstruction) (508.297.2162; email: sylvia@sylverlining.com)
    Acquisitions Editor: Kristine Priddy (composition, theater and film) (618.453.6631; email: mkpriddy)

Editorial, Design, and Production: Barb Martin, EDP Manager (618.453.6614; email: bbmartin)
  Project Editor: Wayne Larsen (618.453.6628; email: wlarsen)
  Book Designer: Linda Buhman (618.453.6612; email: ljbuhman)
Production Assistant: Lola Starck (618.453.6635; email: lolas)
  IT Specialist: Matt MacCrimmon (618.453.6615; email: macc)
Marketing and Sales Manager: Amy Etcheson (618.453.6623; email: aetcheson)
  Marketing Associates: Bridget Brown (618.453.6633; email: bcbrown)
Accounts Payable: Dawn Vagner (618.453.3786; email: dvagner)

Full Member

Established: 1956	Admitted to AAUP: 1980
Title output 2012: 36	Title output 2013: 37
Titles currently in print: 1,200	

Editorial Program

Scholarly books, primarily in the humanities and social sciences. Particular strengths are film studies; theatre and stagecraft; regional and Civil War history, rhetoric, and composition; Beat studies; philosophy; aviation; contemporary poetry. Submissions in fiction and festschriften are not invited.

Special series: Aviation Management; Celebrating the Peoples of Illinois; Civil War Campaigns in the Heartland; The Collected Works of John Dewey; The Concise Lincoln Library; The Crab Orchard Series in Poetry; The Holmes-Johnson Series in Criminology; The Illustrated Flora of Illinois; Landmarks in Rhetoric and Public Address; The Papers of Ulysses S. Grant; Shawnee Classics; Shawnee Books; Studies in Rhetorics and Feminisms; Studies in Writing and Rhetoric; Theater in the Americas; Ulysses S. Grant and the World He Shaped

Southern Methodist University Press

314 Fondren Library West	Orders:
6404 Hilltop Lane	Phone: 800.826.8911
Dallas, TX 75275-0415	

Website and Social Media:
Website: www.tamu.edu/upress/smu/smugen.html

Staff
TBA

Full Member

Established: 1937	Admitted to AAUP: 1946
Titles currently in print: 226	

Editorial Program
The press is undergoing a reorganization, and is not currently acquiring new books.
Special series: Medical Humanities; Sport in American Life

Stanford University Press

425 Broadway
Redwood City, CA 94063

Phone: 650.723.9434
Fax: 650.725.3457
Email: (user I.D.)@stanford.edu

Website and Social Media:
Website: www.sup.org
Blog: stanfordpress.typepad.com
Facebook: www.facebook.com/stanforduniversitypress
Twitter: stanfordpress

Orders:
Chicago Distribution Center
11030 South Langley Avenue
Chicago, IL 60628
Phone: 800.621.2736; 773.702.7000
Fax: (800) 621-8476; 773.702.7212
Email: orders@press.uchicago.edu

European Representative:
Eurospan

Canadian Representative:
Lexa Publishers' Representatives

Staff

Director: Alan Harvey (650.723.6375; email: aharvey)

Rights, Permissions, and Contracts: Ariane de Pree-Kajfez, Senior Rights Manager (650.725.0815; email: arianep)

Acquisitions: Kate Wahl, Publishing Director and Editor-in-Chief (Middle East studies) (650.723.3077; email: kwahl)

Executive Editor: Geoffrey Burn (security studies, international relations, politics) (650.736.1942; email: grhburn)

Senior Editors: Emily-Jane Cohen, (literature, philosophy, religion) (650.725.7717; email: beatrice); Margo Beth Fleming (economics, organizational studies) (650.724.7079; email: mbfleming); Stacy Wagner (history, Jewish studies) (650.725.0845; email: swagner)

Acquisitions Editors: Michelle Lipinski (anthropology, Asian studies, law) (650.736.4641; email: mlipinsk)

Associate Editor: Frances Malcolm (sociology) (650.724.7080; email: fmalcolm)

Editorial Assistant: James Holt (650.736.0924; email: jhholt)

Editorial, Design, and Production: Patricia Myers, EDP Director (650.724.5365; email: pmyers)

Senior Production Editor: Judith Hibbard (650.736.0719; email: jhibbard)

Production Editors: Mariana Raykov (650.725.0835; email: mraykov); John Feneron (650.725.0828; email: johnf); Emily Smith (650.736.0686; email: emilys); Gigi Mark (650.724.9990; email: vmark)

Art Director: Rob Ehle (650.723.1132; email: ehle)

Senior Designer: Bruce Lundquist (650.723.6808; email: brucel)

Production Manager: Harold Moorehead (650.725.0836; email: hmoorehead)

Production Coordinator: Mike Sagara (650.725.0839; email: msagara)

Sales and Marketing: David Jackson, Sales and Marketing Director (650.736.1782; email: david.jackson)

Publicity: Mary Kate Maco, Publicity Manager (650.724.4211; email: mmaco)

Advertising and Direct Mail Coordinator: Ryan Furtkamp (650.725.0823; email: furtkamp)

Exhibits Manager: Christie Cochrell (650.725.0820; email: cochrell)
Marketing Assistant: Sarah Pilat (650.736.1781; email: spilat)
Business: Jean Kim, Director of Finance and Operations (650.725.0838; email: jean.h.kim)
  Royalties/Accounts Receivable: Su-Mei Lee (650.725.0837; email: sumeilee)
  Accounts Payable: Aurelia Hernandez (650.724.8697; email: aureliah)
Systems: Chris Cosner, IT Manager (650.724.7276; email: ccosner)
  Desktop Support Administrator: Meide Guo (650.723.9598; email: meideguo)

Full Member

Established: 1925   Admitted to AAUP: 1937
Title output 2012: 156   Title output 2013: 158
Titles currently in print: 3028

Editorial Program

Anthropology, Asian Studies, Business, Economics, History, International Relations, Jewish Studies, Latin American Studies, Law, Literature, Middle East Studies, Philosophy, Politics, Religion, Security Studies, Sociology.

Special series: Anthropology of Policy; Asian America; Asian Security; Cold War International History Project; The Complete Works of Friedrich Nietzsche; Contemporary Issues in Asia and the Pacific; The Cultural Lives of Law; Cultural Memory in the Present; Emerging Frontiers in the Global Economy; Encountering Traditions; Global Competition Law and Economics; High Reliability and Crisis Management; Innovation and Technology in the World Economy; Jurists: Profiles in Legal Theory; Meridian: Crossing Aesthetics; Post*45; RaceReligion; Social Science History; Square One: First Order Questions in the Humanities; Stanford Business Classics; Stanford Nuclear Age Series; Stanford Series in Comparative Race and Ethnicity; Stanford Studies in Human Rights; Stanford Studies in Jewish History and Culture; Stanford Studies in Law and Politics; Stanford Studies in Middle Eastern and Islamic Societies and Cultures; Studies in Asian Security; Studies in Social Inequality; Studies in the Modern Presidency; Studies of the Weatherhead East Asian Institute; Studies of the Walter H. Shorenstein Asia-Pacific Research Center; Thinking Theory Now

Special imprints: Stanford Briefs; Stanford Business Books; Stanford Economics and Finance; Stanford Law Books, Stanford Security Studies; Stanford Social Sciences

State University of New York Press

22 Corporate Woods Boulevard, 3rd Floor
Albany, NY 12211-2504

Phone: 518.472.5000
Fax: 518.472.5038
E-mail: info@sunypress.edu
Indiv: firstname.lastname@sunypress.edu

<u>Website and Social Media:</u>
Website: www.sunypress.edu
Facebook: www.facebook.com/pages/
   SUNY-Press/112308762113504

<u>UK Representative:</u>
Andrew Gilman
University Presses Marketing

<u>Canadian Representative:</u>
Lexa Publishers' Representatives

<u>Customer Service:</u>
SUNY Press
PO Box 960
Herndon, VA 20172-0960
Phone: 703.661.1575
Toll free: 877.204.6073 (US only)
Fax: 703.996.1010
Toll free: 877.204.6074 (US only)
Email: suny@presswarehouse.com

<u>UK/European Distributor:</u>
NBN International

Staff

Co-Directors: Donna Dixon (518.641.0651); James Peltz (518.641.0668)
   Executive Assistant to the Co-Directors: Janice Vunk (518.641.0674)
   Receptionist: Diana Altobello (518.472.5000)
Acquisitions Editorial:
   Co-Director: James Peltz (518.641.0668) (Excelsior Editions, film studies, Italian American studies, Jewish studies)
   Senior Acquisitions Editors: Nancy Ellegate (518.641.0679) (Asian studies, religious studies, transpersonal psychology); Michael Rinella (518.641.0664) (African American studies, environmental studies, political science)
   Acquisitions Editors: Beth Bouloukos (518.641.0666) (education, Hispanic studies, women's and gender studies); Andrew Kenyon (518.641.0661) (philosophy)
   Assistant Acquisitions Editor: Amanda Lanne (518.641.0662) (New York State studies, native and indigenous studies)
   Editorial Assistants: Rafael Chaiken (518.641.0681); Jessica Kirschner (518.641.0658)
Production:
   Co-Director: Donna Dixon (518.641.0651) (journals)
   Senior Production Editors: Diane Ganeles (518.641.0678); Laurie Searl (518.641.0671); Eileen Nizer (518.641.0665)
   Senior Journals and Accelerated Publishing Editor: Ryan Morris (518.641.0667)
   Assistant Production Editor: Jenn Bennett (518.641.0647)
   Production Assistant: Emily Keneston (518.641.0669)
Marketing and Publicity:
   Director of Marketing and Publicity: Fran Keneston (518.641.0660)
   Executive Promotions Manager: Anne Valentine (518.641.0673)
   Senior Promotions Manager: Michael Campochiaro (518.641.0680)

Exhibits and Awards Manager: Michelle Alamillo (518.641.0677)
Promotions Manager: Kate McDonnell (518.641.0663)
Revenue and Business Operations:
  Associate Director-Revenue and Business Operations: Dan Flynn (518.641.0676)
  Accounting Manager: Sharla Clute (518.641.0653)
  Sales Assistant: Renee Jones (518.641.0659)
  Digital Programs Manager: Greg Smith (518.641.0672)
Digital Programs Coordinator: Paula Weaver (518.641.0675)

Full Member

Established: 1966	Admitted to AAUP: 1970
Title output 2012: 143	Title output 2013: 146
Titles currently in print: 5,281	Journals published: 7

Editorial Program

Scholarly titles and serious works of general interest in many areas of the humanities and the social sciences, with special interest in African American studies; Asian studies; education; gender studies; Hispanic studies; native and indigenous studies; philosophy; political science; psychology; queer studies; religious studies; transpersonal psychology; and women's and gender studies.

SUNY Press distributes books from the Albany Institute of History and Art, Codhill Press, Global Academic Publishing, Hudson River Valley National Heritage Area, Mount Ida Press, Muswell Hill Press, New Netherland Institute, Parks & Trails New York, Rockefeller Institute Press, Samuel Dorsky Museum and the Uncrowned Queens Institute.

Journals: *AUDEM*; *Binghamton Journal of Philosophy*; *International Journal of Servant-Leadership*; *The Journal of Japanese Philosophy*; *Mediaevalia*; *Palimpsest*; *philoSOPHIA*
Imprints: Excelsior Editions

Syracuse University Press

621 Skytop Road, Suite 110
Syracuse, NY 13244-5290

Phone: 315.443.5534
Fax: 315.443.5545
Email: (user I.D.)@syr.edu

Website and Social Media:
Website: syracuseuniversitypress.syr.edu
Blog: syracusepress.wordpress.com/
Facebook: www.facebook.com/pages/
  Syracuse-University-Press/224301261901
Twitter: twitter.com/supress

Canadian Distributor:
Scholarly Book Services, Inc.

Warehouse:
Maple Press Company
Lebanon Distribution Center
704 Legionnaire Drive
Fredericksburg, PA 17026

Orders:
Longleaf Services
Phone: 800.848.6224
Fax: 800.272.6817

UK Distributor:
Eurospan

Staff
Director: Alice R. Pfeiffer (315.443.5535; email: arpfeiff)
  Office Coordinator: Erica Sheftic (315.443.5541; email: esheftic)
Acquisitions Editorial: Suzanne E. Guiod, Editor-in-Chief (315.443.5539; email: seguiod)
  Acquisitions Editors: Jennika Baines (315.443.5647; email: jsbaines); Deanna McCay (315.443.5543; email: dhmccay)
  Editorial Assistant: Kelly Balenske (315.443.5541; email: klbalens)
Editorial and Production Manager: Kay Steinmetz (315.443.9155; email: kasteinm)
  Senior Designers: Victoria Lane (315.443.5540; email: vmlane); Fred Wellner (315.443.5540; email: fawellne)
  Editorial & Production Assistant: Marcia Hough (315.443.5542; email: mshough)
  Editorial Assistant: Ruthnie Angrand (315.443.5544; email: rangrand)
Marketing: Mona Hamlin, Marketing Analyst (315.443.5547; email: mhamlin)
  Design Specialist: Lynn Wilcox (315.443.1975; email: lphoppel)
  Marketing Coordinator: Lisa Kuerbis (315.443.5546; email: lkuerbis)
Business: Karen Lockwood, Senior Business Manager (315.443.5536; email: kflockwo)
  Customer Service Liaison: Lori Lazipone (315.443.5538; email: ljlazipo)

Full Member
Established: 1943   Admitted to AAUP: 1946
Title output 2012: 47   Title output 2013: 47
Titles currently in print: 1,623

Editorial Program
Scholarly books and works of general interest in the areas of Middle East, Irish, Jewish, New York State, women's, Native American, ethnic, and disability studies; religion; television; popular culture; sports history; journalism; human and urban geography; politics; peace and conflict resolution; and selected fiction.

The Press distributes books bearing the imprints of Adirondack Museum; Moshe Dayan Center for Middle Eastern and African Studies (Tel-Aviv University); New Netherlands Project; Jusoor; National Library of Ireland; Arlen House; Dedalus Press; Blackhall Publishing; NUI Galway, Women's Studies Centre; Litteraria Pragensia; Ethnic Heritage Studies Center of Utica College; New City Community Press; Syracuse University In Florence; Graduate School Press; Syracuse University; Point of Contact; Syracuse University; and the Pucker Gallery, Boston.

Special series, joint imprints, and/or copublishing programs: The Adirondack Museum; The Albert Schweitzer Library; America in the Twentieth Century; Arab-American Writing; Contemporary Issues in the Middle East; Critical Perspectives on Disability; Gender, Culture, and Politics in the Middle East; Gender and Globalization; Irish Studies; Iroquois and Their Neighbors; Judaic Traditions in Literature, Music, and Art; Library of Modern Jewish Literature; The Martin Buber Library; Medieval Studies; Middle East Beyond Dominant Paradigms; Middle East Literature in Translation; Modern Intellectual and Political History of the Middle East; Modern Jewish History; Mohamad El-Hindi Books on Arab Culture and Islamic Civilization; New York State Studies; Religion and Politics; Religion, Theology and the Holocaust; Space, Place, and Society; Sports and Entertainment; Syracuse Studies in Geography; Syracuse Studies in Peace and Conflict Resolution; Television and Popular Culture; Women in Religion; Writing American Women

Teachers College Press

1234 Amsterdam Avenue
New York, NY 10027-6696

Phone: 212.678.3929
Fax: 212.678.4149
Email: (user I.D.)@tc.edu
(unless otherwise indicated)

Orders:
Teachers College Press
PO Box 20
Williston, VT 05495-0020
Phone: 800.575.6560
Fax: 802.864.7626

Website and Social Media:
Website: www.tcpress.com
Facebook: www.facebook.com/TCPress
Twitter: TCPress

European Representative:
Eurospan

Canadian Representative:
University of Toronto Press

Staff

Director: Carole Pogrebin Saltz (212.678.3927; email: saltz)
  Assistant to the Director: Laura Popovics (212.678.3965; email: popovics)
  Rights and Permissions Manager/Special Sales Coordinator: Christina Brianik
  (212.678.3827; email: brianik)
Acquisitions Editorial: Brian Ellerbeck, Executive Acquisitions Editor (administration, school
  change, leadership, policy, special and gifted education, multicultural education, teacher
  research, curriculum studies) (212.678.3908; email: ellerbeck)
  Senior Acquisitions Editor: Marie Ellen Larcada (early childhood education, sociology,
  educational research, school reform, higher education) (212.678.3928; email: larcada)
  Acquisitions Editor: Emily Spangler (language and literacy, technology and education)
  (212.678.3909; email: spangler)
  Consulting Senior Acquisitions Editor: Jean Ward (curriculum, professional development,
  literacy) (847.224.02785; email: ward)
  Assistant Acquisitions Editor: Noelle De-La-Paz (212.678.3905; email: de-la-paz)
Production: Michael Weinstein, Production Manager (212.678.3926; email: weinstein)
  Senior Production Editor: Karl Nyberg (212.678.3806; email: nyberg)
  Production Editors: Aureliano Vazquez (212.678.3945; email: vasquez); Lori Tate
  (212.678.3907; email: tate); John Bylander (212.678.3914; email: bylander); Jennifer
  Baker (212.678.3902; email: baker)
  Production Assistants: Debra Jackson-Whyte (212.678.3926; email: jackson-whyte)
Marketing: Leyli Shayegan, Director, Sales and Marketing and Assistant Director
  (212.678.3475; email: shayegan)
  Marketing Manager: Nancy Power (212.678.3915; email: power)
  Graphic Arts Manager: David Strauss (212.678.3982; email: strauss)
  Publicity Coordinator: Emily Renwick (212.678.3963; email: renwick)
  Outreach Coordinator: Michael McGann (212.678.3919; email: mcgann)
Business: TBA, Financial Controller (212.678.3913)
  Secretary/Receptionist: Marcia Ruiz (212.678.3929; email: myr3@columbia.edu)

Full Member

Established: 1904   Admitted to AAUP: 1971
Title output 2012: 66   Title output 2013: 767
Titles currently in print: 767

Editorial Program

Scholarly, professional, text, and trade books on education, education-related areas, and parenting. Multimedia instructional materials, tests, and evaluation materials for classroom use at all levels of education.

Specific areas of interest in education are: curriculum; early childhood; school administration and educational policy; counseling; mathematics; philosophy; psychology; language and literacy; multicultural education; science; sociology; special education; social justice; social studies; teacher education; cultural studies; technology and education; women and higher education.

Special series: Advances in Contemporary Educational Thought; Between Teacher & Text; Counseling and Development; Critical Issues in Educational Leadership; Disability, Culture, and Equity; Early Childhood Education; Education and Psychology of the Gifted; International Perspectives on Education Reform; John Dewey Lecture; Language and Literacy; Multicultural Education; Practitioner Inquiry; Professional Ethics in Education; Reflective History; The Series on School Reform; Teaching for Social Justice; Technology, Education—Connections (TEC); Ways of Knowing in Science and Mathematics

Temple University Press

Mailing Address:
TASB
1852 N. 10th Street
Philadelphia, PA 19122

Street Address:
TASB
2450 West Hunting Park Avenue
Philadelphia, PA 19129

Phone: 215.926.2140
Fax: 215.926.2141
Email: firstname.lastname@temple.edu

Orders:
Chicago Distribution Center
11030 South Langley Avenue
Chicago, IL 60628
Phone: 800.621.2736
Fax: 800.621.8471

Website and Social Media:
Website: www.temple.edu/tempress
Blog: templepress.wordpress.com
Facebook: www.facebook.com/pages/
   Temple-University-Press/21638877349
Twitter: TempleUnivPress

UK Distributor:
Combined Academic Publishers

Canadian Distributor:
Lexa Publishers' Representatives

Staff

Director: Alex Holzman (215.926.2145)
Rights and Permissions: Sara Cohen (215.926.2146)

Electronic Publishing Manager: Barry Adams (215.926.2150)
Acquisitions: Janet M. Francendese, Assistant Director (215.926.2144)
   Senior Editor: Micah Kleit (215.926.2157)
   Assistant Editor: Sara Cohen (215.926.2146)
Production: Charles H. E. Ault, Assistant Director and Director of Production and
   Electronic Publishing (215.926.2142)
   Senior Production Editor: Joan Vidal (215.926.2148)
   Production Coordinator/Designer: Kate Nichols (215.926.2167)
Marketing: Ann-Marie Anderson, Assistant Director and Director of Marketing
   (215.926.2143)
   Advertising and Promotion Manager: Irene Imperio (215.926.2153)
   Publicity Manager: Gary Kramer (215.926.2154)
Business: Barry Adams, Assistant Director and Financial Manager (215.926.2150)
   Customer Service/Operations Manager: Karen Baker (215.926.2156)

Full Member

Established: 1969	Admitted to AAUP: 1972
Title output 2012: 57	Title output 2013: 45
Titles currently in print: 1,360	

Editorial Program

African American studies; American studies; anthropology; Asian studies; Asian American studies; cinema and media studies; communication; criminology; disability studies; education; ethnicity and race; gay and lesbian studies; gender studies; geography; health; labor studies; Latin American studies; law and society; Philadelphia regional studies; political science and public policy; religion; sociology; sports; urban studies; US and European history; women's studies.

Temple University Press distributes books for the Asian American Writers' Workshop.

Special series: America in Transition: Radical Perspectives; American Subjects; Animals, Culture, and Society; Asian American History and Culture; Critical Perspectives on the Past; Emerging Media; Gender, Family, and the Law; Labor in Crisis; Mapping Racisms; The New Academy; Place, Culture, and Politics; Politics, History, and Social Change; Queer Politics, Queer Theories; Rhetoric, Culture, and Public Address; Sound Matters; Studies in Latin American and Caribbean Music; Teaching/Learning Social Justice; Voices of Latin American Life; Wide Angle Books

University of Tennessee Press

Mailing Address:
110 Conference Center
Knoxville, TN 37996-4108

Shipping Address:
600 Henley Street
Suite 110 Conference Center
Knoxville, TN 37902-2911

Phone: 865.974.3321
Fax: 865.974.3724
Email: custserv@utpress.org
Indiv: (user I.D.)@utk.edu

Orders:
Chicago Distribution Center
11030 South Langley Ave.
Chicago, IL 60628
Phone: 800.621.2736
Fax: 773.702.7212

Website and Social Media:
Website: utpress.org
Blog: utpress.org/utpressblog
Facebook page: www.facebook.com/pages/
   University-of-Tennessee-Press/80814711590?ref=ts
Twitter: utennpress

Staff
Director: Scot Danforth (email: danforth)
Acquisitions Editorial: Kerry Webb (email: webbke)
   Editorial Assistant: Thomas Wells (email: twells)
   Production Coordinator: Stephanie Thompson (email: sthomp20)
Marketing: Cheryl Carson, Manager (email: ccarson3)
Exhibits/Publicity Manager: Tom Post (email: tpost)
Business: Lisa Davis, Manager (email: ldavis49)
   Receptionist/Bookkeeper: Linsey Sims (email: lsims9)
IT Manager: Jake Sumner (email: jsumner2)

Full Member
Established: 1940
Title output 2012: 33
Titles currently in print: 825

Admitted to AAUP: 1964
Title output 2013: 38

Editorial Program
American studies; Appalachian studies; African American studies; history; religion; folklore; vernacular architecture; historical archaeology; material culture; literature; and literary fiction. Submissions in poetry, textbooks, and translations are not invited.
Special series, joint imprints, and/or copublishing programs: Appalachian Echoes; Charles K. Wolfe American Music Series; Correspondence of James K. Polk; Legacies of War, Outdoor Tennessee; The Papers of Andrew Jackson; Sport and Popular Culture; Tennessee Studies in Literature; Vernacular Architecture Studies; Voices of the Civil War; and The Western Theater in the Civil War

University of Texas Press

Street Address:
2100 Comal Street
STOP E4800
Austin, TX 78712-1303

Mailing Address:
PO Box 7819
Austin, TX 78713-7819

Phone: 512.471.7233
Fax: 512.232.7178
Email: info@utpress.utexas.edu
Indiv: firstinitiallastname@utpress.utexas.edu

Orders:
Phone: 800.252.3206
Fax: 800.687.6046

Website and Social Media:
Website: www.utexaspress.com
Blog: utpressnews.blogspot.com/
Facebook: www.facebook.com/utexaspress
Twitter: UTexasPress

Staff

Director: David Hamrick (512.232.7604)
  Assistant to the Director: Allison Faust (512.232.7603)
Assistant Director and Rights and Permissions Manager: John McLeod (512.232.7605)
  Rights and Permissions Assistant: Peggy Gough (512.232.7624)
Editor-in-Chief: Robert Devens (American studies, art, photography, Texas history) (512.232.7615)
  Senior Editor: Jim Burr (humanities) (512.232.7610)
  Acquisitions Editors: Casey Kittrell (music, natural history, environmental studies, food culture) (512.232.7616); TBA (Latin American studies, social sciences)
  Editorial Assistants: Angie Lopez, Sarah Rosen (512.232.7608)
Managing Editor: Leslie Tingle (512.232.7614)
  Manuscript Editors: Lynne Chapman (512.232.7607); Bruce Bethell (512.232.7688)
  Assistant Manuscript Editor: Molly Frisinger (512.475.9187)
Design & Production Manager: Ellen McKie (512.232.7640)
  Designers: Derek George (512.232.7642); Lindsay Starr (512.232.7641)
  Production Editor: Regina Fuentes (512.232.7639)
  Production Coordinator: Kaila Wyllys (512.232.7637)
  Production Assistant: Andy Sieverman (512.232.7638)
  Production Fellow: Angie Calderon (512.232.7643)
Marketing and Communications Manager: Brady Dyer (512.232.7627)
  Assistant Marketing Manager: Nancy Bryan (512.232.7628)
  Digital Publishing Manager: Sharon Casteel (512.232.7631)
  Publicist: Victoria Davis (512.232.7634)
  Advertising and Exhibits Manager: Christopher Farmer (512.232.7630)
  Marketing Assistant: Brian Contine (512.232.7633)
Sales Manager: Gianna LaMorte (512.832.9111)
  Sales Representative: Chris Hoyt (512.232.7632)

Assistant Director and Journals Manager: Sue Hausmann (512.232.7620)
  Journals Production Coordinators: Karen Broyles (512.232.7622); Stacey Salling (512.232.7622)
  Journals Marketing and Advertising Coordinator: Sheila Scoville (512.232.7618)
  Journals Circulation and Rights and Permissions Manager: Rebecca Frazier (512.232.7617)
  Journals Customer Service: Elizabeth Fairman (512.232.7621)
Assistant Director and Financial Officer: Joyce Lewandowski (512.232.7646)
  Accounts Receivable: Allie Lambert (512.232.7602)
  Royalties Accountant: Kristin Duvall (512.232.7648)
  Accounts Payable Manager: Linda Ramirez (512.232.7649)
  Office Manager: Andrea Prestridge (512.232.7647)
  Customer Service Supervisor: Brenda Jo Hoggatt (512.232.7650)
  Customer Service Assistant: Dawn Bishop (512.232.7652)
Warehouse (512.471.3634)
  Warehouse Supervisor: George Mill (512.232.7654)
  Warehouse Staff: Rogelio Rocha Jr. (512.232.7658); Rey Renteria (512.232.7655); Paul Guerra (512.232.7657)
Information Systems Manager: William Bishel (512.232.7609)
  Website and Digital Marketing Coordinator: Bailey Morrison (512.471.1728)

Full Member

Established: 1950   Admitted to AAUP: 1954
Title output 2012: 95   Title output 2013: 103
Titles currently in print: 2,000   Journals published: 11

Editorial Program

American music, American studies, anthropology, applied language, architecture, art, Chicano/a studies, classics and the ancient world, conservation, cookbooks and gardening, Egyptology, environmental studies, film and media studies, fine art and documentary photography, food studies, Jewish studies, Latin American and pre-Columbian studies, Latina/o studies, literary modernism, Middle Eastern studies and translations of Middle Eastern literature, natural history, New and Old World archaeology, ornithology, Texas and the Southwest, and women's studies. Original fiction, poetry, and children's books are not invited.

The Press distributes publications for the Jack S. Blanton Museum of Art; Center for Mexican American Studies; Center for Middle Eastern Studies; Dolph Briscoe Center for American History; Harry Ransom Center; and Teresa Lozano Long Institute of Latin American Studies.

Journals: *Archaeoastronomy; Asian Music; Cinema Journal; The Journal of Individual Psychology; Journal of Latin American Geography for the Conference of Latin Americanist Geographers; The Journal of the History of Sexuality; Latin American Music Review; Studies in Latin American Popular Culture; Information and Culture; Texas Studies in Literature and Language; The Velvet Light Trap*

Special series, joint imprints, and/or copublishing programs: American Music; Center for Creative Photography; Center for Mexican American Studies History, Culture, and Society; Center for Middle Eastern Studies (CMES) Binah Yitzrit Foundation Series in Israel Studies; CMES Emerging Voices from the Middle East; CMES Modern Literatures in Translation; CMES Modern Middle East; Chicana Matters; Cognitive Approaches to Literature and Culture; Discovering America; Focus on American History; Handbook of Latin American Studies; Harry Ransom Humanities Research Center (HRC) Imprint; HRC Photography; Inter-America; Literary Modernism; Teresa Lozano Long Institute of Latin American Studies (LLILAS) New Interpretations of Latin America; LLILAS Translations from Latin America; Oratory of Classical Greece; Schusterman Center for Jewish Studies; Southwestern Writers Collection; Texas Field Guides; Texas Archaeology and Ethnohistory; Texas Film and Media Studies; Wittliff Gallery Series of Southwestern and Mexican Photography

Endowed book series: Ashley and Peter Larkin Series in Greek and Roman Culture; Bill and Alice Wright Photography Series; Brad and Michele Moore Roots Music Series; Bridwell Texas History Series; Charles N. Prothro Texana Series; Clifton and Shirley Caldwell Texas Heritage Series; The Corrie Herring Hooks Series; Ellen and Edward Randall Series; Jack and Doris Smothers Series in Texas History, Life, and Culture; Jamal and Rania Daniel Series in Contemporary History, Politics, Culture, and Religion of the Levant; Jess and Betty Jo Hay Series; Jewish History, Life, and Culture; Joe R. and Teresa Lozano Long Series in Latin American and Latino Art and Culture; Linda Schele Series in Maya and Pre-Columbian Studies; Louann Atkins Temple Women and Culture Series; M. Georgia Hegarty Dunkerley Contemporary Art Series; Mildred Wyatt-Wold Series in Ornithology; Peter T. Flawn Series in Natural Resources; Roger Fullington Series in Architecture; Terry and Jan Todd Series on Physical Culture and Sports; William and Bettye Nowlin Series in Art, History, and Culture of the Western Hemisphere

Texas A&M University Press

Street Address:
John H. Lindsey Building, Lewis Street
College Station, TX 77843

Mailing Address:
4354 TAMU
College Station, TX 77843-4354

Phone: 979.845.1436
Fax: 979.847.8752
Email: upress@tamu.edu
Indiv: (user I.D.)@tamu.edu

Orders:
Phone: 800.826.8911
Fax: 888.617.2421
Email: bookorders@tamu.edu

Website and Social Media:
Website: www.tamupress.com
Blog: tamupress.blogspot.com/
Facebook: www.facebook.com/tamupress
Twitter: TAMUPress
YouTube: www.youtube.com/user/TAMUPressConsortium

European Representative:
Eurospan

Staff

Press Director: Charles Backus (979.458.3980; email: charles.backus)

Acquisitions Editorial: Shannon Davies, Editor-in-Chief (natural history & natural sciences; agriculture; gardening & horticulture; conservation & the environment) (979.458.3976; email: sdavies)

Senior Acquisitions Editor: TBA (Texas and Western history, military history, borderland studies, presidential studies, anthropology, archaeology) (979.845.0759)

Acquisitions Assistant: Katie Cowart (979.458.3975; email: katie.cowart)

Manuscript Editorial: Thom Lemmons, Managing Editor (Texas music) (979.845.0758; email: thom.lemmons)

Assistant Editor: Patricia Clabaugh (979.458.3979; email: pclabaugh)

Design/Production: Mary Ann Jacob, Design & Production Manager (979.845.3694; email: m-jacob)

Assistant Design and Production Manager: Kevin Grossman (979.458.3995; email: k-grossman)

Marketing: Gayla Christiansen, Marketing Manager (979.845.0148; email: gayla-c)

Publicity and Advertising Manager: Holli Koster (979.458.3982; email: holli.koster)

Promotional Design and Electronic Marketing Manager: Kyle Littlefield (979.458.3983; email: k-littlefield)

Marketing Communications and Exhibit Manager: Kathryn Krol (979.458.3984; email: k-krol)

Sales Manager: David Neel (979.458.3981; email: d-neel)

Financial Manager: Dianna Sells (979.845.0146; email: d-sells)

Business Operations Manager: Sharon Pavlas-Mills (979.458.3994; email: sharon-mills)

Accounts Receivable Manager: Wynona McCormick (979.845.0136; email: wynona)

Order Fulfillment Supervisor: Christin Wuensche (979.458.3991; email: christin.wuensche)

Warehouse Manager: Mike Martin (979.458.3986; email: mike.martin)

Assistant Warehouse Manager: Cliff O'Connell (979.458.3987; email: c-oconnell)

Full Member

Established: 1974

Admitted to AAUP: 1977

Title output 2012: 64

Title output 2013: 66

Titles currently in print: 1,251

Editorial Program

American and Western history; natural history; the environment; agriculture; natural resource science; nautical archaeology; women's studies; military history; business; architecture; art; veterinary medicine; presidential studies; borderland studies; Texas and the Southwest. Submissions are not invited in poetry or fiction.

Special series: AgriLife Research and Extension; Brannen Series in Military Studies; Centennial Series of the Association of Former Students; Dickson Series in Texas Music; Fay Series in Analytical Psychology; Foreign Relations and the Presidency; Environmental History; Gulf Coast Books; Harte Research Institute for Gulf of Mexico Studies; Hughes Presidency and Leadership Studies; Library of Presidential Rhetoric; Lindsey Series in the Arts and Humanities; Meadows Center for Water & the Environment; Moore Texas

Art; Merrick Natural Environment; Montague Business and Oil History; Moody Natural History; Peoples and Cultures of Texas; Perspectives on South Texas; Presidential Rhetoric and Political Communication; Prothro Texas Photography; Rachal Foundation Series in Nautical Archaeology; Red River Valley Books; Rio Grande/Rio Bravo; Sam Rayburn Rural Life; Spencer Series in the West and Southwest; Tarleton State University Southwestern Studies in the Humanities; Texas A&M Agriculture; Texas A&M Economics; Texas A&M University Anthropology; University of Houston Mexican American Studies; Wardlaw Books; West Texas A&M University; Williams-Ford Series in Military History; Williams Texas Life

TCU Press

Mailing Address:
Box 298300
Fort Worth, TX 76129

Street Address:
3000 Sandage
Fort Worth, TX 76109

Phone: 817.257.7822
Fax: 817.257.5075

Orders:
Phone: 800.826.8911

Website and Social Media:
Website: www.prs.tcu.edu
Facebook: www.facebook.com/pages/
   Fort-Worth-TX/TCU-PRESS/291943790611

Staff
Director Dan Williams (email: d.e.williamms@tcu.edu)
Editor: Susan Petty (email: s.petty@tcu.edu)
Production Manager: Melinda Esco (email: m.esco@tcu.edu)

Full Member
Established: 1966
Title output 2012: NR
Titles currently in print: 376

Admitted to AAUP: 1982
Title output 2013: NR

Editorial Program
Humanities and social sciences, with special emphasis on Texas and Southwestern history and literature; American studies; fiction; and women's studies.
Special series: Chaparral Books for Young Readers; The Chisholm Trail Series; Literary Cities; The Texas Tradition Series; The Texas Biography Series; TCU Texas Poets Laureate; Texas Small Books

Texas Tech University Press

Street Address:
Media and Communication Building
9th Floor
3003 15th Street
Lubbock, TX 79409-1037

Phone: 806.742.2982
Fax: 806.742.2979
Email: firstname.lastname@ttu.edu

Website and Social Media:
Website: www.ttupress.org
Facebook: www.facebook.com/pages/
   Lubbock-TX/Texas-Tech-University-Press/
   46737328830
Twitter: TTUPress

Mailing Address:
Box 41037
Lubbock, TX 79409-1037

Orders:
Chicago Distribution Center
11030 South Langley Ave.
Chicago, IL 60628
Phone: 800.621.2736; 773.702.7010;
International 773. 702.7000
Fax: 800.621.8476
International fax: 773.702.7212

UK and European Distributor:
Eurospan

Staff
Director: Robert Mandel
   Editor/Assistant to the Director: Karen M. Clark
Acquisitions: Joanna Conrad, Assistant Director and Editor-in-Chief
Managing Editor: TBA
Design and Production Manager: Kasey McBeath
Marketing Coordinators: John Brock, Jada Rankin
Office Manager: Isabel Williams
   Customer Service: LaTisha Roberts

Full Member

Established: 1971
Title output 2012: 29
Titles currently in print: 415

Admitted to AAUP: 1987
Title output 2013: 28
Journals published: 4

Editorial Program

American liberty and justice; costume and textile studies; history and culture of Texas and the West, the Great Plains, and modern Southeast Asia during and after the Vietnam War; Jewish studies and literature; Latin American and Latino fiction; natural history and natural science; poetry (by invitation only); fiction and nonfiction for young readers; and sport in the American West.

Journals: *Conradiana*; *Helios*; *Intertexts*; *The William Carlos Williams Review*

Special series: American Liberty and Justice; The Americas; Costume Society of America; Grover E. Murray Studies in the American Southwest; Modern Jewish History; Modern Jewish Literature and Culture; Modern Southeast Asia; Modern Southeast Asian Literature; Plains Histories; Sport in the American West; Walt McDonald First-Book Series in Poetry; Voice in the American West; Women, Gender, and the West

University of Tokyo Press

4-5-29 Komaba, Meguro-ku
Tokyo 153-0041, Japan

US Representative:
Columbia University Press

Phone: +81-3-6407-1921, +81-3-6407-1904
Fax: + +81-3-6407-1582, +81-3-6407-1991
Email: info@utp.or.jp

Staff

President: Junichi Hamada
Chairman of the Board: Hiroshi Watanabe
Managing Director: Takuya Kuroda (email: kuroda@utp.or.jp)
Editorial Director: Mika Komatsu
Marketing Director: Hiroki Hashimoto
Production Director: Hiroshi Takagi
Editor-in-Chief & International Liaisons Executive: Kensuke Goto
(email: gauteau@utp.or.jp)

International Member

Established: 1951
Title output 2012: 124
Titles currently in print: 4,600

Admitted to AAUP: 1970
Title output 2013: 130

Editorial Program

Titles published in Japanese reflect the research carried out at the university in the humanities, social sciences, and natural sciences. Continuing series are published in biology, earth sciences, sociology, economics, philosophy, and Japanese art and historical studies. Special projects include publication of textbooks and reprinting of historical source materials.

English-language publishing began in 1960; special strengths include Japanese and Asian studies (including art, history, economics, law, and sociology). English-language publications also include translations of historical and important literary works and diaries.

University of Toronto Press

Scholarly Publishing Division:
10 St. Mary Street, Suite 700
Toronto, ON M4Y 2W8 Canada
Phone: 416.978.2239
Fax: 416.978.4738
Email: publishing@utpress.utoronto.ca

Journals Division:
5201 Dufferin Street
North York, ON M3H 5T8 Canada
Phone: 416.667.7810
Fax: 416.667.7881; 800.221.9985
Email: journals@utpress.utoronto.ca

Higher Education Division:
199 Woolwich Street, 2nd Floor
Guelph, ON N1H 3V4 Canada
Phone: 519.837.1403
Fax: 519.767.1643
Email: requests@highereducation.com

UTP Distribution Centre:
5201 Dufferin Street
North York, ON M3H 5T8 Canada
Phone: 416.667.7791; 800.565.9523
Fax: 416.667.7832; 800.221.9985
Email: utpbooks@utpress.utoronto.ca

P-Shift:
10 St Mary Street, Suite 700
Toronto, ON M4Y 2W8 Canada
Phone: 416.978.2239

Websites and Social Media:
Publishing: www.utppublishing.com
Blog: utpblog.utpress.utoronto.ca/
Journals: www.utpjournals.com
P-Shift: www.utpshift.com
Facebook: www.facebook.com/utpress; www.facebook.com/utpjournals
Twitter: utpress; utpjournals

UK Representative:
Oxford Publicity Partnership Ltd.
gary.hall@oppuk.co.uk

US Warehouse:
2250 Military Road
Tonawanda, NY 14150
Phone: 716.693.2768

UK/Europe Distribution:
NBN International

Staff

Administration
Indiv. email: firstinitiallastname@utpress.utoronto.ca
President, Publisher and CEO: John Yates (ext. 222)
Senior Vice President, HR & Administration: Kathryn Bennett (ext. 224)
Vice President, Finance: Shawn O'Grady (416.667.7765)
Scholarly Publishing
Indiv. email: firstinitiallastname@utpress.utoronto.ca
Vice President, Scholarly Publishing: Lynn Fisher (ext. 243)
Publishing Coordinator: Charley LaRose (ext. 237)
Permissions & Rights Coordinator: Lisa Jemison (ext. 226)

Acquisitions Editorial

Executive Editor: Suzanne Rancourt (classics, medieval, renaissance studies, Erasmus) (ext. 239)

Acquisitions Editors: Len Husband (Cdn history, native studies, philosophy) (ext. 238); Siobhan McMenemy (film, Cdn literature, cultural studies, book history, communications) (ext. 231); Richard Ratzlaff (history, literature, semiotics) (ext. 233); Daniel Quinlan (political science & law) (ext. 254); Jennifer DiDomenico (business & economics) (ext. 259); Doug Hildebrand (anthropology, education, geography, sociology, urban studies (ext. 251); Eric Carlson (social work, medicine & health) (ext. 230)

Manuscript Editorial & Production

Managing Editor: Anne Laughlin (ext. 236)

Production Manager: Ani Deyirmenjian (ext. 227)

Electronic Publishing

Electronic Publishing Coordinator: Barry Miekle (ext. 232)

Sales & Marketing

Sales and Marketing Manager: Brian MacDonald (ext. 253)

Publicist: Chris Reed (ext. 248)

Advertising, Journal Review Coordinator: Deepshikha Dutta (ext. 247)

Sales & Electronic Marketing Coordinator: Taylor Berry (ext. 250)

Catalogue & Copy Coordinator: Stephen Shapiro (ext. 257)

Exhibits & Examination Copies Coordinator: Elizabeth Glenn (ext. 260)

Data & Web Coordinator: Bob Currer (ext. 249)

Journals (5201 Dufferin St.)

Indiv. email: firstinitiallastname@utpress.utoronto.ca

Vice-President, Journals: Anne Marie Corrigan (416.667.7838)

Editorial Manager, Journals: Sylvia Hunter (416.667.7777 ext. 7806)

Supervisor, Circulation & Distribution: Adele D'Ambrosio (416.667.7777 ext. 7781)

Permissions Coordinator, Journals: Carrie MacMillan (416.667.7777 ext. 7849)

Advertising and Marketing Coordinator: Audrey Greenwood (416.667.7777 ext. 7766)

Higher Education

Indiv. email: @utpress.utoronto.ca

Vice President: Michael Harrison (519.837.1403 ext. 222; email: mharrison)

Acquisitions: Anne Brackenbury, Executive Editor (anthropology; sociology; social work; education; development studies; environmental studies; women's studies; indigenous studies; Latin American studies & Canadian & North American studies) (416.537.0847; email: brackenbury)

Editor: Natalie Fingerhut (history, Medieval & Renaissance studies; religious studies; international political science) (416.922.2171; email: fingerhut)

Assistant Editor: Megan Pickard (519.837.1403 ext. 227; email: mpickard)

Sales & Marketing

Marketing Manager: Anna Del Col (519.837.1403 ext. 224; email: adelcol)

Sales Manager: Michelle Lobkowicz (519.837.1403 ext. 231; email: mlobkowicz)

Senior Publisher's Representative and ebook Sales: Mat Buntin (519.837.1403 ext. 223; email: mbuntin)

Production & Editorial: Beate Schwirtlich, Production Editor (519.837.1403 ext. 228; email: bschwirtlich)

P-Shift

Using Word files, P-Shift generates XML code within your manuscript that marks key information, validates and crosschecks references, and properly formats your document to give you an active, user-friendly file. It is then all easily stored and accessed in our data asset management system.

President, Publisher & CEO: John Yates (416.978.2239 ext. 222 email: jyates@utpress. utoronto.ca)

UTP Distribution Centre
Indiv email: firstinitiallastname@utpress.utoronto.ca
Vice President, Distribution & MIS: Hamish Cameron (416.667.7773)
  Manager, Client Publisher Services: Carol Trainor (416.667.7845)
  Credit Manager: Clive Williams (416.667.7774)

Full Member

Established: 1901	Admitted to AAUP: 1937
Title output 2012: 175	Title output 2013: 179
Titles currently in print: 3,800	Journals published: 37

Editorial Program

Scholarly books, serious non-fiction, course books and books for business professionals with a particular focus on: Business & economics; classical studies; medieval studies; renaissance studies; Slavic studies; environmental studies; Erasmian studies; Victorian studies; english literature; Canadian studies; North American Studies; Canadian literature; cultural studies; literary theory and criticism; modern languages and literatures; philosophy; political science; law and criminology; religion and theology; education; Canadian and international history; history of science and medicine; sociology; anthropology; gender studies; Native studies; social work; geography; urban studies; and women's studies. Submissions are not invited in poetry or fiction.

Higher Education: The aim at UTP Higher Education is to publish materials in History and the social sciences, (notably Anthropology, Politics, Sociology, Environmental Studies, Indigenous Studies, Canadian and North American Studies, Women's Studies, History of Science, Medieval Studies and Social Work) for course use that are pedagogically valuable and that also contribute to ongoing scholarship. Higher Education provides an alternative to larger textbook publishers, both for instructors looking for a refreshing change from the standard course book offerings and for potential authors who value creative and editorial licence as well as the personal attention provided by our editors. The possibilities for rethinking how texts can be used in the classroom, along with new formats for their delivery, are endless, and UTP Higher Education looks to partner with instructors and scholars in this innovative endeavour.

Journals: *Anthropologica*; *ArsMedica*; *Canadian Historical Review*; *Canadian Journal of Criminology and Criminal Justice*; *Canadian Journal of Human Sexuality*; *Canadian Journal of Information and Library Sciences*; *Canadian Journal of Linguistics*; *Canadian Journal of Mathematics*; *Canadian Journal of Program Evaluation*; *Canadian Journal of Women and the Law*; *Canadian Mathematical Bulletin*; *Canadian Modern Language Review*; *Canadian Public Policy*; *Canadian Review of American Studies*; *Canadian Theatre Review*; *Cartographica*; *Diaspora: A Journal of Transnational Studies*; *Eighteenth Century Fiction*; *Histoire Sociale*; *INFOR Information Systems and Operational Research*; *International Journal of Canadian Studies*; *Journal of Canadian Studies*; *Journal of Religion and Popular Culture*, *Journal of*

Scholarly Publishing; Journal of Veterinary Medical Education; Lexicons of Early Modern English; Modern Drama; Physiotherapy Canada; Rotman International Journal of Pension Management; Seminar; The Tocqueville Review; Toronto Journal of Theology; Ultimate Reality and Meaning; University of Toronto Law Journal; University of Toronto Quarterly; Yearbook of Comparative and General Literature

Special series, joint imprints and/or copublishing programs: Rotman-UTP Publishing Imprint. New series include: The Munk Series on Global Affairs; UTP Insights; and Innovation, Creativity, and Governance in Canadian City-Regions, Ongoing series include: Anthropological Horizons; Asian Canadian Studies; Benjamin Disraeli Letters; Business & Sustainability Series; Canadian Cinema; Canadian Social History Series; Collected Works of Bernard Lonergan; Collected Works of Erasmus; Collected Works of Northrop Frye; Cultural Spaces; Dictionary of Canadian Biography; Digital Futures; Erasmus Studies; European Union Studies; Frye Studies; IPAC Series in Public Management and Governance; Japan and Global Society; Joanne Goodman Lectures; The Kenneth Michael Tanenbaum Series in Jewish Studies; Lonergan Studies; Lorenzo DaPonte Italian Library; Medieval Academy Books; Medieval Academy Reprints for Teaching; New Studies in Phenomenology and Hermeneutics; Osgoode Society for Canadian Legal History; Phoenix Supplementary Volumes; Renaissance Society of America Reprint Texts; Robson Classical Lectures; Selected Correspondence of Bernard Shaw; Studies in Book and Print Culture; Studies in Comparative Political Economy and Public Policy; Studies in Gender and History; Themes in Canadian History; Toronto Anglo Saxon Series; Toronto Iberic; Toronto Italian Studies; Toronto Old Norse-Icelandic Series; Toronto Studies in Medieval Law; Toronto Studies in Philosophy; Toronto Studies in Semiotics and Communication; UCLA Clark Memorial Library Series; University of Toronto Romance Series.

Higher Education: Teaching Culture: UTP Ethnographies for the Classroom (see www.utpteachingculture.com); Readings in Medieval Civilizations and Cultures; Companions in Medieval History; Rethinking the Middle Ages; CHA/UTP International Themes and Issues (see www.utphistorymatters.com).

United States Institute of Peace Press

2301 Constitution Avenue, NW
Washington, DC 20037

Phone: 202.457.1700
Fax: 202.223.9320
Email: (user I.D)@usip.org

<u>Website and Social Media:</u>
Website: bookstore.usip.org
Facebook: United States Institute of Peace
Twitter: U.S. Inst. of Peace

<u>Orders:</u>
PO Box 605
Herndon, VA 20172
Phone: 800.868.8064; 703.661.1590
Fax: 703.661.1501
Email:
usipmail@presswarehouse.com

<u>UK/European Representative:</u>
University Presses Marketing

<u>Canadian Representative:</u>
Renouf Books

Staff
Director of Publications: Valerie Norville (202.429.4147; email: vnorville)
Managing Editor: Michelle Slavin (202.429.3821; email: mslavin)
Production Manager: Marie Marr (202.429.3815; email: mmarr)
Sales and Marketing Manager: Kay Hechler (202.429.3816; email: khechler)

Associate Member
Established: 1991
Title output 2012: 5
Titles currently in print: 183

Admitted to AAUP: 1993
Title output 2013: 8

Editorial Program
The Press publishes books that are based on work supported by the Institute. Created by Congress in 1984, the Institute is an independent, nonpartisan institution that works to prevent, mitigate, and resolve violent international conflicts. The Institute's publications range across the spectrum of international relations, including conflict prevention, management, and resolution; diplomacy and negotiation; human rights; mediation and facilitation; foreign policy; gender; ethnopolitics; political science; and religion and ethics.
Special series: Academy Guides; Cross-Cultural Negotiation Series; Peacemaker's Toolkits

W. E. Upjohn Institute for Employment Research

300 South Westnedge Avenue
Kalamazoo, MI 49007-4686

Orders:
Phone: 888.227.8569

Phone: 269.343.4330
Fax: 269.343.7310
Email: publications@upjohn.org
Indiv: lastname@upjohn.org

<u>Website and Social Media:</u>
Website: www.upjohn.org

Staff
Director of Publications: Kevin Hollenbeck (269.343.5541)
  Assistant to the Director: Claire Black (269.343.5541)
Manager of Publications and Marketing: Richard Wyrwa (269.343.5541)
Editor: Ben Jones (269.343.5541)
Production Coordinator: Erika Jackson (269.343.5541)

Associate Member
Established: 1945
Title output 2012: 7
Titles currently in print: 218

Admitted to AAUP: 1997
Title output 2013: NR

Editorial Program
Scholarly works on employment-related issues; labor economics; current issues in the social sciences, with an emphasis on public policy. Books are authored by resident research staff and other scholars in the academic and professional communities. The Institute also publishes working papers, policy papers, and technical reports authored by the resident research staff and grantees; a quarterly journal on the West Michigan economy, Business Outlook for West Michigan, and a quarterly newsletter, *Employment Research.*

University of Utah Press

295 South 1500 East, Suite 5400
Salt Lake City, UT 84112-0860

Fax: 801.581.3365
Indiv: (user I.D.)@utah.edu

Orders:
Chicago Distribution Center
11030 South Langley Ave.
Chicago, IL 60628
Phone: 800.621.2736
Fax: 800.621.8476

Website and Social Media:
Website: www.UofUpress.com
Facebook: www.facebook.com/uofupress
Twitter: UofUPress

UK/European Representative:
Eurospan University Press Group

Staff

Director: Glenda Cotter (801.585.0083; email: glenda.cotter)
Acquisitions: John Alley, Editor-in-Chief (American history; American West, Mormon
   studies, folklore, Middle East studies, environment, trade) (801.585.3203;
   email: john.alley)
   Editor: Reba Rauch (anthropology and archaeology, linguistics, natural history, regional
   guidebooks) (801.585.0081; email: reba.rauch)
   Assistant Editor: Stephanie Warnick (email: stephanie.warnick)
Managing Editor: Glenda Cotter (email: glenda.cotter)
Production Manager: Jessica Booth (email: jessica.booth)
Marketing Manager: Hannah New (email: hannah.new)
Business Manager, Rights and Permissions: Sharon Day (email: sharon.day)

Full Member

Established: 1949
Title output 2012: 30
Titles currently in print: 500

Admitted to AAUP: 1979
Title output 2013: 30

Editorial Program

Anthropology and archaeology, linguistics, Mesoamerica, America Indian studies, history of
the North American West, environmental history, Utah and Mormon studies, Middle East
studies, natural history, nature writing, regional guidebooks, and general titles of regional
interest.
Special series: Agha Shahid Ali Prize in Poetry; Foundations of Archaeological Inquiry; Don
D. and Catherine S. Fowler Prize (Anthropology & Archaeology); The Juanita Brooks Prize
in Mormon Studies; Perspectives on the Mormon Experiencee; Tanner Lectures on Human
Values; Utah Series in Middle East Studies; University of Utah Anthropological Papers; The
Wallace Stegner Prize in Environmental and American Western History

Vanderbilt University Press

Street Address:
2014 Broadway
Suite 320
Nashville, TN 37203

Mailing Address:
VU Station B 351813
Nashville, TN 37235

Phone: 615.322.3585
Fax: 615.343.8823
Email: vupress@vanderbilt.edu
Indiv: firstname.lastname@vanderbilt.edu

Customer Service/Order Fulfillment:
OU Press Book Distribution Center
2800 Venture Drive
Norman, OK 73069
Phone: 800.627.7377
Fax: 800.735.0476

Website and Social Media:
Website: www.vanderbiltuniversitypress.com

Canadian Distributor:
Scholarly Book Services

UK/European Distributor:
Eurospan

Staff
Director: Michael Ames
Acquisitions Editor: Eli J. Bortz
Managing Editor: Joell Smith-Borne
Editing, Design, and Production Manager: Dariel Mayer
Marketing Manager: Sue Havlish
Marketing and New Media Associate: Betsy Phillips
Business Manager: Bethany Graham

Full Member
Established: 1940
Title output 2012: 24
Titles currently in print: 305

Admitted to AAUP: 1993
Title output 2013: 20

Editorial Program
Scholarly books and serious nonfiction in most areas of the humanities, the social sciences, health care, and higher education. Special interests include health care and social issues; caregiving and family policy; studies of race, class, gender, and sexuality; human rights and social justice; public policy; Hispanic and Latin American studies; African American studies; sociology and anthropology; and regional books.
Copublishing program: Country Music Foundation

The University of Virginia Press

Street Address:
Bemiss House
210 Sprigg Lane
Charlottesville, VA 22903-0608

Phone: 434.924.3468
Fax: 434.982.2655
Email: vapress@virginia.edu
Indiv: (user I.D.)@virginia.edu

Website and Social Media:
Website: www.upress.virginia.edu
Facebook: www.facebook.com/uvapress
Twitter: uvapress

Mailing Address:
PO Box 400318
Charlottesville, VA 22904-4318

Warehouse Address:
500 Edgemont Road
Charlottesville, VA 22903-0608
Phone: 434.924.6305
Fax: 434.982.2655

UK/European Representative:
Eurospan

Canadian Representative:
Scholarly Book Services

Staff

Director: Mark H. Saunders (434.924.6064; email: msaunders)
  Rights and Permissions Manager/Assistant Editor: Angie Hogan (434.924.3361; email: arh2h)
Acquisitions Editorial: Cathie Brettschneider (humanities) (434.982.3033; email: cib8b); Richard K. Holway (history and social sciences) (434.924.7301; email: rkh2a); Boyd Zenner (architecture, environmental studies, ecocriticism, and regional) (434.924.1373; email: bz2v); Angie Hogan (eighteenth-century studies)
  Editorial Assistant: Raennah Mitchell (434.924.4725; email: rm3xa)
Electronic Imprint: Mark H. Saunders, Manager (434.924.6064; email: mhs5u)
  Editorial and Technical Manager: David Sewell (434.924.9973; email: dsewell)
  Programmer/Analyst: Shannon Shiflett (434.924.4544; email: shiflett)
Manuscript Editorial: Ellen Satrom, Managing Editor (434.924.6065; email: egs6s)
  Assistant Managing Editor: Mark Mones (434.924.6066; email: emm4t)
  Project Editor: Morgan Myers (434.924.6067; email: jm3yg)
Design and Production: Martha Farlow, Design and Production Manager (434.924.3585; email: mfarlow)
  Assistant Design and Production Manager: Chris Harrison (434.924.6069; email: crh4w)
  Design and Production Assistant: Lindsey Saxby (434.982.2704, les4yg@virginia.edu)
Marketing: Mark H. Saunders, Director of Marketing (434.924.6064; email: msaunders)
  Marketing and Promotions Manager: Jason Coleman (434.924.4150; email: jcoleman)
  Marketing and Publicity Manager: Emily Grandstaff (434.982.2932; email: egrandstaff)
  Advertising and Exhibits Associate: Stephanie Lovegrove (434.924.6070; email: stephanie.lovegrove)
Chief Accountant: Duncan Pickett (434.924.6068; email: fdp7e)
  Customer Service Manager: Brenda Fitzgerald (434.924.3469; email: bwf)
  Warehouse Manager: Johnny Tyler (434.924.6305; email: jrt3u)
  Warehouse Assistant: Willie Clark (434.924.3712; email: wec8e)

Full Member

Established: 1963

Title output 2012: 67

Titles currently in print: 1,322

Admitted to AAUP: 1964

Title output 2013: 71

Editorial Program

Scholarly publications in humanities and social sciences, with concentrations in American history; African American studies; Southern studies; political science; literary and cultural studies, with particular strengths in African and Caribbean studies; Victorian studies; religious studies; architecture and landscape studies; environmental studies; animal studies; regional trade; Virginiana.

The Press also publishes digital publications, primarily critical and documentary editions, and an architectural dictionary, through Rotunda. Documentary editions (ongoing): The Dolly Madison Digital Edition; The Papers of George Washington; The Papers of James Madison; The Papers of Abraham Lincoln; The Eleanor Roosevelt Papers; Selected Papers of John Jay; The Diaries of Gouverneur Morris.

Special series: The American Literatures Initiative; The American South; Buildings of the United States; CARAF Books (Caribbean and African Literature translated from the French); The Carter G. Woodson Institute Series in Black Studies; Constitutionalism and Democracy; Cultural Frames, Framing Culture; Early American Histories; Jeffersonian America; The Modern Language Initiative; A Nation Divided: Studies in the Civil War Era; New World Studies; The Page-Barbour and Richard Lecture Series; Race, Ethnicity, and Politics; Reconsiderations in Southern African History; Studies in Early Modern German History; Studies in Pure Sociology; Studies in Religion and Culture; Under the Sign of Nature: Explorations in Ecocriticism; Victorian Literature and Culture; Walker Cowen Memorial Prize in Eighteenth-Century Studies

University of Washington Press

Street Address:

4333 Brooklyn Avenue NE

Seattle, WA 98195

Mailing Address:

PO Box 50096

Seattle, WA 98145-5096

Phone: 206.543.4050

Fax: 206.543.3932

Email: (user I.D.)@u.washington.edu

Orders:

Hopkins Fulfillment Services

Phone: 410.516.6956

Fax: 410.516.6998

Website and Social Media:

Website: www.washington.edu/uwpress

Facebook: www.facebook.com/pages/
  University of Washington Press

Twitter: UWAPress

YouTube: YouTube.com/uwashingtonpress

Pinterest: pinterest.com/uwapress/

UK Representative:

Combined Academic Publishers

Canadian Sales Group:

University of British Columbia Press

Staff
Administration:
  Director: Nicole Mitchell (206.685.9373; email: nfmm)
  Assistant to Director and Permissions Manager: Denise Clark (206.543.4057;
  email: ddclark)
  Chief Financial Officer: Tom Helleberg (after 3/10/14)
  Advancement Officer and Grants Manager: Beth Fuget (206.616.0818; email: bfuget)
Acquisitions:
  Executive Editor: Lorri Hagman(206.221.4989; email: lhagman)
  Senior Acquisitions Editors: Ranjit Arab (206.221.4984; email: rarab); Regan Huff (206-
  543-4053; email: rhuff); Marianne Keddington-Lang (206.450.5383; email: mkedlang)
  Assistant Acquisitions Editor: Tim Zimmermann (206.221.4940; email: tjz)
Editorial, Design, and Production:
  EDP Manager: Jacqueline Volin (206.221.4987; email: jsvolin)
  Assistant Managing Editor: Mary Ribesky (206.685.9165; email: ribesky)
  Production Manager: Pamela Canell (206.221.4993; email: pcanell)
  Production Coordinator: Diane Murphy (206.221.4992; email: kdm)
  Senior Designer: Tom Eykemans (206.685.9877; email: eykemans)
  Designer: Dustin Kilgore (206.685.9877; email: mrdustin)
Marketing and Sales:
  Marketing and Sales Director: Rachael Levay (617.871.0295; email: remann)
  Publicity Manager: Natasha Varner (206.221.4994; email: nvarner)
  Direct Mail Coordinator: Phoebe Daniels (206.221.4996; email: phoebea)
  Marketing Associate and Ebook Coordinator: Kathleen Pike Jones (206.221.5986; email:
  kpike)
Business:
  Accounts Receivable: Linda Tom (206.543.4722; email: lindatom)
  Accounts Payable: Heidi Olson (206.543.2858; email: hoatar)

Full Member

Established: 1915	Admitted to AAUP: 1937
Title output 2012:56	Title output 2013: 66
Titles currently in print: 2500	

Editorial Program

Art history, architecture and sustainable design, Asian studies, American Studies, Asian American studies, Native American and indigenous studies, anthropology, Western and environmental history, environmental studies, and regional history and culture of the Pacific Northwest.

Special series and imprints: Art History Publication Initiative (AHPI); Capell Family Books; Center for Korea Studies Publications; China Program Books; Classics of Chinese Thought; Classics of Tlingit Oral Literature; Critical Dialogues in Southeast Asian Studies; Culture, Place, and Nature: Studies in Anthropology and Environment; Donald R. Ellegood Publications in International Studies; Emil and Kathleen Sick Lecture-Book Series in Western History and Biography; Franklin D. Murphy Lecture Series; Gandharan Buddhist Texts; Global Re-Visions; A History of East Central Europe; In Vivo: The Cultural

Mediations of Biomedical Science; Jackson School Publications in International Studies; Jacob Lawrence Series on American Artists; Korean Studies of the Henry M. Jackson School of International Studies; Literary Conjugations; McLellan Books in the Humanities; Modern Language Initiative (MLI); Naomi B. Pascal Books; New Directions in Scandinavian Studies; Pacific Northwest Poetry Series; Weinstein Series in Post-Holocaust Studies; Robert B. Heilman Books; Samuel and Althea Stroum Lectures in Jewish Studies; Samuel and Althea Stroum Books; Scott and Lauri Oki Series in Asian American Studies; Studies on Ethnic Groups in China; Studies in Modernity and National Identity; Sustainable Design Solutions from the Pacific Northwest; Thomas Burke Memorial Washington State Museum Monographs; V Ethel Willis White Books; Weinstein Series in Post-Holocaust Studies; Weyerhaeuser Environmental Books

Publishing partners (sales rights in parentheses): Canadian Museum of Civilization (US); Fowler Museum at UCLA (world); Hearst Museum of Anthropology (world); International Sculpture Center (world); Museum for African Art (world); National Gallery of Australia (North America); Power Publications (North America); Silkworm Books (world outside Southeast Asia); UCLA Chicano Studies Research Center (CSRC) Press (world); University of British Columbia Press (US)

Washington State University Press

Cooper Publications Building
Grimes Way
PO Box 645910
Pullman, WA 99164-5910

Phone: 509.335.3518
Fax: 509.335.8568
Email: wsupress@wsu.edu
Indiv: (user I.D.)@wsu.edu

Website and Social Media:
Website: wsupress.wsu.edu
Facebook: www.facebook.com/pages/
    Washington-State-University-Press/121327661093

Orders:
Phone: 800.354.7360; 509.335.7880

Canadian Representatives:
Ingram Book Company
Baker & Taylor Books

Staff

Director: Edward Sala (509.335.3518; email: sala)
Permissions: Marc Lindsey (509.335.3518; email: lindseym)
Editor-in-Chief: Robert Clark (509.335.3518; email: robert.clark)
Production Editor: Nancy Grunewald (509.335.3518; email: grunewan)
Marketing Manager: Caryn Lawton (509.335.3518; email: lawton)
Editorial Assistant/Order Fulfillment Coordinator: Beth DeWeese (509.335.7880; email: wsupress)

Full Member

Established: 1927
Title output 2012: 3
Titles currently in print: 126

Admitted to AAUP: 1987
Title output 2013: 4
Journals published: 2

Editorial Program
Pacific Northwest; natural history; history, science, politics, and culture relating to the region; Western American history; ethnic studies; Native American studies; women's studies; and environmental issues. The Press distributes publications for the Hutton Settlement, Oregon-California Trails Association, Oregon Writers Colony, Pacific Institute, Tornado Creek Publications, Wenatchee Valley Museum and Cultural Center, WSU Center to Bridge the Digital Divide, WSU Museum of Art, WSU School of Hospitality Business Management, WSU Thomas S. Foley Institute, and Washington State Historical Society.
Journals: *Northwest Science; We Proceeded On*

Wayne State University Press

The Leonard N. Simons Bldg.
4809 Woodward Avenue
Detroit, MI 48201.1309

Orders:
Phone: 800.WSU.READ (978.7323)

Phone: 313.577.6126
Fax: 313.577.6131
Email: (user I.D.)@wayne.edu

Website and Social Media:
Website: wsupress.wayne.edu
Facebook: www.facebook.com/wsupress
Twitter: WSUPress

Canadian Distributor:
Scholarly Book Services

UK/European Distributor:
Eurospan

Staff
Director: Jane Hoehner (313.577.4220; email: jane.hoehner)
Community Engagement and Development: Gabe Gloden (313.577.6130; email: ggloden)
Acquisitions Editorial: Kathryn Wildfong, Editor-in-Chief (313.577.6070; email: k.wildfong) (Great Lakes, Judaica, citizenship studies)
   Senior Editor: Annie Martin (313.577.8335; email: annie.martin) (film, fairy tale studies, Africana, speech language pathology)
   Assistant Editor, Rights and Permissions: Kristina Stonehill (313.577.6127; email: as8399) (television)
Editorial, Design, and Production: Kristin Harpster, EDP Manager (313.577.4604; email: khlawrence)
   Assistant Editorial Manager and Reprints Manager: Carrie Downes Teefey (313.577.6123; email: carrie.downes)
   Assistant Design and Production Manager: TBA (313.577.4600)
Marketing/Sales: Emily Nowak, Marketing and Sales Manager (313.577.6128; email: aj3076)
   Promotion and Direct Mail Manager: Sarah Murphy (313.577.6077; email: murphysa)
   Advertising and Exhibits Manager: Jamie Jones (313.577.6054; email: eh3495)

Journals: Lauren Crocker (313.577.4607; email: lauren.crocker)
  Journals Marketing and Sales Coordinator: Julie Markowitz (313.577.4603;
  email: julie.markowitz)
Business: Andrew Kaufman, Business Manager (313.577.3671; email: ae4245)
  Fulfillment Manager: Theresa Martinelli (313.577.6126; email: theresa.martinelli)
  Customer Service: Colleen Stone (313.577.6120; email: colleen.stone)
  Accounts Receivable: DeLisa Fields (313.577.6257; email: ak2081)
  Warehouse Manager: Todd Richards (313.577.4619; email: aa5624)
  Shipping: John Twomey (313.577.4609; email: ai7331)
Technical Project Manager: Bonnie Russell (313.577.1283; email: dt2877)

Full Member

Established: 1941   Admitted to AAUP: 1956
Title output 2012: 34   Title output 2013: 32
Titles currently in print: 914   Journals published: 10

Editorial Program
Scholarly books and serious nonfiction, with special interests in regional and local history
and literature; Africana; Judaica; film and media studies; fairy tales and folklore; speech and
language pathology; citizenship studies; and gender and ethnic studies.
Journals: *Antipodes; Criticism; Discourse; Fairy Tale Review; Framework; Human Biology;
Marvels and Tales; Merrill Palmer Quarterly; Jewish Film & New Media; Storytelling, Self,
Society*
Special series: African American Life; Citizenship Studies; Contemporary Approaches to
Film and Media; Fairy Tale Studies; Great Lakes Books; Made in Michigan Writers Series;
Painted Turtle Books; Raphael Patai Series in Jewish Folklore and Anthropology; TV
Milestones; William Beaumont Hospital Series in Speech and Language Pathology
Joint imprints, copublishing, and distribution programs: Cranbrook Institute of Science;
Detroit Institute of Arts; Lotus Press; University of Alberta Press

Wesleyan University Press

Editorial Offices: Book Distribution Center:
215 Long Lane   Wesleyan University Press
Middletown, CT 06459   c/o University Press of New England
                                    1 Court Street, Suite 250
Phone: 860.685.7711   Lebanon, NH 03766-1358
Fax: 860.685.7712   Phone: 800.421.1561
Email: (user I.D.)@wesleyan.edu   Fax: 603.643.1540

Website and Social Media:
Website: www.wesleyan.edu/wespress/
Facebook: www.facebook.com/pages/Middletown-CT/
  Wesleyan-University-Press/101994439844863
Twitter: weslpress

UK/European Representative: Canadian Representative:
Eurospan   University of British Columbia Press

Staff

Director/Editor-in-Chief: Suzanna Tamminen (860.685.7727; email: stamminen)
Acquisitions Editor: Parker Smathers (860.685.7730; email: psmathers)
Marketing: Leslie Starr, Assistant Director/Marketing Manager (860.685.7725; email: lstarr)
Publicist: Stephanie Elliott (860.685.7723; email: selliott)

Full Member

Established: 1957

Admitted to AAUP: 2001
(Former membership: 1966-1991)

Title output 2012: 30
Titles currently in print: 495

Title output 2013: 27

Editorial Program

The current editorial program focuses on poetry, music, dance, science fiction studies, film/TV/media studies, regional studies, and American studies.
Special series: Early Classics of Science Fiction; Music/Culture; Music/Interview; Wesleyan Poetry; Wesleyan Film; Garnet Books

University of the West Indies Press

7A Gibraltar Hall Road
Kingston 7
Jamaica West Indies

US and Caribbean Orders:
Longleaf Services
P.O. Box 8895
Phone: 800.848.6224

Phone: 876.977.2659
Fax: 876.977.2660

Website and Social Media:
Website: www.uwipress.com

UK/European Distributor:
Eurospan

Canadian Distributor:
Scholarly Book Services

Staff

Director: Linda Speth (email: lspeth@cwjamaica.com)
Editorial & Production Manager: Shivaun Hearne (email: shivearne@gmail.com)
Marketing & Sales Manager: Donna Muirhead (email: uwipress_marketing@cwjamaica.com)
Finance Manager: Nadine Buckland (email: nbuckland@cwjamaica.com)

International Member

Established: 1992
Title output 2012: 25
Titles currently in print: 300

Admitted to AAUP: 2005
Title output 2013: 26
Journals published: 1

Editorial Program
Scholarly books in the humanities and social sciences with lists emphasizing a Caribbean context in the fields of cultural studies, gender studies, history, literature, economics, education, environmental studies, sociology, and political science.
Journal: *Journal of Caribbean History*

West Virginia University Press

Street Address:
Bicentennial House
1535 Mileground Road
Morgantown, WV 26506

Mailing Address:
PO Box 6295
Morgantown, WV 26506-6295

Phone: 304.293.8400
Fax: 304.293.6585

Website and Social Media:
Website: www.wvupress.com
Facebook: www.facebook.com/
   westvirginiauniversitypress

Order Fulfillment and Distribution:
Chicago Distribution Center
11030 South Langley Ave.
Chicago, IL 60628
Phone: 800.621.2736
Fax: 800.621.8476

Staff
Director: Carrie Mullen (ext. 202; email: carrie.mullen@mail.wvu.edu)
Marketing Manager: Abby Freeland (ext. 206; email: abby.freeland@mail.wvu.edu)
Production Manager/Art Director: Than Saffel (ext. 204; email: than.saffel@mail.wvu.edu)
Journals Manager/Editor: Hilary Attfield (ext. 205; email: hilary.hattfield@mail.wvu.edu)
Office Manager: Floann Downey (ext. 201; email: floann.downey@mail.wvu.edu)

Full Member
Established: 1963
Title output 2012: 15
Titles currently in print: 145

Admitted to AAUP: 2003
Title output 2013: 12
Journals published: 5

Editorial Program
Serious works of nonfiction in American history, with an emphasis on West Virginia and Appalachia; art history, economic history; ethnic studies; West Virginia and Appalachian fiction; medieval studies, especially Anglo-Saxon studies; regional studies in Appalachia; American studies; natural history. A second imprint, Vandalia Press, publishes fiction and non-fiction of interest to the general reader concerning Appalachia and, more specifically, West Virginia.
Journals: *Education and Treatment of Children; Essays in Medieval Studies; Tolkien Studies; Victorian Poetry; West Virginia History*
Special series: Medieval European Studies; Regenerations: African American Literature and Culture; Rural Studies; West Virginia University Sound Archive Series; West Virginia and Appalachia Series, West Virginia Classics

Wilfrid Laurier University Press

75 University Avenue West
Waterloo, ON N2L 3C5 Canada

<u>Canadian & US Distributor:</u>
UTP Distribution

Phone: 519.884.0710 ext. 6124
Fax: 519.725.1399
Email: press@wlu.ca
Indiv: (user I.D.)@press.wlu.ca

<u>UK/European Distributor:</u>
Gazelle Book Services Limited

<u>Website and Social Media:</u>
Website: www.wlupress.wlu.ca
Blog: nestor.wlu.ca/blog/
Facebook: www.facebook.com/wlupress
Twitter: wlupress

Staff
Director: Brian Henderson (ext. 6123; email: brian)
Acquisitions Editor: Lisa Quinn (ext. 2843; email: quinn)
Managing Editor: Rob Kohlmeier (ext. 6119; email: rob)
Production and Editorial Projects Manager: Heather Blain-Yanke (ext. 6122; email: heather)
Marketing Manager: Penny Grows (ext. 6605; email: pgrows)
   Web Page and Marketing Coordinator: Leslie Macredie (ext. 6281; email: leslie)
   Publicist: Clare Hitchens (ext. 2665; email: clare)
Permissions & Distribution Coordinator (Books & Journals): Cheryl Beaupré
   (ext. 6124; email: cheryl)
Financial Administrator: Phillip McTaggert (ext. 6030; email: phil)
Information Systems: Steve Izma, Computing Systems Administrator (ext. 6125;
   email: steve)

Full Member
Established: 1974

Admitted to AAUP: 1986

Title output 2012: 40

Title output 2013: 39

Titles currently in print: 460

Journals published: 5

Editorial Program
Art and art history; Canadian literature; cultural studies; environmental studies; family studies; film and media studies; history; indigenous studies; life writing; literary criticism; literature in translation; military history; music; philosophy; poetry; politics; religious studies; social work; sociology/anthropology; women's studies.

Journals: *Canadian Bulletin of Medical History; Canadian Military History; Canadian Social Work Review; Florilegium; Indigenous Law Journal*

Special series and joint imprints: Bahá'í Studies (with the Association for Bahá'í Studies); Canadian Commentaries; Collected Works of Florence Nightingale; Comparative Ethics (CCSR); Cultural Studies; Early Canadian Literature; Editions SR (CCSR); Environmental Humanities; Film and Media Studies;; Indigenous Studies; Laurier Military History; Laurier Poetry; Laurier Studies in Political Philosophy; Life Writing; SickKids Community and Mental Health; Studies in Childhood and Family in Canada; Studies in Christianity and

Judaism (CCSR); Studies in International Governance; Studies in Women and Religion (CCSR); Toronto International Film Festival; TransCanada, WCGS German Studies

The University of Wisconsin Press

1930 Monroe Street, 3rd Floor
Madison, WI 53711-2059

Phone: 608.263.1110
Fax: 608.263.1120
Email: uwiscpress@uwpress.wisc.edu
Indiv: (user I.D.)@wisc.edu

<u>Website and Social Media:</u>
Website: uwpress.wisc.edu
Facebook: university of wisconsin press

<u>UK Distributor:</u>
Eurospan

<u>Orders:</u>
Chicago Distribution Center
11030 South Langley Ave.
Chicago, IL 60628-3892
Phone: 800.621.2736; 773.702.7000
Fax: 800.621.8476; 773.702.7212

Staff

Director: Sheila Leary (608.263.1101; email: smleary)
   Subsidiary Rights: Anne McKenna (608.263.1131; email: rights@uwpress.wisc.edu)
   Permissions: permissions@uwpress.wisc.edu
Acquisitions Editorial:
   Executive Editor: Raphael Kadushin (608.263.1062; email: kadushin) (biography, Classical studies, creative writing, dance, film, gay/lesbian interest, 20th-C European history, Jewish interest, poetry contest, regional Wisconsin food and travel)
Editorial Director: Gwen Walker (608.263.1123; email: gcwalker) (African and African American studies, agriculture, American history and politics, botany, environmental studies, Irish history, human rights, Latin American studies, Russian/East European studies, Southeast Asian studies, regional Wisconsin history and natural history)
   Editor: Sheila Leary, Press Director (email: smleary) (folklore)
Manuscript Editorial: Adam Mehring, Managing Editor (608.263.0856; email: amehring)
   Editor: Sheila McMahon (608.263.1133; email: samcmahon)
Design and Production: Terry Emmrich, Production Manager (608.263.0731; email: temmrich)
   Assistant Production Manager: Carla Marolt (608.263.0732; email: marolt)
   Senior Compositor: Scott Lenz (608.263.0794; email: sjlenz)
Marketing: Andrea Christofferson, Marketing Manager (608.263.0814; email: aschrist)
   Publicity Manager: Elena Spagnolie (608.263.0734; email: publicity@uwpress.wisc.edu)
   Exhibits and Data Coordinator: Lindsey Meier (608.263.1136; email: lnmeier)
   Advertising: (608.263.0733; email: advertising@uwpress.wisc.edu)
Journals: Jason Gray, Journals Manager (608.263.0667; email: jmgray5)
   Production Manager: John Ferguson (608.263.0669; email: jtferguson)
   Advertising: (608.263.0534; email: journal.ads@uwpress.wisc.edu)
   Marketing: Toni Gunnison (608.263.0753; email: gunnison)
   Customer Service: Debra Rasmussen (608.263.1135; email: dlrasmussen)

Bookkeeper: Rebecca Forbes (608.263.0654; email: rlforbes)
Business: Dave Stange, Accountant: (608.263.1137; email: dmstange)
  Office Manager: Jim Hahn (608.263.1128; email: jhahn3)
  Business Assistant: Rebecca Forbes (608.263.1137; email: rlforbes)
Business office fax: (608.263.1120)

Full Member

Established: 1937	Admitted to AAUP: 1945
Title output 2012: 61	Title output 2013: 62
Titles currently in print: 2,081	Journals published: 11

Editorial Program
Scholarly and general-interest works in African and African American studies; agriculture; American history and politics; Classical studies; environmental studies and botany; fiction; film studies; folklore; foreign language learning; dance; gay/lesbian studies and memoirs; human rights; Jewish studies; Latin American studies and Latino/a memoirs; modern European and Irish history; Russian and East European studies; Southeast Asian studies; and Wisconsin and the Upper Midwest/Great Lakes. For our three poetry series (Brittingham, Felix Pollak, and Four Lakes series), contest guidelines are available online at www.wisc.edu/wisconsinpress/poetryguide.html

Journals: *American Orthoptic Journal; Arctic Anthropology; Contemporary Literature; Ecological Restoration; Journal of Human Resources; Land Economics; Landscape Journal; Luso-Brazilian Review; Monatshefte; Native Plants Journal; SubStance*

Special series: Africa and the Diaspora: History, Politics, Culture; Brittingham Prize in Poetry, Felix Pollak Prize in Poetry, Four Lakes Poetry Series; Critical Human Rights; Folklore Studies in a Multicultural World; George L. Mosse Series in Modern European Cultural and Intellectual History; Harvey Goldberg Series for Understanding and Teaching History; History of Ireland and the Irish Diaspora; Languages and Folklore of the Upper Midwest; Living Out: Gay and Lesbian Autobiographies; New Perspectives in Southeast Asian Studies; Print Culture History in Modern America; Publications of the Wisconsin Center for Pushkin Studies; Sources in Modern Jewish History; Studies in American Thought and Culture; Studies in Dance History; Wisconsin Film Studies; Wisconsin Land and Life; Wisconsin Studies in Autobiography; Wisconsin Studies in Classics; Women in Africa and the Diaspora; Writing in Latinidad

Imprints: Terrace Books, Popular Press

The Woodrow Wilson Center Press

Woodrow Wilson International Center for Scholars
One Woodrow Wilson Plaza
1300 Pennsylvania Avenue, N.W.
Washington, DC 20004-3027

Phone: 202.691.4042
Fax: 202.691.4001
Email: press@wilsoncenter.org
Indiv: (user I.D)@wilsoncenter.org

Website and Social Media:
Website: www.wilsoncenter.org/press

Staff

Director: Joseph Brinley (202.691.4042; email: joe.brinley)
Editor: Shannon Granville (202.691.4192; email: shannon.granville)
  Editorial Assistant: Cherie Worth (202.691.4029; email: cherie.worth)

Associate Member

Established: 1987	Admitted to AAUP: 1992
Title output 2012: 16	Title output 2013: 16
Titles currently in print: 262	

Editorial Program

Woodrow Wilson Center Press publishes work written at or for the Woodrow Wilson International Center for Scholars, the official memorial of the United States to its twenty-eighth president. The Center was created by law in 1968 as a living memorial "symbolizing and strengthening the fruitful relation between the world of learning and the world of public affairs." The Press's books come from both the work of the Center's scholars in residence and from some of the eight hundred meetings held at the Center each year.

The Center's interests range widely in areas associated with questions of public policy. The Press has published in American studies; history; international relations; political science; economics and finance; religious studies; urban studies; women's studies; and the study of Africa, Asia, Europe, Latin America, and the Middle East.

All the Press's books are copublished. Partners include Johns Hopkins University Press, Stanford University Press, Indiana University Press, University of California Press, University of Pennsylvania Press, and Columbia University Press. The Cold War International History Project Series is copublished with Stanford.

Yale University Press

Street Address:
302 Temple Street
New Haven, CT 06511

Mailing Address:
PO Box 209040
New Haven, CT 06520-9040

Main: 203.432.0960
203.432.6129 (Receptionist)
203.432.0900 (Acquisitions Editorial)
203.432.4060 (Design/Production)
203.432.0961 (Marketing)
203.432.0163 (Publicity)
Email: (firstname.lastname)@yale.edu

Distribution/Customer Service:
Triliteral LLC
Customer Service Toll Free: 1.800.405.1619
Customer Service Fax 800.406.9145

Yale Press Fax Numbers
203.432.6862 (Accounting)
203.432.0948 (Administration)
203.436.1064 (Acquisitions 1st Floor)
203.432.2394 (Acquisitions 2nd Floor)
203.432.8485 (Marketing 3rd Floor)
203.432.5455 (Promotion)
203.432.4061 (Design/Production)
401.658.4193 (Warehouse)

London Office:
47 Bedford Square
London WCIB 3DP
United Kingdom
Phone: 9-011-44-20-7079-4900
Fax: 9-011-44-20--7079-4901
Email: firstname.lastname@yale.co.uk

Website and Social Media:
Website: www.yale.edu/yup/
Blog: yalepress.typepad.com/yalepresslog/
Facebook: www.facebook.com/yalepress
Twitter: yalepress

Staff

Director: John E. Donatich (203.432.0933)
  Executive Assistant to the Director: Danielle Di Bianco (203.432.4301)
  Chief Operating Officer: Katherine Brown (203.432.8496)
  Chief Financial Officer & Assistant Director: John D. Rollins (203.432.0938)
  Director of Legal Affairs: Pam Chambers (203.432.0936)
  Permissions and Ancillary Rights Manager: Donna Anstey (203.432.0932)
  Margellos Series Coordinator: Elina Bloch (347.282.9568)
  Acquisitions Editorial: Christopher Rogers, Editorial Director/Executive Editor (history, current events) (203.432.0935); Jean E. Thomson Black, Executive Editor (life sciences, physical sciences, environmental sciences, medicine) (203.432.7534); Eric Brandt, Senior Editor (humanities, literary studies, cultural studies, history of ideas, performing arts) (203.432.8010); William Frucht, Executive Editor (law, political science international relations, and economics) (203.432.7571); Patricia Fidler, Art Publisher (art and architectural) (203.432.0927); Jennifer Banks, Senior Editor (religion, classics, philosophy) (203.432.6807); Joseph Calamia, Editor (physical sciences, environmental sciences, geology, applied mathematics, engineering (203.432.0904); Laura Davulis, Digital Projects

Editor/Associate Editor, History (203.432.5701); Michelle Komie, Senior Acquisitions Editor (art and architecture) (203.432.8420); Sarah Miller, Editor (college course-books (203.432.0901); Tim Shea, Editor (foreign languages and ESL) (203.432.4921); Vadim Staklo, Associate Editor (Annals of Communism, Reference) (203.432.0631); Steve Wasserman, Executive Editor-at-Large (Trade) (203.432.9698)

Director of Publishing Operations: Christina Coffin (203.432.4062)

Manuscript Editorial: Jenya Weinreb, Managing Editor (203.432.0914)

  Assistant Managing Editor: Mary Pasti (203.432.0911)

  Editors: Laura Jones Dooley (804.714.4466); Dan Heaton (203.432.1017); Ann-Marie Imbornoni (203.432.0903); Phillip King (203.432.1015); Susan Laity (203.432.0922); Margaret Otzel (203.432.0918); Jeffrey Schier (203.432.4001); Heidi Downey (203.432.2390)

Art Workshop: Kate Zanzucchi, Managing Editor (203.432.0916); Heidi Downey, Assistant Managing Editor (203.432.2390)

Production: Associate Production Manager: Maureen Noonan (203.432.4064)

  Reprint Controller: Orna Johnston (203.432.4060)

  Design and Production Manager Art Books: Mary Mayer (203.432.0925)

  Production Controller: Katherine Golden (203.436.8022)

  Senior Production Controller: Aldo Cupo (203.432.7484)

  Design: Art Director: Nancy Ovedovitz (203.432.4067)

  Designers: Lindsey Voskowsky (203.432.4065); James L. Johnson (203.432.4068); Sonia Scanlon (203.432.4066); Mary Valencia (203.432.8092)

Sales: Jay Cosgrove, Sales Director (203.432.0968)

  General Sales Queries: (203.432.0966)

  Academic and Library Sales Manager: (203.432.7350)

  Art & Digital Sales Manager: Stephen Cebik (203.432.2539)

Marketing and Promotions Director: Heather D'Auria (203.432.8193)

  Publicity Director: Brenda King (203.432.0917)

  Publicists: Robert Pranzatelli (203.432.0972); Alden Ferro (203.432.0909); Elizabeth Pelton (410.467.0989); Jennifer Doerr (203.432.0969); Julia Haav (718.715.1081)

  General Publicity Inquiries: Daniel Blanchard (203.432.0163)

  Online Marketing Manager: Ivan Lett (203.432.0961)

  Educational Marketing Manager: Debra Bozzi (203.432.0959)

  Academic Discipline Marketer: Karen Stickler (203.436.8467)

  Direct Mail Assistant: Lisa Scecina (203.432.0957)

  Exhibits/Advertising Manager: Ellen Freiler (203.432.0958)

  Assistant Marketing Director: David Wilfinger (203.432.0974)

Digital Publishing: David Schiffman, Director of Digital Publishing (203.432.2619)

  Digital Product Manager: Sara Sapire (203.432.0965)

  Digital Production Editor: John Carlson (203.436.9298)

Business: John D. Rollins, Chief Financial Officer & Assistant Director (203.432.0938)

  Accounting Manager: Timothy Haire (203.436.1924)

  Senior Accountant: Wendy DeNardis (203.432.0951)

  Accounting Assistant: Stephanie Pierre (203.432.0949)

  Royalty Accountant: Kim Jones (203.432.0946)

  Database Analyst: Marc Benigni (203.432.8446)

  Operations Coordinator: Theresa Donroe: (203.432.0952)

  Inventory & Building Operations Manager: Jim Stritch (203.432.0939)

Computer Information Services Manager: Milton Kahl (203.432.0937)
London Office:
Managing Director, London and Editorial Director (Humanities): Robert Baldock
Publisher, Art and Architecture: Gillian Malpass, History of Art, History of Architecture and
  Fashion
Publisher, Trade Books, London: Heather McCallum, History, Politics, Current Affairs,
  International Affairs, Biography, History of Science
Publisher, Pevsner Architectural Guides: Sally Salvesen, Decorative Arts, Art and Architecture
Head of Marketing: Noel Murphy
Foreign Rights Manager: Anne Bihan
Editor: Phoebe Clapman, Politics, Economics, Current Affairs

Full Member

Established: 1908   Admitted to AAUP: 1937
Title output 2012: 485   Title output 2013: 427
Titles currently in print: 6,055

Editorial Program

Humanities, social sciences, natural sciences, physical sciences, medicine. Poetry is not
accepted except for submissions to the Yale Series of Younger Poets contest, held annually.
Festschriften and collections of previously published articles are not invited and very rarely
accepted.

Special series, joint imprints and/or co-publishing programs: Agrarian Studies; Anchor
Bible and Commentaries; Annals of Communism; The Annotated Shakespeare; Babylonian
Collection; Bard Graduate Center; Carnegie Endowment for International Peace; The
Castle Lectures in Ethics, Politics, and Economics; A Century Foundation Book; Complete
Prose Works of John Milton; Complete Works of St. Thomas More; Council on Foreign
Relations; Cowles Foundation; Culture and Civilization of China; Darden Innovation and
Entrepreneurship; David Brion Davis Lectures; Democracy in America; The Diary of Joseph
Farington; Dodge Lectures; Dura-Europos; Economic Census Studies; Economic Growth
Center; Economic History; Elizabethan Club; English Monarchs; Faith and Globalization;
George Elliot Letters; The Henry McBride Series in Modernism and Modernity; Henry Roe
Cloud Series for American Indigenous Peoples and Modernity; History of the Soviet Gulag
System; Horace Walpole Correspondence; Institute for Social and Policy Studies; Institute
of Far Eastern Languages; Institution of Human Relations; Intellectual History of the
West; Italian Literature and Culture; James Boswell; Jewish Lives; Lamar Series In Western
History; Library of Medieval Philosophy; Neighborhoods of New York City; Margellos
World Republic of Letters; New Directions In Narrative History; The New Republic; Oak
Spring Garden Library; Okun; Open University; Page Lectures; The Papers of Benjamin
Franklin; The Papers of Benjamin Latrobe; Papers of Frederick Douglass; Papers on Soviet
& East European, Economic & Political Science; Paul Mellon Centre for Studies in British
Art; Pelikan History of Art; Percy Letters; Petroleum Monographs; Pevsner Series: Buildings

of England, Scotland, and Ireland; Phillips Andover Archaeology; Philosophy and Theory and Art; Poems of Alexander Pope; Posen Library of Jewish Culture and Civilization; Psychoanalytic Study of the Child; The Relations of Canada and the United States; Rethinking the Western Tradition; Russian Classics; Science in Progress; The Selected Papers of Charles Willson Peale and His Family; Silliman Lectures; Society and the Sexes; Stalin Archives; Storrs Lectures; Studies in Comparative Economics; Studies in Hermeneutics; Studies in Modern European Literature and Thought; Terry Lectures; Theoretical Perspectives in Archaeological History; Walpole Series in Eighteenth Century Studies; Why X Matters; The Works of Jonathan Edwards; The Works of Samuel Johnson; Yale Classical Monographs; Yale Classical Studies; Yale Contemporary Law Series; Yale Drama Series; Yale Edition of the Unpublished Works of Gloria Stein; Yale French Studies; Yale Guide to English Literature; Yale Health and Wellness; Yale Historical Publications; Yale Judaica; Yale Law Library Publications; Yale Law School Studies; Yale Library of Military History; Yale Liebniz; Yale Linguistics; Yale New Classics; Yale Publications in Religion; Yale Romantic Studies; Yale Series of Younger Poets; Yale Studies in Economics; Yales Studies in English; Yale Studies in History & Theory of Religious Education; Yale Studies in Political Science

AAUP PARTNERS

The AAUP Partner Program was launched in 2008. For more details about the AAUP Partner Program, visit www.aaupnet.org/about/partners. The following companies enrolled as Partners in 2013.

Baker and Taylor

<table>
<tr><td><u>New Jersey Office:</u>
1120 US Highway 22 East
Bridgewater, NJ 08807</td><td><u>New Hampshire Office:</u>
999 Maple Street
Contoocook, NH 03229</td></tr>
</table>

<u>Website and Social Media:</u>
Website: www.baker-taylor.com
Facebook: www.facebook.com/pages/Baker-Taylor/140688295944178
Twitter: BakerandTaylor
YouTube: www.youtube.com/user/BakerandTaylorTV?feature=mhw5

Staff Contacts
Vice President-Academic & Higher Education Library Merchandising: David Hetherington (908.458.5928; email: david.hetherington@baker-taylor.com)
Director, Academic Library and Higher Education Merchandising: Sally Neher (908.541.7460; email: sally.neher@baker-taylor.com)
Director, Ad Sales, Co-op and Editorial: Lynn Bond (908.541.7374; email: lynn.bond@baker-taylor.com)
Merchandise Manager, Academic: Lorraine Ferry (908.541.7435; email: lorraine.ferry@baker-taylor.com)

NH Contacts:
Vice President, Operations and Publisher Relations, YBP Library Services: Nat Bruning (603.746.3102 x3304; email: nbruning@ybp.com)

Year enrolled as AAUP Partner: 2009

Company Description
Baker & Taylor is a leading distributor of books, videos, and music products to libraries, institutions and retailers. We have been in business for 181 years and have developed long-term relationships with major book publishers, movie studios and music labels. We have more than 44,000 customers in more than 120 countries. Baker & Taylor is also committed to being an industry leader in digital media delivery. Through best-of-breed technologies, Baker & Taylor offers its publishers and customers bundled physical and digital media distribution services.

Bookmasters

30 Amberwood Parkway
Ashland, Ohio 44805

Phone: 419.281.5100 Toll-free: 800.537.6727
Fax: 419.281.0200
Email: info@bookmasters.com

<u>Website and Social Media:</u>
Website: www.bookmasters.com
Blog: blog.bookmasters.com/
Facebook: www.facebook.com/bookmastersgroup
Twitter: BookMasters

Staff Contacts

General Manager: David M. Hetherington (908.458.5928; email: david.hetherington@ baker-taylor.com)

Senior Vice President, Book Sales: Jon Ackerman (567.303.8454; email: jackerman@ bookmasters.com)

Vice President, Publisher Services Business Development: Deb Keets (800.537.6727 x1140; email: dkeets@bookmasters.com)

Director, Data Management & eBook Services: Claire Holloway (800.537.6727 x1149; email: cholloway@bookmasters.com)

Director, Marketing & Public Relations: Kristen Steele (800.537.6727 x1410; email: ksteele@bookmasters.com)

Year enrolled as AAUP Partner: 2009

<u>Company Description</u>

Bookmasters is one of the largest providers of publisher services in the world. For more than 40 years, Bookmasters has offered services to publishers and authors, including typesetting; editorial and design; marketing; POD and digital printing; offset printing; complete binding services, including smyth sewing, warehousing and fulfillment; eBook conversion; and book trade sales representation, ranging from national accounts to independent book stores.

Bookmasters, along with its sister company, Baker & Taylor, are Castle Harlan portfolio companies.

codeMantra, LLC

600 West Germantown Pike, Suite 400
Plymouth Meeting, PA 19462

Phone: 610.940.1700
Fax: 215.243.6421
Email: cminfo@codemantra.com

<u>Website and Social Media:</u>
Website: www.codemantra.com

Staff Contacts
President: Anantha Tirupati (610.940.1700; email: andy@codeMantra.com)
Director of Content Solutions: Merv L. Samuels (203.357.8150:
  email: merv@codemantra.com)
Director of Technology: Scott Cook (646.290.7557; email: scook@codemantra.com)
Director of Publishing Services: Walter W.J. Walker (914.310.6205; email: wwjwalker@
  codemantra.com)
Director of Global Client Services: Paul DeMarco (508.497.2500; email:
  pdemarco@codemantra.com)

Year enrolled as AAUP Partner: 2008

Company Description
Headquartered in Plymouth Meeting, Pennsylvania with extensive production and
technology facilities located in Chennai, South India, codeMantra provides software and
services for a comprehensive publishing solution. cM now offers Prepress/composition
services and delivers an end-to-end workflow—generating commercial print-ready files
plus digital derivatives and formats. The company serves all disciplines of commercial
publishing (STM, Trade, Academic and Education) and annually processes millions of pages
of content across a broad range of formats—from print-ready PDF and postscript files to
XML, SGML, XHTML, HTML, HTML5, ePub, uPDF™, PDB, iAuthor, Fixed Layout,
Page Perfect, Print Replica and more. The company's BPO services are complemented by
collectionPoint™, its hosted DAM and digital distribution platform, currently used by more
than 40 publishers, including Oxford University Press, Bloomsbury, Hodder Education,
Yale University Press as well as, the International Monetary Fund and the World Bank. The
latest version (collectionPoint 3.0) features cPMetalogic, a powerful Onix-driven metadata
management and real-time editing application.

Credo Reference

 **CREDO**

201 South Street, Fourth Floor
Boston, MA 01890

Phone: 617.426.5202
Fax: 617.426.3103

Website and Social Media:
Website: www.credoreference.com, corp.credoreference.com
Twitter: credoreference

Staff Contacts
President: John Dove (617.292.6111; email: dove@credoreference.com)
Content Product Specialist: Ingrid Becker
 (617.292.6130; email: ingrid.beck@credoreference.com)

Year enrolled as AAUP Partner: 2012

Company Description
Credo is a completely customizable online reference solution for learners and librarians.
Credo's General Reference Collection, Publisher Collections and Subject Collections
combine extensive content from multiple publishers with unique cross-referencing
technology, effortlessly delivering authoritative answers to millions of researchers worldwide.

CrossRef

50 Salem Street
Lynnfield, MA 01940

Phone: 781.295.0072
Fax: 781.295.0072

Website and Social Media:
Webiste: www.crossref.org
Twitter: CrossRefNews

Staff Contacts
Business Development and Marketing: Carol Ann Meyer (email: cmeyer@crossref.org;
  781.629.9782)
Assistant Marketing Manager: Anna Tolwinska (781.295.0072; email: annat@crossref.org)

Year enrolled as AAUP Partner: 2012

Company Description
CrossRef is a not-for-profit association of publishers. Since 2000, it has provided reference linking services for 63 million content items, including journal articles and books chapters among others. CrossRef's other services include Cited-By Linking, CrossCheck originality screening, CrossMark update identification, and FundRef funder identification.

ebrary/EBL

 ebrary

318 Cambridge Ave.
Palo Alto, CA 94306

Phone: 650.475.8700
Fax: 650.475.8881

<u>Website and Social Media:</u>
Website: www.ebrary.com
Facebook: www.facebook.com/pages/ebrary/154346767012
Twitter: ebrary

Staff Contacts
Senior Director of Content Development: Anna Bullard (650.475.8748; email:
    abullard@ebrary.com)
Director, EBL Publisher Relations: Mark Huskission (mark.huskission@eblib.com)
Publisher Relations Manager: Matthew Kull (650.475.8794; email: mkull@ebrary.com)
VP, Content Devlopment: Leslie Lees (650.475.8757; email: leslie@ebrary.com)

Year enrolled as AAUP Partner: 2009

Company Description
ebrary and EBL offer libraries the widest variety of models for acquiring e-books from over
650 leading publishers. By partnering with us, publishers can easily and effectively take
advantage of the growing e-book market using the same PDF files and metadata that are
created in the process of publishing books in print. ebrary/EBL is a member of the ProQuest
family of companies.

Eurospan | group

Partnering publishers since 1967

3 Henrietta Street
Convent Garden
London WC3E 8LU UK

Phone: 44 20724000856
Fax: 44 2073790609

Website and Social Media:
Website: www.eurospangroup.com
Twitter: eurospan

Staff Contacts
Chairman and Managing Director: Michael Geelan (44 2478450802; email: michael.
geelan@eurospangroup.com)
Administration and HR Manager: Sarah Donovan (442402078450849; email: sarah.
odonovan@eurospangroup.com)

Year enrolled as AAUP Partner: 2013

Company Description
Eurospan Group is Europe's leading independent marketing, sales, and distribution agency
for publishers from North America, Africa and Asia-Pacific seeking to expand sales and
imagery in international markets.

Firebrand Technologies

44 Merrimac Street
Newbury, MA 0195

Phone: 978.465.7755

<u>Website and Social Media:</u>
Website: www.firebrandtech.com

Staff Contacts
Director of Sales and Marketing: Steve Rutberg (845.893.8402;
  email: steve.rutberg@firebrandtech.com)
Executive Assistant: Erin Frazier (978.465.7715; email: erin@firebrandtech.com)

Year enrolled as AAUP Partner: 2013

<u>Company Description</u>
Founded in 1987, Firebrand Technologies is dedicated to providing leading software and
services to help publishers achieve success. Firebrand provides steadfast leadership and
seamless information flow throughout the publishing process.

Glatfelter

Corporate Headquarter:
96 South George Street
York, PA 17401

Phone: 717.225.4711
Fax: 717.846.7208

Website and Social Media:
www.glatfelter.com

Chillicothe Facility
232 E. Eighth Street
Chillicoth, OH 45601

Phone: 740.772.3111
Fax: 740.772.0024

Staff Contacts

Book Publishing Product Manager: Derek Robbins (740.772.0781;
  email: derek.robbins@glatfelter.com)
Key Account Manager: Ken Miller (908.889.4175; email: kenneth.miller@glatfelter.com)

Year enrolled as AAUP Partner: 2011

Company Description

Glatfelter manufactures book publishing papers for university presses; free-sheet papers that meet all ANSI permanence standards. We believe that if a book is important enough to go in print, it's important enough to deserve great paper.

Ingram Content Group

INGRAM.

Ingram Content Group
One Ingram Blvd.
LaVergne, TN 37086 USA

Phone: 615.793.5000
Email: inquiry@ingramcontent.com
Website: www.ingramcontent.com

Staff Contacts
Lead Buyer—University Presses: Ron Watson (615.213.5375;
 email: ron.watson@ingramcontent.com)
VP, Content Acquisition, North America: Joe Thomson (615.213.5129; email:
 joe.thomson@ingramcontent.com)
Content Acquisition Account Executive: Jim Heuer (330.220.6552;
 email: jim.heuer@ingramcontent.com)
 VP, Digital Products: Marcus Woodburn (615.213.5628;
 email: marcus.woodburn@ingramcontent.com)

Year enrolled as AAUP Partner: 2010

Company Description
Ingram Content Group Inc. is the world's largest and most trusted distributor of physical and digital content. Thousands of publishers, retailers, and libraries worldwide use our products and services to realize the full business potential of books, regardless of format. Ingram has earned its lead position and reputation by offering excellent service and creating innovative, integrated solutions while anticipating industry changes and creating opportunities for our customers. Our customers have access to best-of-class digital, audio, print, print-on-demand, inventory management, wholesale and full-service distribution programs.

Integrated Books International

Integrated Books International

22883 Quicksilver Dr.
Dulles, VA 20166

Phone: 703.661.1500
Fax: 703.661.1501
Website: www.booksintl.com

Staff Contacts
Vice President: Vartan Ajamian (703.661.1519; email: vartan.ajamian@booksintl.com)
Director of Business Development: Ellen Loerke (703.661.1512; email: ellen.loerke@
booksintl.com)
Director of Database Management: Beth Prester (703.661.1525; email: beth.prester@
booksintl.com)
MIS Director: Sal Signorino (703.661.1514; email: sal@booksintl.com)
Customer Service Manager: Todd Riggleman (703.661.1527; email: todd@booksintl.com)

Year enrolled as AAUP Partner: 2009

Company Description
Books International provides third-party fulfillment services to publishers and distributors using Cats Pajamas software and the new Elan suite of programs. All activity is done under the publisher's name. EDI, PUBNET, website interface all supported. Publishers have daily to their live database to view and export data. On-site digital printing with Integrated Book Technology Inc. (IBT) offers print-to-order and short print run advantages.

ITHAKA

I T H A K A

JSTOR | PORTICO | ITHAKA S+R

<u>Addresses:</u>
ITHAKA: JSTOR, Portico, and Ithaka S+R
151 East 61st Street
New York, NY 10065
Phone: 212.500.2600
Fax: 212.500.2366

ITHAKA: JSTOR, Portico , and Ithaka S+R
2 Rector Street, 18th floor
New York, NY 10006
Phone: 212.358.6400
Fax: 212.358.6499

<u>Website and Social Media:</u>
Websites: www.ithaka.org, www.about.jstor.org
Facebook: www.facebook.com/JSTOR.org
Twitter: JSTOR

Staff Contacts:
EVP, JSTOR Managing Director: Laura Brown (212.500.2600;
   email: Laura.brown@ithaka.org)
Director, Books at JSTOR: Frank Smith (212.358.6400;
   email: Frank.smith@ithaka.org)
Director, Current Journals Program: Mary Rose Muccie (609.986.2200;
   email: Maryrose.muccie@ithaka.org)
Associate Director, Marketing & Communications: Sarah Glasser
   (212.358.6400; email: Sarah.glasser@ithaka.org)
Associate Director, Archive Collections: Barbara Chin
   (212.358.6400; email: Barbara.chin@ithaka.org)

Year enrolled as AAUP Partner: 2011

Company Description
JSTOR (www.jstor.org) is a research and teaching platform for the academic community.
With more than a thousand journals and one million primary sources, JSTOR is one of the
world's most trusted sources for academic content. JSTOR is part of ITHAKA (www.ithaka.
org), a not-for-profit organization that also includes Portico and Ithaka S+R.

klopotek.

Klopotek North America Inc
2001 Route 46
Parsippany, NJ 07054

Phone: 973.331.1010
Fax 973.331.0042

Website: www.klopotek.com

Staff Contacts:
CEO: Ulrich Klopotek (email: u.klopotek@klopotek.com)
SVP Operations: Susan Lehrhaupt (email: s.lehrhaupt@klopotek.com)
VP Sales & Marketing: George Logan (email: g.logan@klopotek.com)
VP Business Development: Steve Waldron (email: s.waldron@klopotekcom)

Year enrolled as AAUP Partner: 2011

Company Description
Klopotek's mission is to provide software solutions built on standardized business processes to publishers worldwide. Klopotek is dedicated to develop solutions offering publishers the best strategic and commercial advantages in their ever changing business models.
Over 350 book and journal publishers on four continents are using the Klopotek Standard Software Solution

Manila Typesetting Company (MTC)

12th Floor, Pet Plans Building 4444 EDSA
Guadalupe Viejo, Makati City 1212, Philippines 1211
Phone: +632 8976629

Website and Social Media
www.mtcstm.com

Staff Contacts
Manilla Owner & Operations: Paul Hartley (+6328976629; email: phhartley@gmail.com)
UK Owner & International Sales: Michael Angless (+441993709513; email: mangless@mtcstm.com)
Manilla Operations: Myrna Ting (email: myrnacting@gmail.com)
Manilla Customer Service: Amor Nanas (email: amornanas@mtcstm.com)

Year enrolled as AAUP Partner: 2012

Company Description
The Manila Typesetting Company is dedicated to providing high quality, reasonably priced, and timely service to publishers of professional, scholarly, scientific, technical, and medical research.

MTC offers:

Copy Editing
Project Management
Proof Reading
Journal and Book Production
Typesetting, Layout and Design - XML first
Indexing
XML Conversion
Data and Legacy Processing, Medical and Legal
Non Destructive/Destructive Scanning
Image Editing and Enhancement
EBook/ePub Creation and Conversion

THOMSON REUTERS CORE PUBLISHING SOLUTIONS

610 Opperman Drive
Eagan, Minnesota 55116

Phone: 651.687.5270

<u>Website and Social Media:</u>
Website: corepublishingsolutions.thomsonreuters.com/

Staff Contacts
Business Development Manager: Mark Pitzele (651.687.5270; email:
  mark.pitzele@thomsonreuters.com)

Year enrolled as AAUP Partner: 2013

<u>Company Description</u>
Thomson Reuters Core Publishing Solutions provides publishers content management,
print, digital and supply chain solutions. Our scalable and flexible solutions for your titles
allows you to efficiently deliver content to your customers which in turn will help grow you
business.

THOMSON-SHORE

Helping you put your best book forward®

7300 West Joy Road
Dexter, MI 48130

Phone: 734.426.3939
Fax: 800.706.4545
Email: info@thomsonshore.com

Website: www.thomsonshore.com

Staff Contacts
VP of Sales & Marketing: Terri Barlow (734.426.6214; email:Terrib@thomsonshore.com)
Sales Manager–University Press Market: Mark Livesay (734.426.6207; email: markl@
thomsonshore.com)
Customer Service Representatives: Kelley Jones (734.426.6237; email: kelleyj@
thomsonshore.com); Dawn Rice (734.426.6299; email: dawnr@thomsonshore.com)

Year enrolled as AAUP Partner: 2008

Company Description
Thomson-Shore is a renowned book manufacturing company. We offer POD, digital and
offset printing in black and white to full color with full binding capabilities. We also offer
e-book conversion, distribution/fulfillment and publicity services.

Virtusales Publishing Solutions

virtusales
PUBLISHING SOLUTIONS

Third Floor, Sheridan House
112-116 Western Road
Brighton & Hove
BN3 1DD   UK

Phone: 212.461.3686
Fax: +44 8454584021
Email: info@virtusales.com

<u>Website and Social Media:</u>
www.virtusales.com

Staff Contacts
Vice President and Commercial Operations: Rodney Elder (212.461.3686;
   email: rodney.elder@virtusales.com)
PA to VP Commercial Operations: Shella Zaidi (212.461.3686;
   email: shella@virtusales.com)

Year enrolled as AAUP Partner: 2013

Company Description
Virtusales develops Biblio3, BiblioLIVE, BiblioRoyalties and BiblioDAM which are used by
many University Press publishers including Harvard University Press, Wayne State University
Press, Syracuse University Press, Penn State University Press and University of Georgia
Press. The software suite is an advanced publishing management system available in the
cloud, allowing publishers to track their data from pre-acquisition to publication. It covers
functional areas including ONIX & eBook feeds, production management, contracts, rights,
royalties and digital asset management.

International Sales Agents and Distributors

Baker & Taylor International
1120 Route 22 East
Bridgewater, NJ 08807 USA
Phone: 800.775.1800; 908.541.7000
Email: btinfo@btol.com
Website: www.btol.com/international.cfm

Bay Foreign Language Books Ltd.
Unit 4, Kingsmead
Park Farm, Folkestone
Kent CT19 5EU United Kingdom
Phone: +44 (0) 1233 720 020
Fax: + 44 (0) 1233 721 272
Email: sales@baylanguagebooks.co.uk
Website: www.baylanguagebooks.co.uk

Boydell & Brewer, Ltd.
Whitwell House
St Audry's Park Road
Melton Woodbridge
Suffolk IP12 1SY United Kingdom
Phone: +44 (0) 1394 610600
Fax: +44 (0) 1394 610316
Email: trading@boydell.co.uk
Website: www.boydellandbrewer.com

Codasat Canada Ltd.
3122 Blenheim Street
Vancouver, BC V6K 4J7 Canada
Phone: 604.228.9952
Fax: 604.222.2965
Email: info@codasat.com
Website: www.codasat.com

Combined Academic Publishers, Ltd.
Windsor House Cornwall Road
Harrogate North Yorkshire
HG1 2PW United Kingdom
Phone: +44 (0) 1423 526350
Email: enquiries@combinedacademic.co.uk
Website: www.combinedacademic.co.uk

David Brown Book Company
PO Box 511 (20 Main Street)
Oakville, CT 06779 USA
Phone: 860.945.9329
Fax: 860.945.9468
Email: queries@dbbconline.com
Website: www.oxbowbooks.com/dbbc

Distribution du Nouveau Monde
30 Gay-Lussac
F-75005 Paris France
France: Phone: +01 43 54 49 02
Fax: +01 43 54 39 15
Belgium and Luxembourg:
Phone: +33 1 43 54 49 02
Fax: +33 1 43 54 39 15
Email: dnm@librairieduquebec.fr
Website: www.exportlivre.com/
w.librairieduquebec.fr

D.A.P. | Distributed Art Publishers, Inc.
155 6th Avenue, 2nd Floor
New York, NY 10013 USA
Phone: 212.627.1999
Fax: 212.627.9484
Website: www.artbook.com

Eurospan Group
3 Henrietta Street, Covent Garden
London WC2E 8LU United Kingdom
Phone: +44 (0) 2072 400856
Fax: +44 (0) 2073 790609
Email: info@eurospangroup.com
Website: www.eurospan.co.uk

Exportlivre
505, Bélanger Street, Suite 223
Montreal QC H2S 1G5 Canada
Phone: 450.671.3888
Fax: 450.671.2121
Email: order@exportlivre.com

Footprint Books
1/6a Prosperity Parade,
Warriewood, NSW 2102, Australia
Phone: +61 2 9997 3973
Fax: +61 2 9997 3185
Website: www.footprint.com.au/

Forest Book Services
6 Forest Road,
Milkwall, Coleford
Gloucestershire GL16 7LB United Kingdom
Phone: +44 (0) 1594 833858
Fax: +4 (0) 1594 837573
Website: www.forestbooks.com

Gazelle Book Services, Ltd.
White Cross Mills
Hightown, Lancaster
Lancashire LA1 4XS United Kingdom
Phone: +44 (0) 1524 68765
Fax: +44 (0) 1524 63232
Email: sales@gazellebooks.co.uk
Website: www.gazellebookservices.co.uk

Georgetown Terminal Warehouses Ltd
34 Armstrong Avenue
Georgetown, Ontario
Canada L7G 4R9
Phone: 905.873.2750
Fax: 905.873.6170
Email: info@gtwcanada.com
Website: www.gtwcanada.com

Libro Co. Italia s.r.l.
Via Borromeo, 48
50026 San Casciano V.P.
Florence, Italy
Phone: +39 055 8228461
Fax: +39 055 8228462
Email: libroco@libroco.it
Website: www.libroco.it

Login Brothers Canada
300 Saulteaux Crescent
Winnipeg, Manitoba R3J 3T2
Phone: 800.665.1148 or 204.837.2987
Fax: 800.665.0103 or 204.837.3116
Email: orders@lb.ca
Website: www.lb.ca

Marston Book Services, Ltd.
160 Eastern Avenue
Milton Park
Oxon OX14 4SB
Phone: +44 (0) 1235 465500
Fax: +44 (0) 1235 465509
Website: www.marston.co.uk

NBN International
10 Thornbury Road
Plymouth PL6 7PP
United Kingdom
Phone: +44 (0) 1752 202301
Fax: +44 (0) 1752 202333
Email: cservs@nbninternational.com
Website: www.nbninternational.com

Orca Book Services
160 Eastern Ave
Milton Park
Abingdon OX14 4SD United Kingdom
Phone: +44 (0) 1235 465500
Email: tradeorders@orcabookservices.co.uk
Website: www.orcabookservices.co.uk/

Oxbow Books
10 Hythe Bridge Street
Oxford, OX1 2EW United Kingdom
Phone: +44 (0) 1865 241249
Fax: +44 (0) 1865 794449
Email: oxbow@oxbowbooks.com
Website: oxbowbooks.com/oxbow

Oxford Publicity Partnership
2 Lucas Bridge Business Park
Old Greens Norton Road
Towcester
NN12 8AX, United Kingdom
Phone: +44 (0) 1327 357770
Email: info@oppuk.co.uk
Website: www.oppuk.co.uk

Publishers Group UK
63-66 Hatton Garden
London EC1N 8LE United Kingdom
Phone: +44 (0) 207 4051105
Fax: +44 (0) 207 2423725
Email: info@pguk.co.uk
Website: www.pguk.co.uk

Renouf Books
22-1010 Polytek Street
Ottawa, ON K1J 9J3 Canada
Phone: 866.767.6766
Fax: 613.745.7660
Email: orders@renoufbooks.com
Website: www.renoufbooks.com

Roundhouse Group
Unit B
18 Marine Gardens
Brighton BN2 1AH United Kingdom
Phone: +44 (0) 1273 603 717
Fax: +44 (0) 1273 697 494
Email: sandy@roundhousegroup.co.uk
Website: www.roundhousegroup.co.uk

Scholarly Book Services, Inc.
289 Bridgeland Avenue, Unit 105
Toronto, ON M6A 1Z6 Canada
Phone: 800.847.9736; 416.504.6545
Fax: 800.220.9895; 416.504.0641
Email: customerservice@sbookscan.com
Website: www.sbookscan.com

Servidis SA
Chemin des Chalets
1279 Chavannes-de-Bogis
Phone: +022 960 95 25
Fax: +022 776 63 64
Website: www.servidis.ch/

University of Toronto Press Inc. Distribution
5201 Dufferin St.
Toronto, ON M3H 5T8 Canada
Phone: 416.667.7791
Fax: 416.667.7832
Email: utpbooks@utpress.utoronto.ca
Website: ww.utpress.utoronto.ca/
    UTP_Distribution/index.ph

University Presses Marketing
The Tobacco Factory
Raleigh Road,
Southville, Bristol BS3 1TF
United Kingdom
Phone: +44 (0) 117 9020275
Fax: +44 (0) 117 9020294
Email: sales@universitypressesmarketing.
    co.uk
Website: www.universitypressesmarketing.
    co.uk

Yale Representation, Ltd.
Andrew Jarmain
47 Bedford Square
London WC1B 3DP United Kingdom
Phone: +44 (0)207079 4900
Fax: +44 (0) 20 7079 4901
Website: www.yalebooks.co.uk/

THE ASSOCIATION

The Association of American University Presses (AAUP) was established by a small group of university presses in 1937. In the subsequent years, the association has grown steadily. Today AAUP consists of 131 member presses, ranging in size from those publishing a handful of titles each year to those publishing more than a thousand.

AAUP is a nonprofit organization. Its sources of financing are limited to membership dues and to revenues derived from such activities as organizing national conferences and seminars, producing publishing-related books and catalogs, and operating cooperative marketing programs. In addition, grants provided by foundations and government bodies help to finance special projects.

AAUP's member presses provide much of the personnel that guide the association and carry out its work. A board of directors sets policy for the organization. Many individuals serve on committees and task forces. Their activities reflect the diverse concerns of the membership, including keeping up with emerging electronic publishing technologies, production and analysis of industry statistics, maintaining copyright protections, professional development, marketing, and scholarly journals publishing.

The AAUP Central Office, located in New York City, consists of an executive director and a small professional staff. The office manages member programs and coordinates the work of the board and committees.

AAUP members currently fall into four categories—full, international, associate, and introductory. For a complete description of membership requirements, consult the "Guidelines on Admission to Membership and Maintenance of Membership," on page 239.

AAUP Central Office

Association of American University Presses
28 W. 36th Street, Suite 602
New York, NY 10018

Phone: 212.989.1010
Fax: 212.989.0275
Email: info@aaupnet.org

Website and Social Media:
Website: www.aaupnet.org
Facebook: www.facebook.com/universitypresses
Twitter: aaupresses

Staff

Executive Director: Peter Berkery (ext. 29; email: pberkery@aaupnet.org)
Assistant Director and Controller: Timothy Muench (ext. 28; email: tmuench@aaupnet.org)
Administrative Assistant: TBA
Marketing and Communications Director: Brenna McLaughlin (518.436.3586; email: bmclaughlin@aaupnet.org)
Membership Manager: Susan Patton (ext. 25; email: spatton@aaupnet.org)
Marketing and Membership Coordinator: Kim Miller (ext. 26; email: kmiller@aaupnet.org)
Communications Strategist: Regan Colestock (ext. 24; email: rcolestock@aaupnet.org)

2013-2014 AAUP Board of Directors

Philip Cercone, McGill-Queen's, President (2013-2014)
Barbara Kline Pope, National Academies, President Elect (2013-2014)
Peter Dougherty, Princeton, Past President (2013-2014)
Erik Smist, Johns Hopkins, Treasurer (2013-2014)
Mike Bieker, Arkansas, Treasurer Elect (2013-2014)
Jane Bunker, Northwestern (2013-2016)
Timothy Doyle, Harvard School of Engineering and Applied Sciences (2013-2014)
Ellen Faran, MIT (2011-2014)
Garrett Kiely, Chicago (2012-2015)
Sheila Leary, Wisconsin (2012-2015)
Leila Salisbury, Mississippi (2013-2016)
Mark Saunders, Virginia (2012-2015)
Charles Watkinson, Purdue (2011-2014)
Peter Berkery, ex officio

2013-2014 AAUP Committees and Task Forces

Admissions and Standards
John Byram, New Mexico, Chair
Susan Doerr, Minnesota
Garrett Kiely, Chicago
Kyla Madden, McGill-Queen's
Leila Salisbury, Mississippi
Eric Schwartz, Princeton

Annual Meeting
Alisa Plant, Louisiana State, Chair
Rob Dilworth, Duke
Susan Doerr, Minnesota
Terri O'Prey, Princeton
Tony Sanfilippo, Penn State
Ellen Satrom, Virginia
John Sherer, North Carolina

Book, Jacket, and Journal Show
Nathan Putens, Nebraska, Chair
Jamison Cockerham, Indiana
Jeffrey Cohen, Getty
Dustin Kilgore, Washington
Joeth Zucco, Nebraska

Business Systems
John Rollins, Yale, Chair
Robbie Dircks, North Carolina
Tom Helleberg, NYU
Roger Hubbs, Cornell
Tom Johnson, New England
Rebecca Schrader, MIT
Ioan Suciu, Georgetown

Copyright
Laura Leichum, Georgetown, Chair
Sara Jo Cohen, Temple
Claire Lewis Evans, Alabama
Peter Froehlich, Indiana
Sean Garrett, Georgia
Kay Hechler, USIP
Vicky Wells, North Carolina

Design and Production
Carol Stein, ASCSA, Chair
Marianne Jankowski, Northwestern
John Long, National Gallery of Art
Katherine Purple, Purdue
Kenneth Reed, Princeton
Lisa Tremaine, New Mexico

Digital Publishing
Toni Gunnison, Wisconsin, Chair
Dana Dreibelbis, Rutgers
Thomas Elrod, North Carolina
Nathan MacBrien, Northwestern
Bill Trippe, MIT
Annette Tanner, Michigan State

Marketing
Laura Baich, Indiana, Chair
Teal Amthor-Shaffer, Florida
Laraine Coates, British Columbia
Fran Keneston, SUNY
Brian MacDonald, Toronto
Amanda E. Sharp, Georgia

Nominating
MaryKatherine Callaway, Louisiana State, Chair
David Hamrick, Texas
Anna Weidman, California
Darrin Pratt, Colorado
Greg Britton, Johns Hopkins
Gita Manaktala, MIT

Library Relations
Donna Dixon, SUNY, Chair
Jane Bunker, Northwestern
Suzanne Guiod, Syracuse
Larin McLaughlin, Illinois
Peter Mickulas, Rutgers
Raina Polivka, Indiana
Peter Potter, Cornell
Lisa Quinn, Wilfred Laurier
Leila Salisbury, Mississippi
Michael Spooner, Colorado/Utah State
Charles Watkinson, Purdue

Professional Development

Amanda Atkins, MIT, Chair
Sara Davis, Pennsylvania
Dianna Gilroy, Purdue
Bobby Keane, Louisiana State
Jessica Pellien, Princeton
A.C. Racette, Northwestern

Scholarly Journals

Anne Marie Corrigan, Toronto, Co-Chair
Lauren Crocker, Wayne State, Co-Chair
Liz Brown, Johns Hopkins
Jason Gray, Wisconsin
Dave Lievens, Pennsylvania
Jeff McArdle, Illinois
Kathryn Purple, Purdue
Jill Rodgers, MIT
Ann Snoeyenbos, Johns Hopkins
Clydette Wantland, Illinois

University Press Week Task Force

Will Underwood, Kent State, Chair
Colleen Lanick, MIT
Melissa Pitts, British Columbia
Michael Roux, Illinois
Leila Salisbury, Mississippi
Mark Saunders, Virginia

By-Laws (As revised June 17, 2010)

ARTICLE I: PREAMBLE

This Corporation, existing under the Not-for-Profit Corporation Law of the State of New York, shall be known as the Association of American University Presses, Inc. (hereinafter referred to as the "Association"). The Association expects members to recruit, employ, train, compensate, and promote their employees without regard to race, ethnic background, national origin, status as a veteran or handicapped individual, age, religion, gender, marital status, or sexual preference.

ARTICLE II: PURPOSES

The purposes of the Association shall be:

a) To encourage dissemination of the fruits of research and to support university presses in their endeavor to make widely available the best of scholarly knowledge and the most important results of scholarly research;
b) To provide an organization through which the exchange of ideas relating to university presses and their functions may be facilitated;
c) To afford technical advice and assistance to learned bodies, scholarly associations, and institutions of higher learning; and
d) To do all things incidental to and in furtherance of the foregoing purposes without extending the same.

ARTICLE III: MEMBERSHIP

The Association admits members in four categories: (1) full membership, (2) associate membership, (3) international membership, and (4) introductory membership.

Section 1: Definition of Full Membership.

The full membership of the Association shall consist of those members who were in good standing at the time of the incorporation of the Association in 1964, except those who have since resigned or whose membership has been otherwise terminated, and all other members who have since been admitted in accordance with the procedures set forth in Section 3 of this Article. Presses with affiliate status as of June 2007 will be instated as full members upon approval of the membership.

Section 2: Definition of a University Press.

A university press eligible for full membership is hereby defined as the nonprofit scholarly publishing arm of a university or college, or of a group of such institutions within a state or geographic region, located within the Americas and publishing primarily in English. A university press as here defined must be an integral part of one or more such colleges and universities, and should be so recognized in the manual of organization, catalogue, website, or other official publication of at least one such parent institution. The organization and functions of the university press must lie within the prescription of its parent institution or institutions.

Section 3: Eligibility for Full Membership.

Any university press satisfying the requirements set forth in the "Guidelines on Admission to Membership and Maintenance of Membership" (hereinafter, the "Guidelines") that are in force at the time of application shall be eligible for election to full membership in the Association. A university press shall be elected to membership by a majority vote of the membership on the recommendation of the Board of Directors at the Annual or a Special Meeting of the membership. Such action shall be taken by the Board only on the prior recommendation of the Committee on Admissions and Standards, which shall be responsible for determining that the applying university press satisfies the minimum requirements for membership. Annual dues for full members shall be set from time to time by the Board of Directors.

Section 4: Associate Membership.

The associate membership of the Association shall consist of those associate members who have been admitted since the time of the incorporation of the Association in 1964, in accordance with the procedures in force at the time of application.

Presses of non-degree-granting scholarly institutions and associations may apply for associate membership, provided that those institutions are incorporated as not-for-profit and that the presses satisfy the requirements for full membership, except that the auspices and structures of the parent organizations of such presses will in all instances be those of non-degree-granting institutions or scholarly associations rather than those of universities. Associate members should be located within the Americas and publishing primarily in English. In the absence of an editorial committee or board, an applicant for associate membership shall observe commonly accepted standards of editorial review.

Admission to associate membership shall be by a majority vote of the membership at an Annual or Special Meeting, a quorum being present, on the prior recommendation of the Committee on Admissions and Standards and the Board of Directors. Associate members shall enjoy such rights and privileges as determined by the Board of Directors, including the right to serve on the Board of Directors or on the Standing Committees of the Association and the right to vote on any business conducted by the Association. Associate members shall not be eligible to participate in the Association's statistical programs for full members. Annual dues for associate members shall be set from time to time by the Board of Directors. The number of associate members shall not exceed thirty-five percent of the number of full members of the Association and no more than one associate member representative may serve on the Board at any one time.

Section 5: International Membership.

The international membership of the Association shall consist of those international members who have been admitted since the time of the incorporation of the Association in 1964, in accordance with the procedures in force at the time of application.

International membership may be applied for by (a) university-affiliated scholarly publishers and presses of non-degree-granting scholarly institutions and associations in parts of the world not embraced by the Americas and (b) such presses within the Americas that publish primarily in languages other than English. To qualify for international membership in the Association, a publisher in either class must submit the same application as applicants for full and associate member status but will not be expected to meet precisely the staffing and organizational requirements for those members. Admission to international membership shall be by a majority vote of the membership at an Annual or Special Meeting, a quorum being present, on the prior recommendation of the Committee on Admissions and Standards and the Board of Directors.

International members shall enjoy all rights and privileges of membership except the right to vote in any business being conducted by the Association, the Board of Directors, or the membership. Any reference elsewhere in these By-Laws to a voting right, therefore, shall be read so as to exclude international members. Annual dues for international members shall be set from time to time by the Board.

Section 6: Introductory Membership.

Eligible for introductory membership are nonprofit scholarly publishers that intend to apply for AAUP membership in one of the other categories either during their introductory term or at the end of that term. Presses may not stay in the introductory category for more than three years.

Candidates for introductory membership will be expected to provide evidence concerning the scholarly character of their publishing programs and information about present staffing, reporting relationships, review processes, and also any changes or developments proposed in these areas, but they will not be expected to meet the publication rate, staffing, or organizational requirements of full membership. Admission to introductory membership shall be made at the discretion of the Executive Director of the Association in consultation with the Board upon receipt by the Membership Manager of a letter of application that includes the requested information.

At any time during the introductory period introductory members may apply for regular membership in the appropriate category. After three years, the introductory membership is automatically terminated.

Introductory members shall enjoy such rights and privileges as determined by the Board of Directors, but in no event shall their rights and privileges extend to service on the Board of Directors or on the Standing Committees of the Association or voting in any business conducted by it. Any reference elsewhere in the By-Laws to a voting right, therefore, shall be so read as to exclude introductory members. Annual dues for introductory members shall be set from time to time by the Board.

Section 7: Voting and Other Privileges.

Each full member and each associate member of the Association shall be entitled to one vote in such business as may come before the Association. Only members in good standing shall be entitled to vote or otherwise enjoy the privileges of membership in the Association.

Section 8: Cancellation of Membership and Resignation.

A university press, by its very nature, must be devoted to scholarly and educational ends; the failure of a university press to pursue such ends as its fundamental business shall constitute grounds for canceling its membership in the Association. Any accusation of such a failure will be brought to the Committee on Admissions and Standards for a recommendation to the Board.

A membership may also be canceled for continued nonpayment of dues or for continued failure, after admission to membership, to meet the minimum requirements set forth in the Guidelines.

Cancellation of full, associate, or international membership shall be effected, on recommendation of the Board of Directors, by a two-thirds vote of the members present and voting at the Annual Meeting or a Special Meeting, a quorum being present.

Any member may resign at any time if its current annual dues are paid, provided its resignation is confirmed in a written communication to the Executive Director and President of the Association from a responsible officer or group of officers of the parent institution or institutions.

Should a member in any class of membership resign after the due date of the annual dues payment and before the next annual dues payment date, the member is responsible for the payment of such dues at the time of resignation.

ARTICLE IV: MEMBERSHIP MEETINGS

Section 1: The Annual Meeting.
The Annual Meeting of members shall be held at such time and place within or without the State of New York as may be designated by the Board of Directors after giving due weight to preferences expressed by members. Such meetings shall be held for the purpose of electing the Board of Directors, approving the annual budget, and transacting such other business as may be properly brought before the meeting. At each Annual Meeting of members, the Board of Directors shall cause to be presented to the membership a report verified by the President and the Treasurer, or by a majority of the Board, in accordance with the requirements of Section 519 of the New York Not-for-Profit Corporation Law.

Section 2: Special Meetings.
Special Meetings of the members shall be held at such time and place within or without the State of New York as may be designated by the Board of Directors. Such meetings may be called by (a) the Board of Directors; or (b) the Executive Committee; or (c) the President, the President-elect, or the Executive Director acting on a request received in writing that states the purpose or purposes of the meeting and is signed by 30 percent or more of the members of the Association.

Section 3: Notice of Meetings.
Notice of the purpose or purposes and of the time and place of every meeting of members of the Association shall be in writing and signed by the President, President-elect, or the Executive Director, and a copy thereof shall be delivered personally or by the U.S. Postal Service not less than ten or more than fifty days before the meeting, to each member entitled to vote at such meeting.

Section 4: Representation by Proxy.
A member may authorize a person or persons to act by proxy on all matters in which a member is entitled to participate. No proxy shall be valid after the expiration of eleven months from the date thereof unless otherwise provided in the proxy. Every proxy shall be revocable at the pleasure of the member executing it.

Section 5: Quorum.
Except for a special election of Directors pursuant to Section 604 of the New York Not-for-Profit Corporation Law, the presence at a meeting in person or by proxy of a majority of the members entitled to vote thereat shall constitute a quorum for the transaction of any business, except that the members present may adjourn the meeting even if there is no quorum.

Section 6: Voting.
In the election of members of the Board of Directors and the election of Officers, a plurality of the votes cast at an Annual Meeting shall elect. Any other action requires a majority of votes cast except as otherwise specifically provided in these By-Laws. A vote may be taken without a meeting if a majority of the members in good standing submit written votes in response to a request to this effect from the President, the President-elect, or the Executive Director.

ARTICLE V: DIRECTORS AND OFFICERS

Section 1: The Board of Directors.
The Association shall be managed by its Board of Directors, and, in this connection, the Board of Directors shall establish the policies of the Association while considering the wishes of the membership and the constituency of the Association (which constituency consists of the employees of the member presses), and shall evaluate the performance of the Executive Director. The Board of Directors shall meet at least three times each year, once in the fall and once in the winter and in conjunction with the Annual Meeting of the membership of the Association. The Board of Directors shall consist of not fewer than nine or more than thirteen Directors, all of whom shall be at least nineteen years of age, at least two-thirds of whom shall be citizens of the United States, four of whom shall be the elected Officers of the Association. Directors other than Officers (Directors-at-Large), like Officers, must be on the staff of a member press, except that the Executive Director is an ex officio (nonvoting) member of the Board of Directors and the Executive Committee.

Section 2: Election Procedure and Term of Office.
Directors shall be elected by a plurality vote of the members present at the Annual Meeting. Candidates may be nominated by the Nominating Committee appointed by the Executive Committee, or from the floor. Officers shall be elected for a one-year term, except that the President shall remain on the Board of Directors for an additional year as Past-President; Directors-at-Large shall be elected for a three-year term. Directors shall not succeed themselves except that (a) Directors who are elected Officers shall continue as Directors as long as they remain Officers, and (b) the Treasurer shall remain on the Board for an additional year as a Director-at-large. Each newly elected Director and Officer shall assume office at the close of the Annual Meeting at which the election is held. Any Director or Officer may resign by notifying the President, the President-elect, or the Executive Director. The resignation shall take effect at the time therein specified. Except as provided for in Article IX ("The Executive Director"), Directors shall not receive any compensation for serving as Directors. However, nothing herein shall be construed to prevent a Director from serving the Association in another capacity for which compensation may be received.

Section 3: Officers.
The elected Officers of the Association, each of whom must be on the staff of a member press, shall be a President, a President-elect, a Treasurer, and a Treasurer-elect, each to be elected for a one-year term by a plurality vote of the members present at the Annual Meeting. Between Annual Meetings of members, a Special Meeting of members may elect, by a plurality vote of the members present, an Officer to complete the term of an Officer who has resigned or otherwise ceased to act as an Officer.

Section 4: Duties of Officers.
The President shall serve as presiding officer at all meetings of the membership and all meetings of the Board of Directors and the Executive Committee. The President, with the Executive Director, serves as spokesperson for the Association. At the Annual Meeting of members, the President and the President-elect shall provide a forum for the Association membership and constituency to discuss and assess the Association's program. The President-elect shall discharge the duties of the President in the President's absence, and shall succeed to the office of President in the event of a vacancy in that office, filling out the unexpired term as well as the term to which he or she is elected President.

The Treasurer shall be custodian of the Association's funds, shall be responsible for the preparation of its financial records as the basis for an annual audit, and shall report at the Annual Meeting of members on the Association's financial condition. The Treasurer-elect shall discharge the duties of the Treasurer in the Treasurer's absence, and shall succeed to the office of Treasurer in the event of a vacancy in that office, filling out the unexpired term as well as the term to which he or she is elected Treasurer.

Section 5: Removal from Office and Replacement.
Any Director or elected Officer may be removed from office at any time, for cause or without cause, by a majority vote of the membership or may be removed for cause by a majority vote of the Board acting at a meeting duly assembled, a quorum being present. If one or more vacancies should occur on the Board for any reason, the remaining members of the Board, although less than a quorum, may by majority vote elect a successor or successors for the unexpired term.

Section 6: Board Meetings.
Meetings of the Board of Directors shall be held at such place within or without the State of New York as may from time to time be fixed by resolution of the Board, or as may be specified in the notice of the meeting. Notice of any meeting of the Board need not be given to any Director who submits a signed waiver of such notice. Special Meetings of the Board may be held at any time upon the call of the Executive Committee, the Executive Director, the President, or the President-elect.

Section 7: Board Quorum.
A majority of the members of the Board of Directors then acting, but in no event less than one-half of the entire board of Directors, acting at a meeting duly assembled, shall constitute a quorum for the transaction of business. If at any meeting of the Board there shall be less than a quorum present, a majority of those present may adjourn the meeting without further notice from time to time until a quorum shall have been obtained. The "entire Board of Directors" shall mean the total number of Directors that the Association would have if there were no vacancies.

Section 8: Board Voting.
Except as otherwise specified in these By-Laws, all decisions of the Board shall be by majority vote of the Directors in attendance, a quorum being present. Any Board action may be taken without a meeting if all members of the Board or committee thereof consent in writing to the adoption of a resolution authorizing the action. The resolution and the written consents thereto shall be filed with the minutes of the proceedings of the Board. Any member of the Board or of any committee thereof may participate in a meeting of such Board or committee thereof by means of a telephone or similar communications equipment allowing all persons participating in the meeting to hear each other at the same time. Participation by such means shall constitute presence in person at a meeting.

ARTICLE VI: EXECUTIVE COMMITTEE
The Executive Committee of the Board of Directors shall consist of the Past-President and President of the Association and the President-elect, Treasurer, Treasurer-elect, and the Executive Director (ex officio, nonvoting). The Executive Committee shall advise and confer with the Executive Director, call Special Meetings of the Board of Directors as necessary, appoint committee members not otherwise appointed pursuant to these By-Laws, and serve as the investment committee for the Association. The Executive Committee shall, if

necessary, act for the full Board of Directors between meetings of the Board, but only in those matters not establishing policy or not requiring a vote of more than a majority of Directors in attendance.

ARTICLE VII: STANDING COMMITTEES

The Standing Committees of the Association (in addition to the Executive Committee) shall be the Committee on Admissions and Standards, the Committee on the Annual Meeting Program, and the Nominating Committee. The Committee on Admissions and Standards shall be constituted as provided in the Guidelines. Appointments to the Committee on the Annual Meeting Program and the Nominating Committee shall be made in accordance with Article VIII of these By-Laws.

ARTICLE VIII: OTHER COMMITTEES AND TASK FORCES

Other committees and task forces may be established by agreement of the Executive Director and the Board. The President-elect shall appoint chairs of said committees (and the Standing Committees) and such of their members as the Executive Committee may care to designate. The President-elect shall charge the said committees with such duties, including reporting duties, as he or she may deem appropriate. Task forces shall be established for a limited time to accomplish a specific goal. The President shall appoint chairs of task forces and provide their charges. Reports of standing and all other committees and task forces shall be made to the Board of Directors, in writing or orally, as requested by the Executive Director.

ARTICLE IX: THE EXECUTIVE DIRECTOR

The Board of Directors may appoint at such times, and for such terms as it may prescribe, an Executive Director of the Association who shall report to the Board of Directors and who is responsible for implementing policy through fiscally sound programs; monitoring the work of committees and task forces; and managing the Central Office (such Central Office consisting of salaried employees hired by the Executive Director in order to carry out the business of the Association). The Executive Director shall prepare an operating plan and budget and shall participate in meetings of the Board of Directors and Executive Committee in an ex officio nonvoting capacity as appropriate. Under the authority of the Board of Directors, the Executive Director shall have responsibility for the execution of Association policy, for the furtherance of the Association's interests, and for the day-to-day operation of the Association's business and programs. The Executive Director shall act as secretary at all Board meetings, Executive Committee meetings, and Annual and Special Meetings of the Association, and shall prepare and distribute minutes of the same. The Executive Director shall serve as Corporate Secretary. The Executive Director's salary shall be fixed annually by the Board.

ARTICLE X: REGIONAL ORGANIZATIONS

The Board of Directors may recognize geographical regions within which members of the Association and others may organize themselves for regional meetings to further the aims of the Association.

ARTICLE XI: DUES

The amount of the annual dues payment by members shall be voted each year at the Annual Meeting on recommendation of the Board of Directors. The fiscal year of the Association shall be April 1 to March 31. Dues shall be payable by September 30, at which time any member press that has not paid its dues shall be subject to suspension at the Board's discretion. When a member is suspended for nonpayment of dues, the President of the Association shall so notify the director of the said member and the responsible officer or officers of its parent institution or group of institutions, and shall further advise them that if such member has not paid its dues by the end of the Association's fiscal year its membership shall be subject to cancellation.

ARTICLE XII: BOOKS AND RECORDS

The Association shall keep at its office within the State of New York correct and complete books and records of account; minutes of meetings of the members, of the Board of Directors, and of the Executive Committee; and an up-to-date list of the names and addresses of all members. These books and records may be in written form or in any other form capable of being converted to written form within a reasonable time.

ARTICLE XIII: CHANGES IN BY-LAWS AND GUIDELINES

Members may propose changes to these By-Laws and Guidelines by submitting the proposed change and its rationale to the Executive Director. S/He will arrange for the Board's review of any such proposal at the next appropriate Board Meeting. If the Board recommends Association approval of the proposed change, the change will be presented with at least thirty days advance notice to the membership at the next Annual or Special Meeting called for that purpose at which a quorum is present. A change to the By-Laws requires a two-thirds majority of all Members eligible to vote (in person or by proxy). A change to the Guidelines requires a majority of all Members eligible to vote (in person or by proxy). Whenever there is a conflict between these By-Laws and the Guidelines, any Statement of Governance, or a resolution of the membership, Board of Directors, or Executive Committee, or any other document published by the Association, these By-Laws shall prevail.

In the event the Board recommends against approval of a proposed change, the member proposing the change may call a vote on the measure at the Annual Meeting or at a Special Meeting for that purpose, provided thirty days notice is given and thirty percent of the Association's voting members sign a request that sign a request that said proposal be voted upon. Requirements for adoption of the measure are as stated in this Article.

Guidelines on Admission to Membership and Maintenance of Membership

As revised June 14, 2007

A. Preamble

The purposes of the Association are to encourage dissemination of the fruits of research and to support university presses in their endeavor to make widely available scholarly knowledge and the most important results of scholarly research; to provide an organization through which the exchange of ideas relating to university presses and their functions may be facilitated; to afford technical advice and assistance to learned bodies, scholarly associations, and institutions of higher learning; and to do all things incidental to and in furtherance of the foregoing purposes without extending the same.

B. Types of Membership

The Association admits members in four categories: (1) full membership, (2) associate membership, (3) international membership, and (4) introductory membership.

1. Full Membership

Eligible for full membership are nonprofit university presses, defined as the scholarly publishing arm of a university or college or a group of such institutions within a state or geographic region, located within the Americas and publishing primarily in English, that satisfy the following criteria:

(a) Eligible presses must be an integral part of one or more such colleges and universities, and should be so recognized in the manual of organization, catalogue, website, or other official publication of at least one such parent institution. The organization and functions of the university press must lie within the prescription of its parent institution or institutions.

(b) A committee or board of the faculty of the parent institution or institutions shall be charged with certifying the scholarly quality of the publications that bear the institutional imprint.

(c) Publication of ten or more scholarly titles in the twenty-four months preceding the date of application shall be required for admission to full membership. Scholarly books, journals, and digital projects that include original scholarly content will all be counted to satisfy this requirement. The word "scholarly" is used here in the sense of original research of a character usually associated with the scholarly interests of a university or college. (Textbooks, manuals of a synthetic character or intended for class use, and publications for which the press serves primarily as a printer and/or distributor for other departments or divisions of the university or college are not to be included in the aforementioned minimum scholarly publishing requirement.)

(d) An acceptable scholarly publishing program shall have the benefit of the service of not fewer than three full-time equivalent employees, of whom one shall have the rank and functions of director. This official shall report, organizationally, to the President of the university or college, or to an officer at the vice-presidential or decanal level (i.e., an officer reporting either to the President or to the chief academic officer) having both academic and fiscal authority, or to the designated representative of a group of such institutions who shall have both kinds of authority.

Any press satisfying these requirements shall be eligible in principle for election to full membership in the Association. Annual dues for full members shall be set from time to time by the Board.

2. Associate Membership

Presses of non-degree-granting scholarly institutions and associations may apply for associate membership, providing those institutions are incorporated as not-for-profit and that the presses satisfy the requirements for membership, except that the auspices and structures of the parent organizations of such presses will in all instances be those of non-degree-granting institutions or scholarly associations rather than those of universities. Applicants for associate membership should be in a state or geographic region located within the Americas and publishing primarily in English. In the absence of an editorial committee or board, an applicant for associate membership shall observe commonly accepted standards of editorial review.

Associate members shall enjoy such rights and privileges as determined by the Board of Directors, including the right to serve on the Board of Directors and on the Standing Committees of the Association and the right to vote on any business conducted by it. Associate members shall not be eligible to participate in the Association's statistical programs for full members. The number of associate members shall not exceed thirty-five percent of the number of full members of the Association and no more than one associate member representative may serve on the Board at any one time. Annual dues for associate members shall be set from time to time by the Board.

3. International Membership

International membership may be applied for by (a) university-affiliated scholarly publishers and presses of non-degree-granting scholarly institutions and associations in parts of the world not embraced by the Americas and (b) such presses within the Americas that publish primarily in languages other than English.

Candidates for international membership will be expected to provide evidence concerning the size and scholarly character of their publishing programs but will not be expected to meet the staffing or organizational requirements of full membership.

International members shall enjoy all rights and privileges of full membership except the right to vote in any business conducted by the Association. Any reference elsewhere in the By-Laws to a voting right, therefore, shall be so read as to exclude international members. International members shall not be eligible to participate in the Association's statistical programs. Annual dues for international members shall be set from time to time by the Board.

4. Introductory Membership

Eligible for introductory membership are nonprofit scholarly publishers that intend to apply for AAUP membership in one of the other categories either during their introductory term or at the end of that term.

Candidates for introductory membership will be expected to provide evidence concerning the scholarly character of their publishing programs and information about present staffing, reporting relationships, review processes, and also any changes or developments proposed in these areas, but they will not be expected to meet the publication rate, staffing, or organizational requirements of full membership. Presses may not stay in the introductory category for more than three years.

At any time during the introductory period introductory members may apply for regular membership in the appropriate category. If a press does not wish to continue as an introductory member for three years, it may resign from the Association after payment of its current annual dues. After three years, the introductory membership is automatically terminated.

Introductory members shall enjoy such rights and privileges as determined by the Board of Directors, but in no event shall their rights and privileges extend to service on the Board of Directors or on the Standing Committees of the Association or voting in any business conducted by it. Any reference elsewhere in the By-Laws to a voting right, therefore, shall be so read as to exclude introductory members. Annual dues for introductory members shall be set from time to time by the Board.

C. Application, Admission, and Cancellation

1. Application

All inquiries from prospective applicants for membership in the Association are to be directed to the Membership Manager of AAUP. The Membership Manager shall advise the candidate of the substance of these Guidelines on Admission to Membership and Maintenance of Membership, and shall require as evidence of satisfactory compliance with them for all membership categories, except the Introductory Membership, the following materials for submission to the Committee on Admissions and Standards:

(a) One copy of each of 10 or more different scholarly titles published by the applicant and certified by its faculty editorial board or committee in the twenty-four months preceding the date on which the application for membership is filed, and full runs of the issues of any journals for the year or years in which a journal serves as one of the titles. If original digital publications are submitted, the applicant will provide access to committee members.
(b) A list of the peer reviewers (names and affiliations) for each of the books or original digital publications submitted as part of the application. Published reviews of the titles and information about scholarly awards received may be submitted as part of the application.
(c) Copies of the applicant press's catalogs for the past two years for each member of the Committee on Admissions and Standards.
(d) A complete list, by name and title, of the staff of the applicant press, to be prepared in that form in which such information is given for active members in the most recent edition of the Directory of the Association of American University Presses. For part-time staff the list should indicate the percentage of time each person devotes to the press.
(e) A statement from a senior administrative officer of the parent institution, or the designated representative of a group of institutions, outlining the immediate and long-term intentions and financial expectations of the institution or group of institutions for its press, and reflecting a realistic appreciation of the cost of supporting a serious program of scholarly publication.
(f) Copies of its financial operating statements for the two most recently completed fiscal years.

With respect to the scholarship of published works, the Association will in general accept the certification of the press's own faculty board or committee and will not pass judgment on the scholarship of any individual work. However, the Committee on Admissions and Standards will take into account the observance by the press of commonly accepted standards of editorial review, ordinarily including at least one positive evaluation by a qualified scholar not affiliated with the author's own institution.

2. Admission

Following the filing of a formal application for full, associate, or international membership and notification by the Membership Manager of AAUP to the applicant of its acceptance for consideration, the candidate press shall be regarded as having entered a period of probation, which will last for a period of time no longer than one year, at the end of which, if not sooner, its candidacy will be acted upon as prescribed under the By-Laws, and during which it shall enjoy the following privileges of membership: (a) the right to send delegates to the Annual Meeting at the member rate, and (b) the right to send representatives to all training sessions, workshops, symposiums, and conferences dealing with professional activities of scholarly publishers and enjoying the support of the Association.

A press shall be elected to full, associate, or international membership by an affirmative vote of a majority of the Association's full members at the Annual Meeting or a Special Meeting, a quorum being present, on the recommendation of the Board of Directors. Such action shall be taken by the Board only on the prior recommendation of the Committee on Admissions and Standards, which shall be responsible for determining that the applying press satisfies the minimum requirements for membership. Admission of a new full, associate, or international member to the Association shall take effect immediately following an affirmative vote of a majority of the Association's full membership at the Annual Meeting or a Special Meeting.

Admission to introductory membership shall be made at the discretion of the Executive Director of the Association in consultation with the Board upon receipt by the Membership Manager of a letter of request that includes information about present staffing, reporting relationships, review processes, and any changes or developments proposed in these areas.

To maintain its active membership status, each member press shall be required to submit each year to the Central Office of the Association, for publication in the annual Directory of members, both a roster of its current staff and an indication of the number of books, journals, and original digital publications that it has published in each of the two calendar years preceding and that have been certified as to scholarship by its editorial board or committee.

3. Cancellation

A university press, by its very nature, must be devoted to scholarly and educational ends; the failure of a press to pursue such ends as its fundamental business shall constitute grounds for canceling its membership in the Association. Any accusation of such a failure will be brought to the Committee on Admissions and Standards for a recommendation to the Board. Cancellation of membership shall be effected, on recommendation of the Board of Directors, by a two-thirds' majority vote of the members present and voting at the Annual Meeting or a Special Meeting, a quorum being present.

It shall be the responsibility of the Membership Manager to review each listing of an active press in each annual edition of the membership Directory, and to undertake action as follows when any member seems to have fallen below the qualifying criteria for membership: (a) to notify the Executive Director and the Committee on Admissions and Standards of a member's apparent delinquency under the Guidelines so that the Executive Director may make an inquiry and, if current standards are not being met, offer the assistance and cooperation of the Association in bringing about satisfactory solutions to the member's problems; (b) to advise the President, the Committee on Admissions and Standards, and the Board when notification of an apparent delinquency has been sent and an offer of assistance made; (c) to inform the President, the Committee on Admissions and Standards, and the

Board of any response received from the member press following the offer of assistance.

Should the delinquent press fail to resolve its difficulties within one year of the Executive Director's notice, the Committee on Admissions and Standards shall submit to the Board of Directors a full report of the situation, and recommend, for endorsement by the Board and transmission to the membership for ratification, that the membership of the delinquent press be terminated. Two years from the date of its expulsion, a press shall be entitled to apply for readmission through initiation of the application procedures herein prescribed.

E. The Committee on Admissions and Standards

The official agency for the administration of these guidelines shall be the Committee on Admissions and Standards, which shall operate under authority delegated by the Board of Directors, and which shall consist of between four and six members, two of whom, at least, shall be the director of a member press. The incoming President will appoint the chair of the committee from among members of the current committee with at least one year of service. The chairs shall each serve a term of one year as part of their three-year term on the committee and may not succeed themselves in office. The chair shall appoint the remaining committee members. Terms of the committee members will normally be three years each except that in the year that these revised Guidelines take effect shorter terms may be established for some of the members. Committee members will not be eligible to serve more than two successive terms.

PERSONNEL INDEX

Kasper, Carol	49, 50	Klose, Lisa	85
Kasprzak, Danielle	110	Knoll, Elizabeth	71
Kass, Gary	113	Knox, Helena	60
Kati, Rebekah	60	Kohlmeier, Rob	198
Kaufman, Andrew	195	Kolman, Amanda	60
Kaur, Manjit	120	Komatsu, Mika	181
Kaveney, Dan	140	Komie, Michelle	203
Kawai, Colins	73	Kondrick, Maureen	96
Kean, Linda Griffin	78	Kopperson, Caitlin	39
Keane, Bobby	229	Kornbluh, Gregory	72
Keane, Kathleen	84	Kosman, Phoebe	72
Keane, Robert	95	Kosowski, Mary Beth	104
Kearn, Vickie	149	Koster, Holli	178
Keating, George	118	Kostova, Julia	139
Keddington-Lang, Marianne	192	Kosturko, Bob	37
Keene, Katie	112	Kozakov, Sergiy	35
Keener, Alix	106	Kracht, Peter	147
Keeran, Katie	158	Kramer, Gary	173
Keets, Deb	207	Kraus, Dennis	51
Kelaher, Christopher	40	Kraus, Donald	139
Keller, Holly	38	Kress, Steven	144
Kelley, Pamela	73	Kriesel, Leslie	54
Kelly, Kathleen	135	Krissoff, Derek	119
Kelly, Melinda	86	Krock, Trista	161
Kendzejeski, Nicole	85	Krol, Kathryn	178
Keneston, Fran	168, 228	Krol, Thomas P.	103
Kennedy, Melinda	49	Kruggel, James C.	47
Kenney, Mary Lou	85	Krum, Jeff	45
Kenyon, Andrew	168	Kuerbis, Lisa	170
Kepler, Judy	125	Kuhn, Kyle	67
Kerr, Karen	58	Kulka, John	71
Kessler, John	50	Kull, Matthew	211
Kiely, Garrett	49, 227, 228	Kuny, Greg	27
Kilgore, Dustin	192, 228	Kuroda, Takuya	181
Killoh, Kathy	34	Kurtz, Kevin	55
Kilmartin, Kerry	39	Kushnirsky, Julia	55
Kim, Charles	115	Kutsko, John F.	161
Kim, Hannah	115	Kwederis, David	45
Kim, Jean	167	LaBrenz, Marcia	106
Kim, Sulah	67	Laet, Veerle De	92
Kimbel, Travis E.	107	Lage, Amy	120
Kimberling, Clint	112	Lail, Tyler	33
Kimm, Kelley	152	Laity, Susan	203
King, Brenda	203	Lake, Kim	63
King, Brian	33	Lamb, Cynthia	46
King, Frederick	40	Lambert, Allie	176
King, John	41	Lambert, Julia	144
King, Melissa	33	Lambert, Ray	60
King, Phillip	203	Lamm, Gigi	143
Kingra, Mahinder	58	LaMorte, Gianna	175
Kirk, Kara	70	Lane, Mary Ann	72
Kirk, Robert	149	Lane, Victoria	170
Kirkpatrick, Kristin	112	Langley, Norris	61
Kirschner, Jessica	168	Langston, John A.	112
Kisilinsky, Stuart	50	Lanick, Colleen	99, 229
Kistler, Steve	153	Lanne, Amanda	168
Kittrell, Casey	175	Lape, Todd	112
Klein, Kathie	161	Laplante, Tanya	139
Kleit, Micah	173	LaPoint, Lisa	72
Klopotek, Ulrich	218	Lara, Greg	55

Ngueha, Hubert	47	Panner, Craig	139
Nicholls, David	67	Pappas, Mari	117
Nichols, Kate	173	Paradise, Avi	149
Nichols, Sally	97	Parker, Lynne	163
Nichols, Suzanne	157	Parker, Nevil	63
Nicolaes, Chantal	31	Parker, Nick	140
Nishimoto, Kiera	74	Parris, Scott	139
Nizer, Eileen	168	Parsons, Joe	127
Noble, Clair	118	Parsons, Thomas	40
Noe, Jason	140	Pasti, Mary	203
Noonan, John	161	Patnaik, Gayatri	37
Noonan, Margaret M.	64	Patrick, Richanna	58
Noonan, Maureen	203	Patton, Susan	227
Norell, Randy	26	Paul, Tammy	51
Norton, Jennifer	144	Pavitt, Irene	54
Norton, Rebecca	69	Pavlas-Mills, Sharon	178
Norton, Scott	43	Pearce, Catherine	139
Norville, Valerie	186	Pearson, Janie	80
Noth, Michael	80	Pearson, Laura	139, 140
Nowak, Emily	194	Peeler, Denise	76
Nyberg, Karl	171	Pellien, Jessica	229
O'Brien-Nicholson, Kate	64	Pelton, Elizabeth	203
O'Connell, Cliff	178	Peltz, James	168
O'Connor, Chris	161	Peluse, Michael	44
O'Connor, Noreen	143	Penman, Paul	31
O'Donnell, Robert	156	Pennefeather, Shannon	109
O'Donovan, Maria	56	Penrose, Denise	43
O'Grady, Shawn	182	Pensak, Susan	55
O'Handley, Robert	99	Perillo, Jennifer	54
O'Hare, Joanne	121	Perkel, Bonnie	59
O'Neill, Brendan	139	Perov, Heidi	128
O'Neill, Kathy	76	Pervin, David	139
O'Prey, Terri	228	Pescatore, John	45
O'Rourke, Kellie	45	Pesek, Diana	144
O'Shea, Patti	49	Petersen, Lorna	156
Oakes, Ian	128	Peterson, Bob	50
Oates, Paula	129	Peterson, Joseph	50
Oblack, Linda	79	Peterson, Ryan	155
Ochsner, Daniel	110	Peterson, Sam	126
Ohlin, Peter	139	Petilos, Randolph	49
Okrent, Marilyn	139, 140	Petty, Susan	179
Olson, Andrea	106	Pfeiffer, Alice R.	170
Olson, Heidi	192	Pfund, Niko	139
Ortiz, Ángel	151	Phillips, Betsy	189
Osterman, Anne	50	Phillips, Peter	44
Otero, Rosa V.	151	Pickard, Megan	183
Otzel, Margaret	203	Pickett, Duncan	190
Ovedovitz, Nancy	203	Piell, Amanda	32
Ovenden, Laurel	102	Pierce, Rich	80
Oweka, Ime	140	Pierre, Stephanie	203
Owen, Susan	42	Pilat, Sarah	167
Owens, Kathryn	120	Pimm, Matthew	115
Pace, Susan	93	Pinchefsky, Andrew	102
Pacheco, Lisa	161	Pinnone, Daniela	31
Pagan, Cristina	78	Pintaudi-Jones, Rose	140
Pakiela, James	55	Pisano, Joanne	101
Palao, Patricia	126	Pitts, Kathryn	133
Pan, Jennifer	157	Pitts, Melissa	38, 229
Pancorbo, Ernesto	151	Pitzele, Mark	220
Pankratz, Sherith	140	Plant, Alisa	94, 228

Wallace, Ivey Pittle	66	White, Rebekah	72
Wallen, Michelle	128	White, Sara Henderson	87
Waller, Mira	60	Whitehorn, Clark	124
Walsh, Bailey	50, 131	Whitmore, Anne M.	85
Walters, Carolyn	79	Whittaker, Jenna	80
Walters, Marthe	63	Wholey, Makiko	115
Waltz, Nikki	113	Wilcox, Bruce	97
Wang, Kinglen	114	Wilcox, Lynn	170
Wantland, Clydette	77, 229	Wildfong, Kathryn	194
Ward, Jean	171	Wilfinger, David	203
Ward, Roy	102	Wilkie, Craig R.	90
Ware, Cynthia	117	Wilkins, Tim	149
Waren, Miriam	32	Willcox, Clair	113
Warlick, Dottie	141	Williams, Clive	184
Warne, Kate	43	Williams, Dan	179
Warnement, Julie	117	Williams, Isabel	180
Warner, Chris	63	Williams, Kimberley	149
Warnick, Stephanie	188	Williams, Lakisha	126
Warren, John W.	67	Williams, Liz	156
Washburn, Amanda	115	Willis, Amy	131
Wasserman, Marlie	158	Willis, Cathy	78
Wasserman, Steve	203	Willis, Kathleen Z.	33
Wasti, Shubhash	35	Willmes, Karen	85
Watanabe, Hiroshi	181	Willoughby-Harris, H. Lee	60
Waterman, Dan	23	Wilson, Andrew	27
Waters, Lindsay	72	Wilson, Carolyn	141
Waters, Suzi	128	Wilson, J.D	23
Watkins, Anne Dean	90	Wilson, Jean L.	96
Watkins, Julie	33	Wilson, Sharon	25
Watkinson, Charles	152, 228	Windsor, Elizabeth R.	85
Watkinson, Peter	227	Wippo, Jacqueline	31
Watson, Ron	215	Wise, Amelia	58
Watters, Latasha	23	Wisniewski, Cassandra	50
Weaver, Caroline	117	Wissink, Jan-Peter	31
Weaver, Paula	169	Wissoker, Ken	59
Webb, Kerry	174	Witchen, Kelly	106
Webster, Allison	90	Witzke, Jennifer	80
Weglinski, Michaela R.	122	Wolfe, Alex	147
Wehmueller, Jacqueline C.	84	Wolfe, Shelly	116
Weidemann, Jason	110	Wong, Angelina	52
Weidman, Anna	42 228	Woodburn, Marcus	215
Weiner, Deborah	67	Woodcock, Kevin	60
Weinreb, Jenya	203	Woodward, Fred	87
Weinstein, Michael	171	Woollen, Susan	40
Welch, Rebecca	134	Worth, Cherie	201
Wellner, Fred	170	Wrenn, Anne	110
Wells, Phyllis	69	Wright, Charlotte	82
Wells, Thomas	174	Wright, John	41
Wells, Vicky	128, 228	Wrinn, Stephen M.	90
Welsby, Alison	93	Wrzesinski, Julie	108
Welsch, Sarah	134	Wu, Nancy	140
Wenzel, Stephanie	127	Wuensche, Christin	178
Werts, Lynn	63	Wyllys, Kaila	175
Wessels, Cindy	147	Wyrwa, Richard	187
West, Linda	85	Yahner, Kathryn	144
Westlund, Laura	110	Yamaguchi Ryo	49
Wheel, Brian	140	Yates, John	182, 184
Whipple, George	58	Yates, Steve	112
Whitaker, Theresa M.	103	Yen, Cindy	74
White, Katherine	124	Yenerich, Pat	130

OTHER PUBLICATIONS AND RESOURCES

AAUP Announce
An informational bulletin for AAUP's wider community. Interested scholarly communications, academic, and publishing professionals are invited to subscribe to this email bulletin to stay up-to-date on Association news and events

AAUP Annual Report
The report provides a summary of association activities.

AAUP Book, Jacket, and Journal Show Catalog
The purpose of the Show is to recognize achievement in the design, production, and manufacture of books, book jackets, and journals. The catalog displays and critiques all titles selected in this annual competition. Gratis to members, $20.00 to non-members.

AAUP bulletin
The bulletin is a monthly news brief on the programs and activities of the association, distributed electronically to AAUP members only.

AAUP Digital Digest
A blog of news and commentary from AAUP,.
aaupdigitaldigest.wordpress.com

AAUPNET.ORG
The association's website features information about AAUP programs, activities, and upcoming events; news about our member presses; a job list; resources for scholars, publishers, and librarians; and much more.

AAUPWiki
The AAUPWiki is a collaborative site designed to help AAUP members learn and share best practices, conference materials, and professional development tools. Hosted by Princeton University Press, and editable by registered AAUP members, the AAUPWiki is open to interested members of the scholarly communications field at:
aaupwiki.princeton.edu/

Books for Understanding
Books for Understanding is an online resource for anyone looking for in-depth background and expertise on today's news. This service features subject-specific bibliographies on critically important news stories. New bibliographies are compiled when a major news story breaks or heated public debate takes place. This resource is available at:
www.booksforunderstanding.org

The Exchange
The association's quarterly public newsletter is now an online-only publication. *The Exchange* is available free to interested members of the public and the scholarly communications community on the AAUP website.

University Press Books for Public and Secondary School Libraries
An annual bibliography that lists more than 400 university press titles in a wide range of disciplines. A committee of public and secondary school librarians selects the titles. The bibliography is published with support from the American Library Association (ALA) and is now also available in print and online at: *www.aaupnet.org/librarybooks*